BOOKS BY DONALD M. STREET, JR.

A Cruising Guide to the Lesser Antilles (1964, revised 1974)
A Yachting Guide to the Grenadines (1971)
The Ocean Sailing Yacht, Volume I (1973)
The Ocean Sailing Yacht, Volume II (1978)
Seawise (1979)
Street's Cruising Guide to the Caribbean
    VOLUME I: Sailing Directions, Charts, Weather, Tides, Reg-
        ulations etc. (1981)
    VOLUME II: Puerto Rico to Dominica (1980)
    VOLUME III: Martinique to Trinidad and Tobago (1980)
    VOLUME IV: Venezuela (1980)

SEAWISE

SEAWISE

Donald M. Street, Jr.

W · W · NORTON & COMPANY · NEW YORK · LONDON

FIRST EDITION

❧ THIS TEXT is composed in photocomposition Primer, with display type in Craw Clarendon Outline and Electra Bold. Manufacturing is by the Maple-Vail Book Manufacturing group. Book design is by Marjorie J. Flock.

Library of Congress Cataloging in Publication Data
Street, Donald M
  Seawise.
  Includes index.
  1. Yachts and yachting—Addresses, essays,
lectures.   I. Title.
GV813.S93   1979   797.1   79–18750

ISBN 0–393–03232–9

2 3 4 5 6 7 8 9 0

To THE LATE W. H. "Bill" Taylor, sailor, raconteur, one-time editor of *Yachting,* who was not afraid to "tell it as it is" and who frequently laid into the yachting industry. Bill not only helped teach me to sail and race when I was growing up but he also bought my first article and thus launched me on my career as a yachting writer.

Contents

V ∗ THE ART OF SEAMANSHIP

VI ∗ STREET SPEAKS OUT

Preface

YACHTING IS an ever-changing scene and some of the articles in this collection date back to 1964. Therefore it must be remembered that a few of them, especially the Caribbean articles, are slightly out of date. However, this book is not a cruising guide. The general cruising articles are still valid even though the islands are changing. Some of the sailing articles have been changed slightly in view of new developments in international regulations regarding lights, radio frequencies, and the like so as not to misguide the reader.

I will not deny that I am an old conservative, but I'm not really *that* old. I claim that so long as I can climb the mast without the aid of a bosun's chair, I'm thirty-eight—and holding. I guess this makes Rod Stephens, on a similar basis, about the age of twenty-five as he goes up a hell of a lot faster!

I am not against new products and developments but it has to be proved to me that the new products, developments, techniques, etc., really work in the conditions for which they were designed. I do not feel that a boat designed specifically for cruising alongshore (like the *Stone Horse*) be capable of making an offshore passage. However, the boat which is allegedly designed, advertised, and sold as an offshore boat must be able to stand the test of a long, offshore passage where a variety of weather conditions can be expected.

I spend every winter in the Caribbean cruising on *Iolaire,* but this is not the limit of my sailing experience. To keep in touch with reality and to see what is new on the market in the way of boats and gear, I always go to the Annapolis Boat Show. After that, as a penance for all my pleasure sailing in the Caribbean, I deliver a boat from the East Coast of the States to the Islands. I also sometimes do the reverse in the spring. I have made about forty trips to and from the States on maybe twenty-five different boats and this, plus four transatlantic passages, gives me an excellent basis for comparisons and judgments.

Because of the varied conditions one encounters on a 1200–1500-mile delivery trip, I get the opportunity to test a boat extensively. This is nothing like the boat tests done by most of the yachting magazines, which are usually based on a sail round Biscayne Bay or Tampa Bay or a cruise out to Catalina Island and back—most often, in light-to-moderate conditions. I have, on the contrary, written my articles, boat tests, and reports (often extremely controversial) as the result of long and frequently harsh passages.

Probably one of the reasons I am considered an old conservative is because I can look back on logs of past trips and compare boats. I realize that some of the boats I delivered in the mid-sixties, though not the best, were *far* superior to the present generation of boats that is being inflicted on owners and delivery skippers. In years gone by, a delivery was usually a pleasant trip, but frequently today, delivery jobs are pure hell. Boats are poorly designed and built, have no quality control, have the windward-going qualities of sand barges, and are loaded down with all the latest fancy gear that doesn't work.

I am not deliberately controversial. I have very definite, though not fixed, opinions which I frequently express. I will gladly change my opinion if proven wrong.

Over the years, I have built a reputation on calling a spade a spade and staking my reputation on what I feel is the truth. I don't say merely what people want to hear. Tact may not be one of my strong points. However, think how boring life would be if we agreed all the time!

D.M.S.

Acknowledgments

THIS BOOK has only come to pass because of the help and encouragement I've had from editors and publishers. Bill Taylor, of course, is the one who launched me on my writing career; Bill Robinson, his successor for many years, bought an article each year for the Caribbean issue of *Yachting*. Monk Farnham also helped by commissioning me to do a number of articles on seamanship for *Boating*.

A special thanks should go to Murray Davis who, while editor of the then quite small but up-and-coming *Sail* magazine, hired me to do a regular series of cruising and seamanship articles. He thus inflicted me upon his long-suffering editorial staff, Jeff Spranger, Chip Mason, and Patience Wales, all of whom worked long and hard at polishing up my articles. Needless to say, this led to many vociferous arguments, but none so vociferous that they couldn't be settled across the street with a couple of beers. Their help over the years is greatly appreciated.

Keith Taylor, current editor of *Sail,* continued buying my articles after Murray left. Gail Anderson and Lydia Orcutt of *Sail* also deserve special thanks for chasing around after copies of old articles and fielding many questions, despite the fact they are very busy.

My special thanks should go to Carleton Mitchell, who urged Vic Jorgenson of *Telltale Compass* to commission articles from me. *Telltale Compass* is one of the few yachting publications in the world that carries no advertising and can, therefore, always level with its readers. Vic publishes the articles regular yachting magazines feel are too hot to handle and won't touch with a ten-foot barge pole. My wife Trich says *Telltale Compass* keeps me from having ulcers, for rather than feeling completely frustrated about a yachting controversy, I simply write an article and sell it to Vic.

My thanks go, as well, to Eric Swenson for publishing this anthology and to Harvey Loomis for excellent and knowledgeable help in selecting the articles, editing, and arranging them into publishable form.

Finally, my thanks to Audrey Semple for cutting, chopping, correcting, and gluing this jigsaw puzzle to make it understandable and readable for the editors and, ultimately, the readers.

D.M.S.

Getting to the
Lesser Antilles

1 ❧ South to the Islands

EACH YEAR more and more people cruise the Caribbean. If they have already done Florida and the Bahamas, and, politics being what they are, they don't want to visit Cuba or the twin republics on Hispaniola, their eyes turn eastward to the Lesser Antilles. In the careful planning required in bringing a boat down, the basic decision is the route south and the landfall to aim for. San Juan, Puerto Rico, and Charlotte Amalie, St. Thomas, are the two major ports in the northern end of the Lesser Antilles chain. San Juan harbor is a big commercial port, and is dead to leeward of the rest of the Lesser Antilles, leaving a beat to windward to reach the other islands. For this reason most boats head directly for St. Thomas, which has a commodious harbor, or rather, a series of harbors with facilities to maintain, repair, and haul all except the largest yachts.

Arrangements can be made to leave a yacht and have her taken care of by various organizations or, with a crew aboard, she can moor at Sheraton Marina in Long Bay. Good mechanics, ship chandlers and sailmakers are here and supplies are generally available. Food is plentiful but expensive, though the opening of new markets has reduced prices. Since it is a free port, there are bargains in liquor, binoculars, cameras, watches, etc., and San Juan is only forty minutes away by air.

Most people plan their Antilles cruise for winter, and coming down in the fall poses a problem. Departure in September, when the weather is good up north, means the chance of running into a West Indian hurricane. Wait too long, and you get caught in winter storms or iced in before leaving. A check of the dates of hurricanes over the past years and a check of pilot charts will show that November is about the best month to come down. In December there is a lot of cold weather and the frequency of gales in the area north of the 30th parallel will increase greatly. Despite the outside possibility of a late season hurricane (records show very few hurricanes starting after Oct. 20), I prefer early November or the last

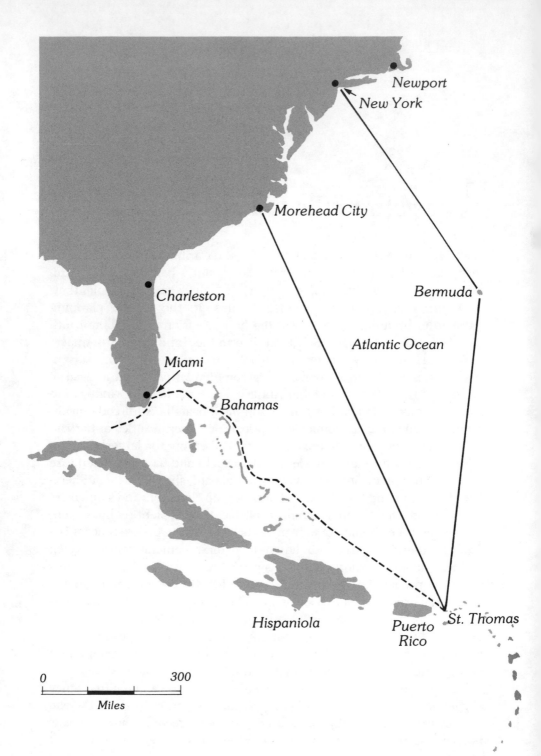

Newport

New York

Morehead City

Charleston

Bermuda

Atlantic Ocean

Miami

Bahamas

Hispaniola

Puerto
Rico

St. Thomas

0   300

Miles

Recommended and alternate routes south.

week in October because, with a good long-range weather forecast, chances of making the trip without getting caught in a gale are good. In December, the chances of not getting caught in a gale diminish rapidly.

In studying the chart it appears at first glance that the safest and easiest route is to go down the Inland Waterway in the fall and then work eastward to St. Thomas through the Bahamas. This is good in that the only long offshore hop is from Turks Island to St. Thomas. However, there are enough disadvantages in this route to discourage most people. From New York to Miami is about 1,300 miles, while St. Thomas is roughly 1,000 miles ESE of Miami. This is mainly in the trade-wind belt, with its constant easterly wind and adverse current. This means that you sail hard on the wind all the way with plenty of extra distance thrown in due to tacking, avoiding islands in the Bahamas, and the leeward set of the current. After leaving Turks Island you have the graveyard of many good ships in the unmarked Mouchoir and Silver Bank. Halfway through the Bahamas many a crew has decided that all this windward work was not worth it. Even a successful passage by this route is a very time-consuming process, probably taking about six weeks. A boat delivered by a crew on a *per diem* basis on this route will eat up a large piece of change.

There are other ways to reach the Lesser Antilles that are pleasanter sailing and faster, however. The choice boils down to three major ones that we should examine carefully. The first is to leave from New York or points east, direct to St. Thomas. The distance is almost the same from New York or any place west of Cape Cod Canal. A stop at Bermuda increases it by about 150 miles. The second is to leave from the Virginia Capes and go direct, or a much longer trip via Bermuda, not really worthwhile, considering the extra miles. The other offshore route is to leave from some place south of Hatteras.

To leave from New York or points east and head for St. Thomas or Bermuda, it is roughly 180 miles to the northern edge of the Gulf Stream and warm water. It is about 700 miles to 30 N latitude, the approximate northern limit of the doldrums and southern limit of Northern Atlantic gales. During November, the area of the first part of the trip has 9 to 12 per cent of days in November with gales (over 40 knots) while in the area around Bermuda the percentage rises to 17. Bermuda attracts gales like a magnet; the percentages rise to 19 in December and 28 in January. Even the direct course to St. Thomas traverses this gale-ridden area, so it is just as sensible to take advantage of the shore-leave, rest, and fresh stores available in Bermuda. By going to Bermuda and then heading south there will probably be no windward work at all. Records indicate little southeast wind in November. It is only about a 5–7 day trip to Bermuda and about

6–7 to St. Thomas from Bermuda. Thus it is possible to do the trip with two different crews, using only a week apiece of vacation.

The two-part trip has another advantage. Bermuda is a good place to avoid in November due to gales, while the West Indies are dangerous before then due to hurricanes. However, if the trip is made in two jumps, it is possible to avoid both the gales and hurricanes. Hurricanes start about Longitude 58 to 59 W and Latitude 11 to 18 S. At their formation, they are a minimum of 800 miles in a straight line from Bermuda. They travel in a curve, usually WNW, gradually turning further north and then east, traveling about 1,100 miles before they finally reach the vicinity of Bermuda. Therefore, it is about five days from the time a hurricane is spotted until it could possibly be dangerous to a boat enroute to Bermuda.

To work the Bermuda stopover route best, carefully check the weather in September just before departure. If no hurricane is reported, you should have clear sailing for four to five days. Continue to check the weather, and, if no hurricane is reported in the first forty-eight hours, you should reach Bermuda before one can approach. If a hurricane is reported forming during the first forty-eight hours, decide immediately whether to continue to Bermuda or turn back to the States, with caution advisable in pressing on.

Once you have reached Bermuda, leave the boat there until the time to begin the final leg of the trip during November. With jet schedules you can get to and from Bermuda in a couple of hours.

During late October or early November, keep a close weather watch and fly to Bermuda when the reports look good. Push south with all speed to the region of the doldrums before any gales arrive. Don't be afraid to use fuel in the beginning of the trip; it is more important to get out of the region of gales than to worry about getting becalmed in the doldrums.

The course is due south. You have made enough easting so that once you hit the trades it should be fast sailing into St. Thomas on a reach. Landfall is a tricky one on this route. The island of Anegada is about 40 miles east of the Bermuda–St. Thomas rhumb line and is the graveyard of many ships. It is low (highest point 40′) and unlit. The first *Ondine* met her end here in 1960 en route from Bermuda to St. Thomas. To the eastward of her presumed position, she hit the outer reefs early in the morning and bounced over into the deep water inside the reef.

If you are tempted to continue from Bermuda to St. Thomas in September, don't do it. You are heading toward the birthplace of hurricanes. One year a hurricane formed due east of Anguilla and flattened that island before any warning was sent out. Boats in St. Thomas harbor had no time to get to Hurricane Hole only twenty miles away, and a boat end-

ing her trip from Bermuda would have been in serious trouble. The islands should not be approached until after November because of this lack
of opportunity for evasive action. Even after then, warnings should be
checked continually. There can be "freaks of nature" in any month.

It is possible to depart from the Virginia Capes at the mouth of the
Chesapeake direct for St. Thomas. An advantage is in being fairly far
south, and the weather will be warmer. The distance is 1,260 miles. A
disadvantage, however, is that the Outer Banks and Cape Hatteras are on
the starboard bow. If a gale springs up out of the northeast, it is a dead lee
shore justly feared as a graveyard of ships. The shoals of Hatteras and
Cape Lookout each extend twenty miles to sea, the currents and tides are
very strong, and your only harbor of refuge would be Morehead City, N.C.
Its channel, with strong tides, is tricky under good conditions, and I
would hate to have to enter on a stormy night. Except with a boat drawing too much water for the Inland Waterway, I would be very much
against departing from the Virginia Capes for this reason.

Morehead City is, despite its channel, the best place to take off from
for St. Thomas. The distance is 1,160 miles, and it is not worthwhile continuing further along the Waterway, as it tends much more west than
south from Morehead. The distance from Charleston is 30 miles more to
St. Thomas, and, more important, 180 miles further west, making it all
that much harder to get easting. A boat can be taken down the Waterway
in easy stages to Morehead City in the fall and be ready to leave for St.
Thomas without using precious vacation time.

Morehead City is an excellent base for the offshore passage. It has
numerous places to leave a boat, excellent stores and plenty of good
mechanics. One word of caution—they don't know what good hard blue
coal is in the South so those with coal stoves should bring a supply. Also,
Morehead City is a fishing port. There is practically nothing in the way of
sailboat fittings available.

Scout around town and find some five-gallon oil tins, as they make
excellent disposable fuel drums to carry on deck. Carry as much fuel as
you can, because the trades may be light or nonexistent in November,
and the doldrums usually extend about 300 miles. One year we spent
eighty-four hours under power and ran out of fuel.

A good long-range weather report is essential and difficult to get. I
have had no success with the Coast Guard or the Weather Bureau, but
have always been able to get a good, accurate, detailed weather report by
calling the FAA weather at Norfolk Airport. Do not call during the day—
they are too busy giving weather reports to airplanes. Call between
0200–0300 in the morning, starting a few days before your planned de-

parture. At this hour of the morning things are slow, and the weatherman is usually most cooperative and will really study the maps and often give a detailed report well beyond the standard one. Even if you have a good weather report, make sure you are well and truly rigged for heavy weather, because anything can—and does—happen in November. Check the tides and leave at high water slack. As noted, the channel has strong currents. The first of the ebb will really boot you along, and may even carry you clear of Cape Lookout. The inner edge of the Gulf Stream is only sixty miles offshore, and the current set to the northeastwards should be used in gaining easting, weather permitting. The best course is ESE until St. Thomas bears SSE, then a rhumb-line course should mean a nice close reach.

If the wind acts the way the pilot charts say it will, and departure from Morehead has no gales in sight, it should be an easy trip. According to the charts, for the first part of the trip the wind will be in the northerly quadrants, NW to NE about Force 4, making it a downhill slide. About latitude 30 or 31, the wind will get light and variable entering the doldrums, so don't forget that big genoa. The final 300 miles should be a fast reach with the wind high on the beam. Landfall on St. Thomas is easy, as there is a very bright light on Culebra Island to the westward, and radio tower lights are atop St. Thomas' 1,550-foot hills. Charlotte Amalie has grown so much that the loom is visible as much as 20–30 miles off.

The one difficulty with the Morehead City route is the Inland Waterway. With more than 7½′ draft I would advise checking what the actual depth is with someone who has recently traveled the Waterway. In 1962 in a boat drawing 6′ we frequently touched bottom in Currituck Sound in mid-channel.

Unless draft rules out the Waterway, I strongly recommend the Morehead City route. If you must do the whole trip offshore I advise going via Bermuda in two sections. In fact, unless one of these two routes can be used at the times mentioned, I would be inclined to advise against the trip. If it is made at other times, in the knowledge that circumstances will probably be unfavorable, make sure that the boat is perfectly equipped and that the crew is experienced. Practically every winter one or more boats have been lost enroute to the Virgin Islands. It is not a trip to be lightly undertaken. On the other hand, certain boats have made this trip numerous times with no difficulty. They are well equipped, well manned, have watched their weather, and, probably most important, the gods have been kind.

A check of various fall trips of 1963 is interesting. One 46′ ketch waited at Great Bridge, Va., near Norfolk for Hurricane Ginny to make up its mind in October and then went on to Morehead in the Waterway, waited until a depression off Antigua dissipated, then left with a favorable weather report and fair tide. She did 901 miles in five days, ran out of wind, turned on the iron genoa, and arrived in St. Thomas seven days, seven hours out of Morehead.

A large motorsailer left New York in early October, spent the next two weeks at sea dodging Hurricane Ginny and the depression off Antigua, and arrived in St. Thomas via Antigua, almost three weeks (and 2,000 miles) out of New York.

Another large yawl took off early in October from the Delaware Capes, was caught by Ginny as the storm went north, then got hit again when it turned south, spent 32 hours with sea anchor over the stern and took 13 days to reach St. Thomas. Another motorsailer left Morehead City with a favorable weather report in late November, carried southwesterlies well down towards 30th parallel, then motorsailed and had an uneventful trip.

As you near the islands, turn on the SSB radio and call WAH 2009 (or Channel 16 VHF). WAH maintains daytime radio communication and can patch through via the telephone and call anywhere in the world.

Coming directly from the States you have no entry to make, but if you have stopped in Bermuda you will have to clear. Hoist your Q flag and proceed to Sheraton Harbor Marina and call Immigration. They will instruct you on the latest clearance procedures. Make sure you moor stern to; the officials won't come out in a dinghy even if you provide it. Once cleared, there are numerous places within a few steps that can provide you with cold drinks. Once refreshed, move to Prince Rupert's Dockyard (western side of the harbor) or Yacht Haven in Long Bay and plan the continuation of your cruise as you contemplate your accomplishment in getting there.

2 ❧ Home Free to St. Thomas

EACH YEAR boats head south to the West Indies. Some boats do it year in, year out, with little or no difficulty, and frequently have a glorious sail. On the other hand, a few boats get in trouble. Boats are lost, sometimes with all hands, and not missed until they are long overdue. Others cry "May-

Sail, September 1974.

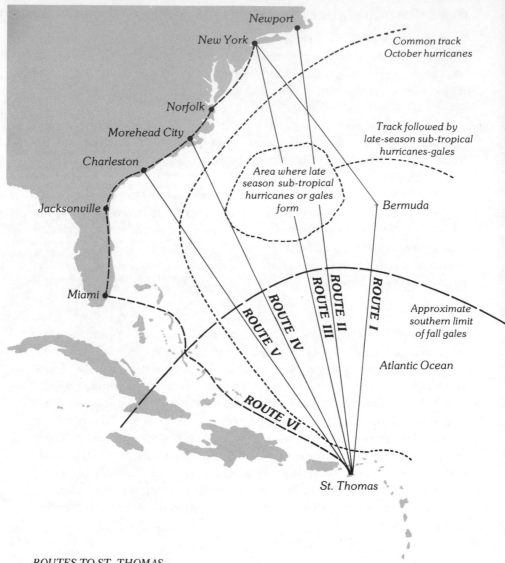

ROUTES TO ST. THOMAS

ROUTE I. New York-Bermuda 790 miles, Bermuda-St. Thomas 800 miles. Sometimes difficult landfall in Bermuda, crosses path of both late-season hurricanes and the small gales—subtropical hurricanes that form between Hatteras and Bermuda.

ROUTE II. Newport-St. Thomas 1,670 miles, crosses hurricane track, passes through area of late-season hurricane-gales that form between Hatteras and Bermuda.

ROUTE III. New York-St. Thomas 1,650 miles, same as II.

ROUTE IV. Morehead-St. Thomas, 1,160 miles, crosses hurricane track and the southeastern corner of the late-season subtropical hurricane-gale area. However, this is so day!" and are then the subject of a massive, expensive air/sea search, followed by a rescue and, at best, a salvage operation.

Some of the disasters and near-disasters can, of course, be blamed on unseaworthy boats and/or incompetent or insufficient crew. However, good boats and good crews have been lost en route to the islands.

When these boats with efficient crews get in trouble it is usually because they left at the wrong time of year, or took the wrong route, or a combination of these two reasons.

Off the East Coast of North America there are three distinct types of storms that can cause trouble for yachts offshore. Fronts come across the North American continent in a regular parade. As they pass off the coast, the wind goes northwest, blows, then slowly swings north, then northeast, east, and finally dies out. Sometimes they produce nothing but a single-reef breeze; at other times, especially from November through April, the front produces gale-force wind, and with it rain, sometimes freezing rain, sleet, or snow.

The second type of storms is hurricanes. These can be encountered off the East Coast from June through November. August and September are the worst hurricane months. July and October have the same frequency of hurricanes. June and November hurricanes are a rarity.

The third type of storm often went unreported prior to the establishment of weather satellites but has caused much trouble. This is a gale, sometimes referred to as a sub-tropical hurricane, that springs up between Cape Hatteras and Bermuda, frequently the result of a low-pressure area deepening and intensifying as it arrives over warm water. In a

---

close to Morehead that one should be able to cross this area on a good weather forecast. Inland from NY to Morehead safe but draft limited to 7'–8', not limited by overhead clearance.

ROUTE V.   Charleston-St. Thomas 1,200 miles, crosses late-season hurricane track, passes south of late-season subtropical hurricane-gale area, but so far west usually a lot of windward work. Draft limited to 7'; overhead bridge clearance limited to approx. 55'. Long waterway trip from NY.

ROUTE VI.   Miami-St. Thomas roughly 1,000 miles, most of it to windward; navigational and draft problems in Bahamas, plus 1,200 miles of inland waterway from NY.

Routes I, II, and *III* for large yachts only, Oct. 28–Nov. 21.

Route IV.   Best route Oct. 28–Nov. 21.

Route V.   After Nov. 21, go farther along the waterway to Charleston, until mid-December; after mid-December continue south to Jacksonville, then to Miami; then Route VI.

matter of hours, with little or no warning, a full gale develops, lasts for 24 to 36 hours, then dissipates or swings farther out to the east. These gales were seldom reported and their frequency vastly underrated prior to the establishment of the weather satellites whose photographs pick up this type of storm almost immediately upon formation. Previously, though intense, they were so small and their track was such that since they did not strike a land mass they often formed and died unreported.

The best months to sail in the island are in April, May, and early June. August and September are obviously out, as they are the height of the hurricane season. Many feel that October is a good month, and head south then. Others feel this is a drastic mistake. An examination of the records shows that almost every year at least one October hurricane passes up the East Coast, usually far enough offshore so that little or no damage is done on shore. However, the track of the hurricane is apt to cross the track of any yacht going south in October.

In 1973, more than a dozen yachts headed south in October. All were caught in or near the two hurricanes that came up the coast. One was lost with all hands, others were badly damaged. Many seamen feel that once it is blowing more than 65 knots, the average yacht's survival depends 65% on good seamanship, and 35% on plain good luck! One goof by a helmsman can do in the best of boats.

From late November through April the time of year is inauspicious to go offshore as the cold-weather gale-force winds just should not be messed with. A gale in summer is bad enough, but trying to handle a boat in freezing conditions when you are encased in multiple layers of clothes and foul-weather gear is difficult and dangerous.

Thus the last few days of October and the first three weeks of November are the only relatively safe periods to head south, unless one does the trip in two separate stages, as described in the preceding article.

Hurricanes. From 1887 to 1952 the following were reported by month: May—1; June—10; July—15; August—59; September—102; October—52; November—8; December—1.

Inspection of the weather charts shows that the percentage of gale frequencies between New York, Boston, and Bermuda is infinitely higher than the percentage of gales found on the rhumb-line route from Morehead City to St. Thomas. Frequency of gales in the fall: Boston, Bermuda, New York triangle is 10% to 15%, and on up, depending on exact location and the month of the year, reaching 23% in January and February. Gale percentages on the Morehead/St. Thomas route are at no time of the year more than 3% or 4%.

Even if they leave at the right time of year, many boats are still done in by taking the wrong route. A yacht leaving from New York or east has a full 800 miles to sail before she is clear of the area of gales. To traverse this distance will take at least six days. Obtaining a long-range weather forecast that can be relied on to cover this period is an impossibility, as the gales that develop often form without warning in a matter of hours.

For example in 1972, a 45′ keel/centerboard yawl left the eastern end of Long Island Sound in early November, had a splendid long-range weather forecast, enjoyed a comfortable trip to a point 300 miles east of Hatteras, and then ran smack into an unpredicted gale. She lay ahull, anemometer registering 90 in gusts, till one greybeard threw her on her beam ends. She came up, but she was minus her mizzenmast and all her winch handles, which had dropped out of the boots and into the bottom of the sea. Luckily no one was injured, but it was an expensive insurance claim.

Leaving from the Virginia Capes—the mouth of the Chesapeake—is the height of folly. Off the starboard bow lie the Outer Banks, with Cape Hatteras, the graveyard of literally thousands of ships, and a deadly lee shore in a northeast gale.

South of Hatteras, three days' easy steaming in the Waterway, lies Morehead City, the ideal spot from which to take a departure heading south. Three hundred miles—36 to 48 hours' sailing time—brings a yacht clear of the gale area. The course only touches the edge of the gale-ridden area between Hatteras and Bermuda. Moreover, six hours out of Morehead City is the Gulf Stream, with water and air warm enough to make snow, freezing rain, or sleet a remote possibility.

Many people who have experienced this route feel the best course is to sail coastwise to Cape May, then head straight for Norfolk, weather permitting. If the weather is so bad as to rule out the outside route between Cape May and Norfolk, one can go up the Delaware River, through the C & D Canal, then down through Chesapeake Bay to Norfolk. From Norfolk to Morehead City is three days in the Waterway with a chance for some good sailing part of the time.

Store ship in Morehead City (great for food, but buy beer in Virginia). Leave Morehead at the top of the tide with a good weather report, and hopefully on the face of a northwest front that will blow you offshore and across the Gulf Stream before it shifts to the northeast. With luck, the front will blow you down to and sometimes across the doldrums, home free to St. Thomas.

3 ❧ How *Not* to Go South

IN THE BOAT, at the right time of the year and via the right route, there is no reason why yachts cannot sail from the mainland to the Caribbean without difficulty. A few boats, and a handful of experienced sailors, are regular commuters each year.

With the increase in interest in southern waters, and with the great growth of chartering in the area, however, more and more boats are coming down the wrong way. Each year in the past ten or twelve, at least two boats a year have been lost, usually with loss of life as well, but these tragedies are not the subject of this article. Instead, this is an account of how some of the boats who got there made it against all odds. One way or another they managed to luck through, and they have no real right to still be alive today. Perhaps the story of some of their mishaps that can be told, instead of becoming lost mysteries of the sea, since they made it, will help to keep other fools from rushing in where angels fear to tread.

Just such was the 110′ schooner that finally arrived off the north coast of Puerto Rico after a tough trip down, suffering numerous breakdowns and the indignity of a tow into Charleston, S.C. Night came on as they neared the northeastern tip of the island, and, beating towards Culebra, fifteen miles east of Puerto Rico, on the port tack, they mistook the light at the eastern end of Puerto Rico for Culebra and sailed straight through La Cordillera, a string of exposed, unlit coral reefs extending eastward from the tip of the island. By pure luck they hit an unmarked gap in the reefs and sailed merrily through, finding themselves in Vieques Sound at daylight having come through a spot no one would try in broad daylight in a vessel half the size. Their luck was better than their navigation.

Luck can play a part in other ways. A delivery skipper picked up a rather tired sloop in New Jersey and took her down the Waterway to Morehead City, N.C. From here he took off for the islands at a later-than-recommended date in early December and had a nice beam reach in a 12-knot breeze to start with. Two days out, it became apparent that the transom and backstay chainplate were very wobbly, and the skipper thought of returning to the mainland, only to hear on the radio that it was blowing hard northwest near the coast, dead on the nose. Where he was it was pleasant and the wind fair, so he rigged a securing tackle around the radio-telephone insulator on the backstay and a strop around the after overhang to bolster up the shaky parts.

From here he held a fair wind for six days to St. Bart's and then had an easy reach to Grenada, where the boat was hauled. On inspection it could be seen that one good strong breeze would have parted the back-stay and transom from the rest of the boat, but a good seaman, with luck to match, managed to get through.

Choice of crew can be important, and sometimes it is hard to make the right estimate of someone's capabilities. A boat from Maine ended up shorthanded in the Chesapeake in November, 1967, and the skipper was able to sign on two officers from the Naval Academy Sailing Squadron. They seemed like good candidates, but shortly after leaving Morehead, the officers discovered that the bridge of a Navy ship is far different from the deck of a small sailboat.

One of the officers retired below and refused to appear on deck again, and the other was completely knocked out by seasickness. He was to have been the navigator, and this left the skipper pretty busy and pretty much in the dark.

On board, he had a transmitter that had an aircraft frequency and he gave a call to "any aircraft." Within a few minutes he had a reply from a Pan Am air freighter on the New York–San Juan route wanting to know his altitude.

The pilot was a bit surprised at the answer "anywhere from zero to thirty feet depending on what part of a wave I'm on." The sailor never could get a direct fix from the plane, but for the next few days he was in contact with passing aircraft and had at least an idea of what general part of the ocean he was in. When he picked up an island after a few days, his reviving navigator was sure it was St. Thomas. None of them had ever seen the Virgins, but it didn't look right to the skipper, and finally, by calling the Coast Guard on 2182, via bearings and descriptions of various islands, they were able to decide he was off Virgin Gorda, and a turn to the right brought him into St. Thomas.

He was lucky, because this is not far from notorious Anegada Reef, graveyard of many a vessel, including two well-known yachts in recent years. Despite these disasters, some people luck through with the most elementary kind of navigation. One system supposedly has it that you "steer east southeast from Morehead City until the butter melts, then south southeast, and you will hit St. Thomas or Puerto Rico."

This theory of navigation was supposedly developed many years ago when two St. Croix natives were hired to bring an old Bar Harbor 30 down from Morehead. They were good seamen and had sailed through all the West Indies, but they had never been north (and were very unhappy at the sight of their first snow in North Carolina, and at the cold during their first two days).

The butter melting rate was perhaps not quite right, because they ended in Haiti, to the west of Puerto Rico, by turning south southeast when the butter went soft. At least they knew where they were then, and just "turned left."

One incredible experience resulted from the November, 1967, storm that caused trouble for many boats on their way to the islands. This was a modern fiberglass sloop whose skipper was a good sailor but no navigator, and the crew consisted of two greenhorns. When the storm hit, they ran before it under storm jib and became completely lost. A wave came aboard and washed out the engine, which was low in the bilge, and with it went all electricity except a battery-operated depth sounder.

Just to see the "warmth of the light flashing round and round," the skipper turned it on and was a bit puzzled to pick up bottom at 60 fathoms, with rapid shoaling, when he thought he was far at sea in 2,000 fathoms. When it got down to ten fathoms he switched to reading the foot scale and got down to depths of as little as six and eight feet.

Checking the chart, he found the Silver Bank and said "Ah. Now I know where I am." So, he made a right turn and headed for San Salvador in the Bahamas, which sent him along the entire length of this notorious patch of water. With only a large-scale chart, he didn't realize that parts of the Silver Bank are almost bare, and it seems unbelievable that he was able to avoid breaking seas. The best reconstruction by those who know the area is that he entered the Bank at the eastern end inside the line of breakers and sailed its whole length behind them. How he managed to miss coral heads, reefs, and breakers and reach San Salvador safely is one of the miracles of the age.

The story I call the "Case of the Potato Lugger" is another one that shows how some people fail to realize the demands of navigation. One day an incredibly crude 35′ schooner sailed into English Harbour, Antigua. She made the native sloops look like yachts, and it turned out she had started life carrying potatoes in Newfoundland. Her owner had singlehanded her down from Canada, leaving in December, with a compass and a "National Geographic" map of the Western Hemisphere as his entire navigation equipment.

By sailing steadily south, he made a landfall on Barbuda, which of course he couldn't identify, saw some yachts heading toward the next island, and followed them into the harbor there. When he got inside he recognized the Dockyard from pictures and stepped ashore, saying, "Well, Antigua is where I wanted to be. There isn't much to this navigation business really, is there?"

Once I was accosted by some sailors who had come direct from St. Thomas to Grenada, and they complained that my sailing directions were not very accurate in my book, *A Cruising Guide to the Lesser Antilles.*

"You didn't say there was an island right on your recommended course."

It seems they had come without charts or navigation checks. They merely took my directions about steering 167′ from the end of St. Croix and hadn't read on to the warning about Avis Island. Setting the course, they did nothing more about navigating until mid-morning of the second day, when the crew called down the hatch to the skipper. "Hey, there's an island right in front of us."

Avis, less than half a mile long and only six feet high, is one of the hardest-to-find spots in the Caribbean and good navigators have spent many a wasted hour trying to locate it. (In 1974 the Royal Navy relocated it approximately 6 miles NW of it's charted position.) Luckily, our own happy-go-lucky characters came onto it in daylight and at least had a lookout of sorts.

Sometimes those who don't make it have luck of sorts, too. An experienced but fairly senior skipper left Buzzards Bay for the islands with a crew of young one-design sailors who proved fairly useless when they got in a gale offshore. Seasickness and exhaustion took their toll and the skipper decided to head back to the mainland.

Under storm jib, they were running before it on a dark night with the skipper asleep below when some talk of seeing lights filtered down from the youngsters who had the watch on deck. Struggling awake from exhausted sleep, to go on deck and check, the watch below realized it was too late when they felt her crunch aground and bounce rapidly forward. At least it was sand, and they drove so far up they could jump ashore from the bow. The boat was lost, but no lives.

A similar "landfall" was made by a trimaran arriving in the islands from Europe. They picked up lights identified as Antigua in very light going and the two most experienced crew members then went below, leaving a novice at the helm with instructions to wake them when the lights came closer. Without his realizing it, the breeze picked up, and the first thing they knew there was a tremendous crash and they were high and dry on a beach. It was near a hotel, so they walked to the bar and celebrated their arrival, toasting the hull conformation of a tri that allows upright beaching in shallow water.

Checking charts could have saved a southward-bound yacht real headaches in the Carolinas. A fixed bridge with 55-foot clearance, too low for the boat's mast, had been built across a channel at Morehead City, and they backtracked all the way to Norfolk. They had a rugged time battling around Cape Hatteras, never realizing that they could have gone back just two miles, taken the channel to Beaufort and gone out another channel with a drawbridge.

And so they come, some with luck despite bad planning and foolish mistakes, but the percentages do catch up, as the figures on boats lost attest: at least one or more boats a year in the twenty-two years I have lived in the islands. A departure from Morehead between October 25 and November 15 with an experienced crew, a well-equipped boat, and a good long-range weather forecast gives the best prospect of a safe and pleasant voyage to the islands.

4 ❧ Westward Across the Atlantic

TIMING PROBLEMS plague the sailor who wants to cross the Atlantic westward to the Lesser Antilles just as they plague him when he decides to head south from the US East Coast to the islands. There is no easy answer.

If you leave northern Europe in early September or late August, you will arrive in the Madeira, Salvage, Canary Island area in mid-September, much too early for a safe transatlantic crossing, since August, September, and October are still hurricane months. Although by the end of October the hurricane danger is largely past, you should not count on the likelihood of a decent passage before late November or early December at which time the trades have settled down to their winter reliability.

In the Lesser Antilles the "Christmas winds" herald the departure of the fall variables and lead to the winter trades. These Christmas winds come in strong and steady, but can arrive any time from mid-November straight through till early or mid-January. And even when the Christmas winds do blow in they can be a false herald. They might blow hard for a few weeks, die out for a few days' calm, then come in again as they did in 1976. I wrote this article on December 20 in a pre-Christmas-, post-Christmas-wind calm. It had blown like mad for two-and-a-half weeks, apparently announcing the arrival of a good windy winter; and then sud-

Sail, September 1977.

denly the fan was turned off. Boats that left the Canaries in the beginning of December probably sat around in mid-Atlantic becalmed.

As each month goes by, the trades become more and more settled, to the point that May, June, and July can be the best sailing months in the Lesser Antilles. When it blows in these months it blows a steady twelve to fourteen knots all day long with no calms whatsoever, whereas in winter it will blow hard, twenty to twenty-five for several days; then it will drop off to a light six to eight for a few days; and then it will build up again. A late March–April calm has arrived every year without fail for the more than twenty years I have been in the Eastern Caribbean. No one can explain why, but it arrives and knocks down windy April's average wind velocity to less than that of May, June, and July.

With few exceptions the fastest transatlantic crossings have been made in April, May, and early July, while many slow, 45- to 60-day passages were made in late October, November, and early December.

On *Arabella*, a ketch aboard which I crossed the Atlantic (as cook and apprentice navigator), we left the Canaries in May, 1956. We would have made a record passage that would still stand today if we had not turned north as we approached the longitude of the Lesser Antilles. Though *Arabella* was only forty-five feet overall, of heavy displacement, and towing a three-bladed "sea anchor," though we were carrying only main, mizzen staysail and windward twin headsail, we logged 2,156 miles in 11½ days, 187 per day, which is really going for a boat of her size and type. We had solid trades all the way across from the minute we left the Canaries until we turned north.

However, few boats leave northern Europe in the spring to summer in the Lesser Antilles. They spend their summer sailing in Europe and then come out. So getting to Madeira in the fall is the first order of business.

Since I live in the Lesser Antilles, I have listened to horror story after horror story about the difficulties of crossing the Bay of Biscay, rounding the corner of Spain, and reaching Madeira and the Canaries. The northern European usually leaves the Baltic during the autumn, works his way down the North Sea, and makes final preparations in the Solent for the jump across the Bay of Biscay. Similarly, the majority of English yachtsmen prepare for their jump across the Atlantic from the Solent, some stopping at Plymouth to make good deficiencies in gear discovered while beating down Channel.

The normal routine from Plymouth is to stand off on the starboard tack to clear Ushant, and then stand south across the Bay of Biscay. Usually it is a tough fight to work the boat far enough to the west to clear

Ushant and, often upon rounding that island, a southwesterly gale springs up, driving you into the Bay of Biscay. All the old seamanship manuals continually warned the merchant seaman never to become embayed (caught between two points of land with the prevailing wind driving the vessel farther and farther into the bay onto a lee shore). This is still the great danger in crossing the Bay of Biscay, as in the autumn, gales come piling into the Bay with alarming frequency.

On leaving Plymouth, far better than trying to clear Ushant, you should work your way down the Cornish coast where harbors are plentiful, at least as far as Falmouth, and here make a decision. If a favorable weather report gives you a good chance of crossing the Bay of Biscay before the next southwest gale comes in, it is best to jump south immediately to Point A, 480 miles southwest magnetic, and to clear Ushant by about fifty miles.

If the wind is southwest, head across to Ireland—the jump across to Ireland is well worthwhile (see Street, "Gateway to Europe," *Sail,* March 1977).

The great advantage of proceeding northwest from Falmouth over to Ireland is that you will be well to the west; and will be able to steer about SSW to Point B, 500 miles away, and clear Finisterre by 240 miles. If you wait until a front passes through and the wind goes west and veers into the northwest, you have a fairly good chance of getting across the Bay of Biscay before the next gale sets in. If a gale does arrive, at least given a few days of decent weather you should be completely off soundings in over 2,000 fathoms of water.

A course of southwest from Cape Clear leads off soundings in only 60 miles' sailing. One reason for the roughness of the Bay of Biscay is the fact that the Bay is relatively shallow. The Atlantic swells, coming on soundings, hump up to greater and greater heights. This route will also give you over 300 miles of sea-room. Thus even if you are caught in a gale and driven 100 or 200 miles into the Bay you are still not in too bad a position.

Once you are across the Bay of Biscay the time has come for you to make an important decision: do you stop at one of the ports along the Spanish or Portuguese coasts or do you continue on to Madeira? In 1975, on my yawl *Iolaire,* we continued south, with the glorious Portuguese trades behind us until we were about 100 miles south of Lisbon, when suddenly the wind switched around to the south and either blew like mad or died out completely. The wind was basically southerly, but when we were driven to the west of the rhumb line and tacked, the wind came in from the southwest; and when we were driven east of the rhumb line and tacked again, the wind came in from the southwest. We finally arrived in

Madeira fourteen days out, feeling very sorry for ourselves. Later we discovered that other boats with engines had taken even longer.

We were discouraged to find that in this instance, had we stopped in Spain or Portugal for a few days, the weather pattern would have switched back to normal since boats four or five days after us enjoyed consistent Portuguese trades right into Madeira. But stopping in Spain or Portugal can be dangerous. You can become weather-bound by westerly gales, and spend week after week waiting for a favorable forecast that will enable you to break free. And once you are south of Finisterre you will have difficulty obtaining a good weather report, as not many boats have bilingual crews that can translate the machine-gun static called Spanish or Portuguese that comes over the air.

We were slightly behind schedule as I had business to take care of and thus we could not tarry in Madeira, the Salvage, and the Canary Islands on this crossing, which was most unfortunate. Most yachtsmen view them merely as stopover points for fuel and water prior to departing across the Atlantic to the Lesser Antilles. But this is a very bad mistake— if you leave Madeira, the Salvage, and the Canary Islands too soon and head off across the Atlantic immediately, you are leaving before the trade winds really start to blow, usually have a slow passage, and miss some good cruising.

Madeira is warm or almost hot in the daytime, but at night the island is so high that cool air drops off the mountain. It is just like opening the door to a really good air-conditioning system to the extent that the normal attire in the evening in Madeira is tie and jacket (if you happen to be male). The temperature is not tropical and the jacket is comfortable.

The Salvage Islands are low and windswept, hot during the day, fairly cool at night, and can be cool during the day if the wind is in the north and it is overcast. Remember that the islands' latitude of 30° N means that they are quite far north.

The Canaries, 90 miles to the south, latitude 28°30′ N, are in normal circumstances not only warm but hot; they cool off in the evening but not so much as Madeira. It can get cool in the Canaries when the weather is bad, but in general the climate is practically the same as that of the Lesser Antilles. If a hard west wind starts blowing directly off the Sahara, it can be stifling, and in fact the Sahara sands can reduce visibility drastically over the Canaries. Also remember that the Canaries are not truly in the trade-wind belt.

The wind pattern of the Canaries is influenced by Africa, which means that violent storms can blow across the islands. In 1975, for example, a brief storm of almost hurricane velocity swept through and put about five yachts up on the beach as total losses.

You definitely ought to spend a few days in the Archipelago de Madeira. The two inhabited islands, Madeira and Porto Santo, are completely different. Porto Santo is lower than Madeira and is surrounded by beautiful white sand beaches. An excellent fishing bank extends off to the north of the island. A word of caution here: I would suggest that you obtain the Portuguese charts (from J. Garraio & Co., Avenida 24 de Julho 2, I.o.D., Portugal; and from Fernand B. Montejo, Lope de Rueda, No. 27. Madrid, Spain), since the locals claim there is a lot less water than the British Admiralty chart shows. If you like mile after mile of deserted beach, Porto Santo is for you, as it was for Columbus. As a young merchant captain he found his bride here in the person of Dona Felipa Perestrello e Moniz, whose father was hereditary governor of Porto Santo.

The islands of Ilheu Chao, Ilheu Deserta Grande, and Ilheu do Bugio are uninhabited, with high cliffs on all sides, and no harbors.

The main harbor in Madeira is Funchal. Anchor just west of the north/south pier at the eastern end of the harbor, and be sure to put down three anchors—two bow anchors to the southeast plus a stern anchor towards the shore. Although you will be dropping your bow anchors in about sixty feet of water, the anchors will hold since the bottom is mud and shelves off so steeply that you will be pulling them uphill with a narrow angle at the anchors. There is good reason for the three anchors. During the day an on-shore wind picks up from the southeast and reaches 12–15, possibly 25, by about 4:00 P.M. Then just at the point when you think the anchorage is becoming untenable someone turns off the fan; it goes flat calm; and within an hour a north or northwest offshore breeze comes down the hills, dropping the temperature about ten degrees.

One of the most interesting things in Funchal is watching the lovely old launches running back and forth to the cruise ships and across the harbor to the south pier. All the launches are long and narrow and beautifully maintained, and one is particularly famous, the *Mosquito,* which I photographed in 1956 when I came through aboard *Arabella.* Twenty years later *Mosquito* looked exactly the same. On checking her history I found that she was originally built as a steam launch and is thought to be over one hundred years old.

You can take tours all over the island, sledge rides down the hillsides, or you can hire a taxi to take you down to Conical to the whaling station where even if they are not actually whaling it is possible to buy all sorts of whale bone, whale teeth, and so on.

The small, picturesque fishing village of Camara de Lobos has an excellent restaurant overlooking the river. The cove is so small that the boats have to be pulled up on the beach every day when they come in from fishing. Since they fish at night, it is worth making a trip there late in the afternoon to watch the boats being launched, or you might arrive very early in the morning to watch them being pulled up.

There are numerous good restaurants in and around Funchal. The open-air market is excellent and a fish called *espada* is one of the ugliest but best-tasting I have ever eaten. The bakery is wonderful; so-called supermarket, merely adequate.

Because not many sailors speak Portuguese, it is lucky that Funchal has always had a large English-speaking colony dating back to the days when the island was important as a wireless and coaling station.

At eleven o'clock every morning, at the tourist office in Madeira, the meteorological bureau delivers a weather map which covers the whole Atlantic Ocean, so you can check the weather before you sail, and delay departure if necessary.

On the route from Madeira to Tenerife (160 miles, course south) lie the Salvage Islands (Ilheus Selvagens), so called because they are on a direct line from Madeira to Tenerife, Canary Islands. They are small and unlit and rise steeply from extremely deep water. The "salvage" islands have been nailing ships for the past 500 years. We had hoped at least to take a look at them in passing but, unfortunately and fortunately, we left with a good hard easterly and had the old *Iolaire* screaming along at 7½ knots. It was completely overcast, thus we had no hope of obtaining a sun line that afternoon or the following morning to ascertain whether we were steering a straight course or whether we were being set westward by the current. When the sun finally broke through we were twenty miles to leeward of the rhumb line and did not feel like beating back to windward to examine the islands. This we discovered subsequently was a mistake. Despite numerous inquiries, I have spoken to no one who has stopped at or even seen the islands, but have only picked up third-hand information which leads me to believe that they look like the Grenadines.

If the weather is good, why rush on to the Lesser Antilles when you can enjoy almost the same climate, same water and fishing conditions on the eastern side of the Atlantic as you will find in the Grenadines? The Salvages are completely unspoiled: no local inhabitants; no visiting yachts; no charter boats or tourists from cruise ships. And stopping at the Salvage Islands also gives you a chance to practice eyeball navigation before you arrive in the Lesser Antilles.

Salvagen Pequeno is dominated by Pic de Veads, 150 feet high, but the rest of the island is low and windswept with sparse, prickly vegetation. There are some coves where you can anchor with a moderate degree of shelter in settled conditions. An 85,000-ton tanker is aground off the northwest corner of the island. Reputedly, a good anchorage can be had in two fathoms off the southwest corner, but is strictly a case of eyeball navigation.

Salvagen Grande according to my source, an article in *Neptune Nautisme,* January 1976, by Patrick Van God, has an anchorage protected from the prevailing wind in Anse de Coyonas on the southwest corner of the island and has a dinghy landing in the dry stream bed.

The island is high, filled with puffins, and has good fishing (though not so good as Salvagen Pequeno) and excellent snorkeling.

I also heard that one yacht poked its nose into the Salvage Islands (more third-hand information, so I have not been able to ascertain whether they stopped at Salvagen Grande or Pequeno) and discovered that the islands were semi-inhabited during the fishing season. The owner or his representative was there, met the crew on landing, showed them around the island. He then sat them down at his house and fed them a great and glorious lunch—to me they sound like a group of islands which definitely need exploring! Consult French chart 5771, and British 365, and both American and British pilot books for more information. Since the above was written, the islands have been declared a bird sanctuary and permission must be gained at Funchal to visit the islands. If you are caught anchored in the islands without a permit, it means a fat fine and forced return to Funchal for a court hearing before one's yacht is released.

From the Salvage Islands you head south or southeast to the Canaries, depending which island you intend to visit. When Malcolm Horsely of *Stormvogel* was asked which islands in the Canaries should be visited, he said, "All of them."

While in the Canaries we met the crew of the motorsailing ketch *Hanover* from Hamburg, who have spent the last five years chartering throughout the Canaries, up to Madeira and back to the Canaries. Why *Hanover* never stopped at the Salvage Islands as they passed north and south from the Canaries to Madeira is beyond me; no one could offer any good explanation. They stated that all the Canaries were worth visiting, and also brought out their German charts to show me where visiting yachts should go. These German charts were much more up to date than our British ones, but when after reaching Antigua I ordered copies of Nos. 841 and 844 from Eckhardt and Messtorff, 2 Hamburg 11, Rodingsmarkt 16 (telephone 334374) we were sent uncorrected charts, older than the ones *Hanover* had on board in November and which were obviously not new then.

As with the Lesser Antilles, do not try to enter harbor at night. Spanish lights are rather unreliable at the best of times; and the Spanish government is in the midst of expanding and rebuilding the harbors in the Canaries. This means that the charts are completely out of date. Frequently, although they build a breakwater, they still leave the old leading lights without discontinuing them which leads the unwary into the new breakwater rather than into the harbor.

The commercial harbors are Las Palmas, Grande Canaria, and Santa Cruz de Tenerife. Don't use the main harbor in Tenerife but rather a smaller fishing harbor just to the east. The entrance is marked by the seven big oil tanks at the eastern end of the harbor. In general they are likely to be filthy with oil, especially if the wind goes to the southeast. The best thing to do in both places is to come in, secure, do your business, and get out to one of the new yacht harbors that are rapidly being built on the islands, or to one of the smaller Canaries.

Having last visited the Canary Islands in 1956, and having heard that we would be unable to stock a boat in the Canaries, we were pleasantly surprised when in Santa Cruz we discovered this information to be untrue. Although supplies were not cheap, you could more than adequately stock a boat with no trouble at all. The population of the Canaries is a mixture of French, German, Spanish, Portuguese, Italian, and Scandinavian, so if you go to the main supermarket you have a complete variety of types of meat, canned goods and dry goods to choose from. We even found the Kerrygold whole dried canned milk which we were unable to find in Ireland or England. If you spend a few hours at the supermarket (which delivers) plus a morning at the fresh-food market your yacht can be completely stored up for the transatlantic passage.

Get yourself stored, take a few bus tours around the islands, and depart the main commercial harbors. Then spend a week, two weeks or maybe even three exploring the Canaries and waiting for the trades to settle down. Obtain a good weather report verifying the fact, and take off.

Before you decide to leave the Canary Islands check the weather carefully to make sure that there will be wind enough to push you down into the trade-wind belt. It is most discouraging to leave the Canary Islands and spend three or four days becalmed in sight of the islands. It is better to stay ashore than to roll in the swell offshore.

Once you get a good weather report take off directly for the Lesser Antilles. Some boats attempt to head for the Cape Verde Islands and then across to shorten the longest leg of the trip. Practically everyone who has taken that route, except powerboat people who need to stop for fuel, has advised against it. The Cape Verde islands are dry, barren, almost a desert, singularly unattractive. They are one of the few places where peo-

ple arrive, get their fuel, take a look ashore, go back to the boat, and
depart immediately.

Also, you have the problem of very strong currents and poor visibility
to the point where boats have suddenly found themselves in the breakers
where they can't see a 5,000-foot-high island a few miles off. If you
wonder about going to the Cape Verde Islands, just read the description
of the Cape Verde Islands in the American and British pilot books and you
will avoid them like the plague.

Rather, when departing the Canary Islands, head roughly southwest; forget about the great circle course. You are interested in getting
down to the trades and carrying the trades across rather than in minimizing the distance. Check the pilot charts for the month and the
average barometer reading; work your way southwestwards watching
your barometer. When the barometer begins to rise above normal, take a
more southerly course, as the rising barometer will probably mean that
the Azores high has moved south of this position. The Azores high will
obliterate your wind.

When crossing the Atlantic you should be rigged for all conditions. A
description of *Iolaire*'s crossing is rather typical: We left the Canaries
under reefed main and staysail; once clear of the islands we swung off to
a southwesterly course, doused the main, set a roller-furling staysail on
the spinnaker pole, and surged off at seven-and-a-half to eight knots
under staysail only. After a day and a half of this, the wind moderated and
we set a light, reaching staysail on the other side to the other spinnaker
pole. As days went by, the wind moderated. We rolled up one staysail and
attached the pole to the medium genoa. The wind moderated more and
we sheeted the large genoa out to the end of the mainboom, replacing the
light, reaching staysail. Then we added the mizzen staysail and we
chugged along, averaging a little over 160 miles a day for nine days,
seeing only the occasional whitecap. The wind picked up for a few days,
swung around to the southwest and suddenly died out almost completely.
We found ourselves beating hard to windward on port tack, rail down
under normal working canvas and unable to lay west. Then the wind died
again; then it came in dead aft, so we set the light spinnaker. After about
eighteen hours the wind began to increase. We doused spinnaker,
switched to twin genoas, and slowly reversed the process of sail changing
we had experienced on the other side of the Atlantic until we were back
down to roller-furling staysail alone on one pole. We were at hull speed
when we made our landfall in Desirade eighteen days out of the Canaries.

Remember that self-steering gear takes a terrible beating on the trip
across. You should carry spare parts and should check your gear carefully
before you leave the Canaries.

Two of the biggest problems you will encounter when crossing the "Pond" are sunburn and heat. To minimize damage from the former, buy some big straw hats in Madeira or the Canaries, tie strings to them, tie them to the shirt you are wearing, and, even if they blow off, they will still be attached to the shirt. Secondly don't worry—no matter how much you cover up, by the time you reach the Lesser Antilles, you will be tanned. When in doubt cover up. Bring plenty of cream to bar all suntan, for use on face, back of the hands, and top of the feet.

Sailing across in the trade-wind route the sun comes up dead astern; by 10:00 it is shining down on the deck with an awful lot of heat and stays up overhead, blazing down on the deck until late in the afternoon when it disappears behind the headsails. Thus, for about four to six hours a day, you should rig a small cockpit awning so that the helmsman and anyone relaxing on deck can do so in the shade.

Heat below decks is always a problem, especially if the boat is not well ventilated. Crews heading to the Lesser Antilles should really attack the ventilation problem before they leave, but even the best ventilated boats get hot when they are running dead downwind.

On *Iolaire* (an extremely well-ventilated boat) we opened the forecastle hatch and rigged our large galley staysail into the forecastle and left it there continually. As rain squalls came by we tied a sailstop around it and flipped the hatch closed, opening the hatch immediately after the squall passed. This produced a good air flow through the entire boat, cooling it off drastically at night and making it cool during the day to the point that the thermometer hanging in the overhead in the main cabin never rose above 79 from the Canaries to the Lesser Antilles. Surging along at hull speed in the low-freeboard *Iolaire,* there was always a lot of water on deck aft—but the foredeck was usually dry. And seldom did any water come down the forecastle hatch from the Canaries to Desirade.

Despite the fact that it is hot during the day, remember that at night if it is blowing hard, especially if it is squally, good foul-weather gear, a light wool sweater, a watch cap, sneakers, and socks or seaboots and socks (depending on the weather conditions) make life comfortable.

Regarding fishing: counting on catching fish all the way across the Atlantic is a dead loss as an idea—since the only thing you usually catch is a log line (your own) which can make a godawful mess. On boats with high bulwarks, especially if they are painted white and the boat is fairly low freeboard, you can expect four or five flying fish on board every night. Cooking them so that they taste good is difficult unless you have a Bajan cookbook on board. In Barbados, flying fish is a delicacy, but if you don't use a Bajan recipe the flying fish taste rather oily.

However, you should keep fishing gear handy because if you become becalmed or are sailing slowly, very likely a large dolphin—*dorado* in Spanish—will come by, attracted by the shade under the bilge of the boat. This happened to us when we were becalmed, but by the time we got out the fishing gear stowed in the bottom of the lazarette, we made so much noise banging around that the *dorado* was scared off.

Do not be tempted to go swimming overside if you are becalmed in mid-Atlantic as, although the sharks in the Lesser Antilles know the rule: "Don't bite visiting tourists or visiting yachtsmen," sharks in mid-Atlantic don't know that rule and will swallow up anything.

Regarding landfalls and direction-finder stations, check the light list and the frequencies on your radio as you will not be able to receive some of the DF stations in the Lesser Antilles on the average direction-finder frequency. However, it is not too difficult as you can always use the commercial radio stations in the islands as DF beacons but make sure you have the right station attached to the right island.

The Lesser Antilles are not particularly well lit and in fact when you are coming across the Atlantic the only lights you can really rely on are those of Desirade on the eastern end of Guadeloupe, Tartante, midway down the east coast of Martinique, Vieux Fort on the southern end of St. Lucia, and the lights of Barbados.

Tartante and Vieux Fort are not good landfalls, as once the light is picked up and a landfall is made the harbors are a long day's sail away from the light. Thus Barbados and Desirade are the two best. The lights of Barbados are close to the normal yacht anchorage; the lights of Desirade form a good landfall for continuing on fifty-odd miles on a reach or run from Desirade direct to English Harbour, Antigua. Do not attempt to enter English Harbour at night.

If you arrive at Barbados, swing around the south end of the island, sail up to the anchorage off the Careenage, hoist your flag, and hope. Do not go into the main steamer dock under any circumstances. If no one comes out, row ashore to the harbor master's office and make inquiries. In years gone by, Barbados was the most pleasant island in the Lesser Antilles to clear into. Shortly after you got in, a long lean launch would come alongside with the harbor police, dressed as the sailors were dressed in Nelson's day, accompanied by smartly uniformed customs and immigration officers. They would promptly and efficiently clear you in very short order. Today, one hears various reports from Barbados: sometimes they are supremely efficient; sometimes supremely inefficient. Cross your fingers and hope.

If you are entering English Harbour, sail in and anchor or warp stern-to if space is available and hoist your Q flag. Then the skipper should go down to the police station inside the dockyard gate to find the customs and immigration.

No landfall in the Lesser Antilles should be made north of Desirade, as north of that point there is not a single reliable light visible from the east. Remember that Barbuda has approximately 250 wrecks on its reefs, Anguilla probably 150, Anegada well over 300. Don't add to the total.

If your landfall is Barbados, remember that one of the nicest islands in the Lesser Antilles is Tobago. This island is seldom visited because a beat to windward out to Tobago from the main chain in the Lesser Antilles is difficult in the extreme; however, it is a nice easy reach from Barbados. Be sure to enter at Scarborough and stop nowhere until you have entered. Spend some time cruising the island. It is incomparably beautiful and quite unspoilt. When you tire of Tobago you then have an easy beam-reach over to Grenada. From there you can work your way northwards through the chain.

In crossing the Pond westward you should remember that the hardest part of the trip is from northern Europe to Madeira. Once you reach Madeira, it is really duck soup from there on. If decent weather— steady trades—is encountered leaving the Canaries and if you have a boat that is equipped to sail in light airs, you should be able to sail the approximately 2,700 miles at not too far below hull speed, probably 1.2 × the square root of the waterline length, or for heavy cruising boats towing big propellers, the square root of the waterline length, *provided* the boat will sail well in light airs. If the boat is a dog in light airs, load stores for a long trip. The traffic you will encounter in coming across the Atlantic from the Canaries to the Lesser Antilles is minimal. The chance of stopping a freighter to pick up additional supplies is virtually nonexistent.

The longest jump across the Atlantic westward is considerably longer than across the Pond eastward, but it is a much easier and much more relaxing trip—good sailing.

II

Cruising the
Lesser Antilles

5 ❧ Little Known Anchorages

The Virgin Islands

THE SOUTH COASTS OF Puerto Rico, the Passage Islands, Vieques and
Culebra, provide an excellent cruising area. East of Puerto Rico lie the incomparable cruising grounds of the U.S. and British Virgin Islands. The
Virgins consist of six major islands and numerous small islands and cays,
all overlapping. They are small enough not to break the force of the
trades, but large enough to break the force of the sea, and close enough
so that one can limit the jumps between coves to short sails of two to
three hours.

Puerto Rico and the U.S. Virgin Islands are fortunate in that most of
the islands were resurveyed in the 1930s and 1940s and detailed charts of
1:10,000 are available. Unfortunately, this cannot be said for most of the
other Caribbean islands to the east and south.

In the Virgin Islands, it has been said that finding an anchorage all to
yourself is a thing of the past. I will have to agree with that statement, if
you insist on sticking to the major, well-known anchorages. Actually,
there are literally hundreds of other anchorages in these islands, many
more than might be apparent by looking at the government charts.

So, while there may be crowded anchorages in the Virgins there are,
at the same time, practically unlimited opportunities to get away from the
crowd for the good sailor who wants to explore a little. But you must
remember that these "out-of-the-way" harbors often are either improp-
erly charted or are charted to such a small scale that it is difficult to figure
out the exact location of the rocks. Therefore, when you enter one of
these out-of-the-way harbors, you should enter and leave only between
the hours of ten in the morning and three in the afternoon—while the
sun is high. Remember, an overcast day can make it impossible to use
these habors, even during midday, for a heavy overcast can distort the
color of the water and water color is by far the best indication of available
depth.

Despite what some cruising guides say to the contrary, I feel strongly
that cruising the Virgin Islands with only chart NOS 905 on board is fool-

ish. Doing so may be the cause of many of the groundings suffered by
strangers to the area.

Normal procedure in St. Thomas, after picking up a boat, is to depart
immediately for Christmas Cove on the west side of Great St. James
Island. However you can often arrive some time in the afternoon and discover twelve boats anchored. A much better first afternoon run in my
mind is to leave Long Bay, run westward through St. Thomas Harbor
through Haulover Cut, through Gregerie Channel and on to Little Saba
Island (Fig. 1). Off the sand beach at the north end is a secluded anchorage that is good in all normal weather. It may be a little bit rolly but you
will be almost guaranteed to have the anchorage to yourself. There is
good snorkeling off the beach, and, if the weather is calm, snorkel on Dry
Rocks, a few hundred yards to the west.

Fig. 1.

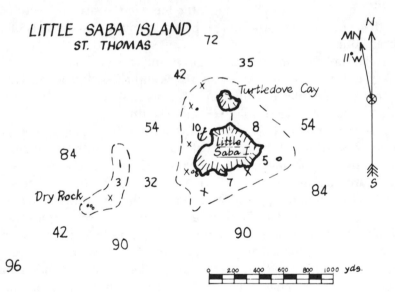

People who don't want to sail to leeward on leaving Long Bay, stand
to the south to Buck Island (NOS 933) where the anchorage off the small
dock underneath the lighthouse is excellent. Sail in as close as possible to
the dock, (there is ten feet of water right up to the dock) and anchor. In
late spring and summer if the wind is in the southeast, there is a good anchorage on the north side of Buck Island, off the white sand beach; not
usable in winter at all.

Moving eastward, there is a good anchorage at the northeast corner
of Great St. James (Fig. 2). The chart does not show either enough

Fig. 2.

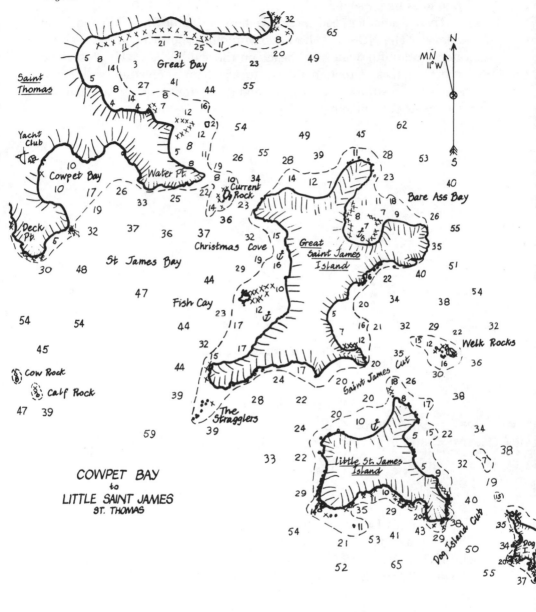

COWPET BAY
to
LITTLE SAINT JAMES
ST. THOMAS

shelter or enough water to anchor; however, it is a favorite spot of refuge for the oldtimers, especially those with a girlfriend in tow. Locally, it is referred to as Bare Ass Bay.

There is another good anchorage between Little St. James and Great St. James. The NOS 938 shows no soundings; however, there is ample water, a beautiful white sand beach on the south side of the passage on Little St. James. Although this is an excellent anchorage, remember, there is a very strong reversing tide and if you are spending the night set up a proper Bahamian moor (Fig. 3).

Fig. 3.

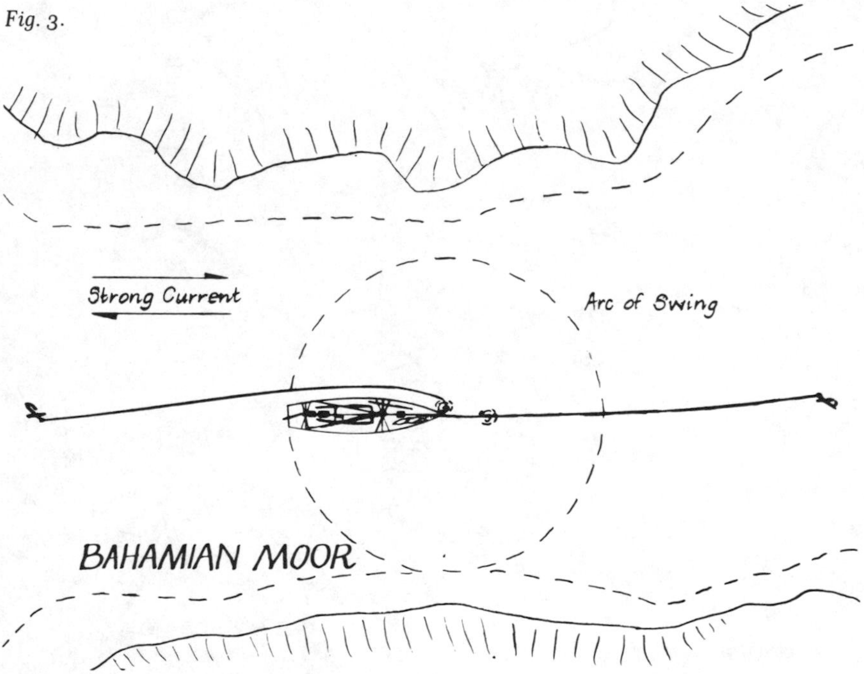

Strong Current

Arc of Swing

BAHAMIAN MOOR

St. John's Island has two small bays on the north side that do not show on the chart. Haul Over Bay (Fig. 4) was frequently used by local sloops. They would pick up cargo in St. Thomas, sail up through Current Cut to Pillsbury Sound, up Sir Francis Drake Channel, moor in Haul Over Bay, offload cargo to be discharged at Coral Harbor, cart it over the low land to Round Bay where it would be transferred into waiting small boats to be rowed downwind to Coral Bay.

When you are sailing along the coast, there doesn't appear to be any shelter in Haul Over Bay. But there is an excellent anchorage in the

Fig. 4.

EASTERN END of SAINT JOHN

southeast corner in all normal weather. Boats drawing up to eight feet
can easily use this Bay. But you *must* be in the southeast corner, and a
proper Bahamian moor is urged. If, however, you arrive at Haul Over Bay
and discover it is already occupied, do not despair. Just east of the Bay is
another tiny bay. It cannot be used if the wind is north of east. But if it's
east or south of east and you draw less than five feet, try New Found Bay
(Fig. 4). Entering is not easy, for you must run-in downwind between the
reefs; it's strictly eyeball navigation on a course approximately southeast.
Make sure you are under short sail and on port tack. Once you have
passed between the reefs, round up to port, douse the sail, and drop
anchor. This is definitely a place to use a Bahamian moor, and, I must tell
you, there is only room for one boat.

Roadtown Harbor is completely changed. Do *not* use NOS 137, but
the British chart (2020) is relatively correct.

Everyone knows the popular anchorages on Peter Island, Great Harbor, Little Harbor, Sprat Bay, and Dead Man's Bay. Dead Man's is over-
rated for there is almost always a swell rolling in, which makes the anchorage rather uncomfortable. Few sailors know about the excellent
anchorages on the south side of Peter Island which are impossible to find
on the normal charts. One of the best is what I call South Sprat Bay
(Fig. 5). Reefs extend out on both sides from both points of land, and you
must round up smartly and anchor in the middle. There is eight feet of
water, and again there's only room for one boat. Use a Bahamian moor.
If the wind is north of east, there is a good anchorage eastwards of South
Sprat Bay behind Key Point. There is a good sand bottom for anchoring
off the white beach. Just feel your way and anchor when Carrot Rock
appears before Key Point and Key Island.

East of Key Point lies White Bay, another excellent anchorage close
in to shore. It has a beautiful white sand beach, but is not an all-weather
anchorage, for at times the ground swell does roll in which has built up
that wonderful sand beach.

South of White Sand Bay lies Whelk Bay with a gravelly beach. It's
an excellent anchorage in all weather and a wonderful spot to find
whelks, those delicious seagoing snails.

Norman Island has a very popular overnight anchorage in the Bight,
and some people use the anchorage south of Water Point. However, two
other anchorages seldom have any boats. Benures Bay (Fig. 6), on the
north side, has an excellent anchorage off the beach in the southeast
corner of the Bay as long as the wind stays in the east, or south of east.
Feel your way in and anchor at suitable depth. The wind sweeps across
the low land between twin 250′-high peaks making the area cool and bug-
free.

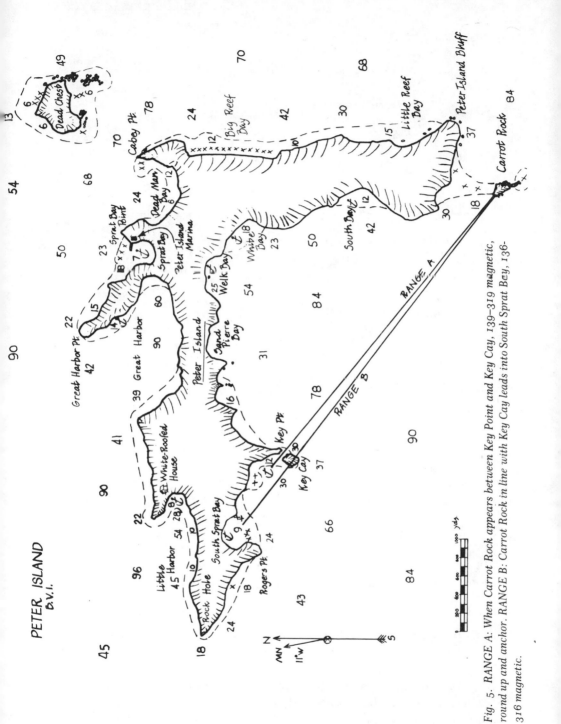

Fig. 5. RANGE A: When Carrot Rock appears between Key Point and Key Cay, 139–319 magnetic, round up and anchor. RANGE B: Carrot Rock in line with Key Cay leads into South Sprat Bay, 136–316 magnetic.

Fig. 6.

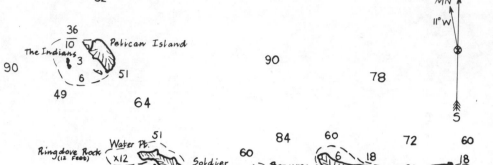

NORMAN ISLAND
B.V.I.

If the wind is north of east, especially northeast, sail around the eastern end of Norman Island and enter Money Bay. There is a white sand beach, and you can anchor in two fathoms of sand with good holding bottom. This is a restricted anchorage, and you must use a Bahamian moor.

West of Money Bay is a reef-sheltered cove accessible to those with skill, guts and a little luck thrown in.

Bluff Bay on the south side of Beef Island is another seldom-used anchorage that is excellent in all weathers. But again it's only for the skillful.

Most of the remaining British Virgin Islands are well covered by the charts. Little need be said about them if one is careful to look at the chart and use it. However, the charts do not discuss weather conditions and this is a big factor. The entire western coast of Virgin Gorda, for example, is exposed to ground swell, and anchorages there should be considered accordingly.

The western entrance to Virgin Gorda between Mosquito Island and Virgin Gorda should not be used under any circumstances when a ground swell is running, for it will frequently break almost all the way across the entrance. With a ground swell running, use the northwestern entrance to Gorda Sound. And be careful, for even well-sailed bare-boat charters are continually going windward when entering Gorda Sound. The groundings usually are caused by carelessness and the fact that they are probably using NOS 905 rather than detailed chart OS 25244 or BA 2016.

There is one good anchorage on the eastern side of Virgin Gorda. It is not well marked on the chart and should only be used by experienced sailors who are accustomed to operating in the tropics and judging depth by the color of the water. Many experienced Virgin Island sailors will be angry when I mention South Sound, their private anchorage (Fig. 7). However, I must point out that the seven-mile beat from Round Rock passage to South Sound will soon separate the men from the boys; for there is nothing to windward to break the 3,000-mile sweep of wind and sea across the Atlantic.

South Sound is indeed a beautiful, windswept anchorage. You enter by finding the break in the reef west of Lance's Bluff; the course is approximately northwest. Pass through the break in the reef and stay on either side of the one-fathom patch in mid-channel. Follow around to port behind the reef heading south to Matte Point. You can anchor a little south of that point behind the reef. This is a good anchorage when the wind is either in the north, or in the summer when it is not blowing particularly hard. Never attempt it in heavy weather.

Ross Norgrove, an experienced charter skipper, sounded this area in a whaler and found twelve feet until he reached South Creek. There he still found six to eight feet inside, and he regards South Creek as a good hurricane hole; but again for one boat only.

There are the ruins of an old Spanish estate house overlooking the anchorage and cattle graze on the hillsides. An unusual feature here uncommon in the Virgin Islands is the fact that fresh water can be had by digging a hole three to four feet deep.

If you are heading back to St. Thomas and the wind is not out of the south, this is a good time to investigate the south coast of St. John (Fig. 8) which is not shown in detail on any British or U.S. chart.

These short descriptions have outlined just a few of the many undis-

Fig. 7.

to Great Hill

SOUTH SOUND
VIRGIN GORDA

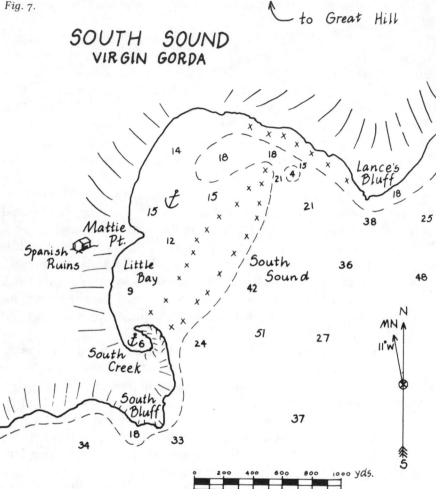

covered anchorages that do exist in the Virgin Islands. Many more are equally good, but there is just not enough space to discuss them here. But hopefully you can see that many quiet places do still exist; it just takes a little bit longer to find them than it used to.

Anguilla to Antigua

Many sailors who are familiar with the Virgin Islands are intrigued by the area to the eastwards; but relatively few people are familiar with the interesting cruising area from Anguilla to Antiqua.

This area has been neglected by sailors in the past for a variety of

Fig. 8.

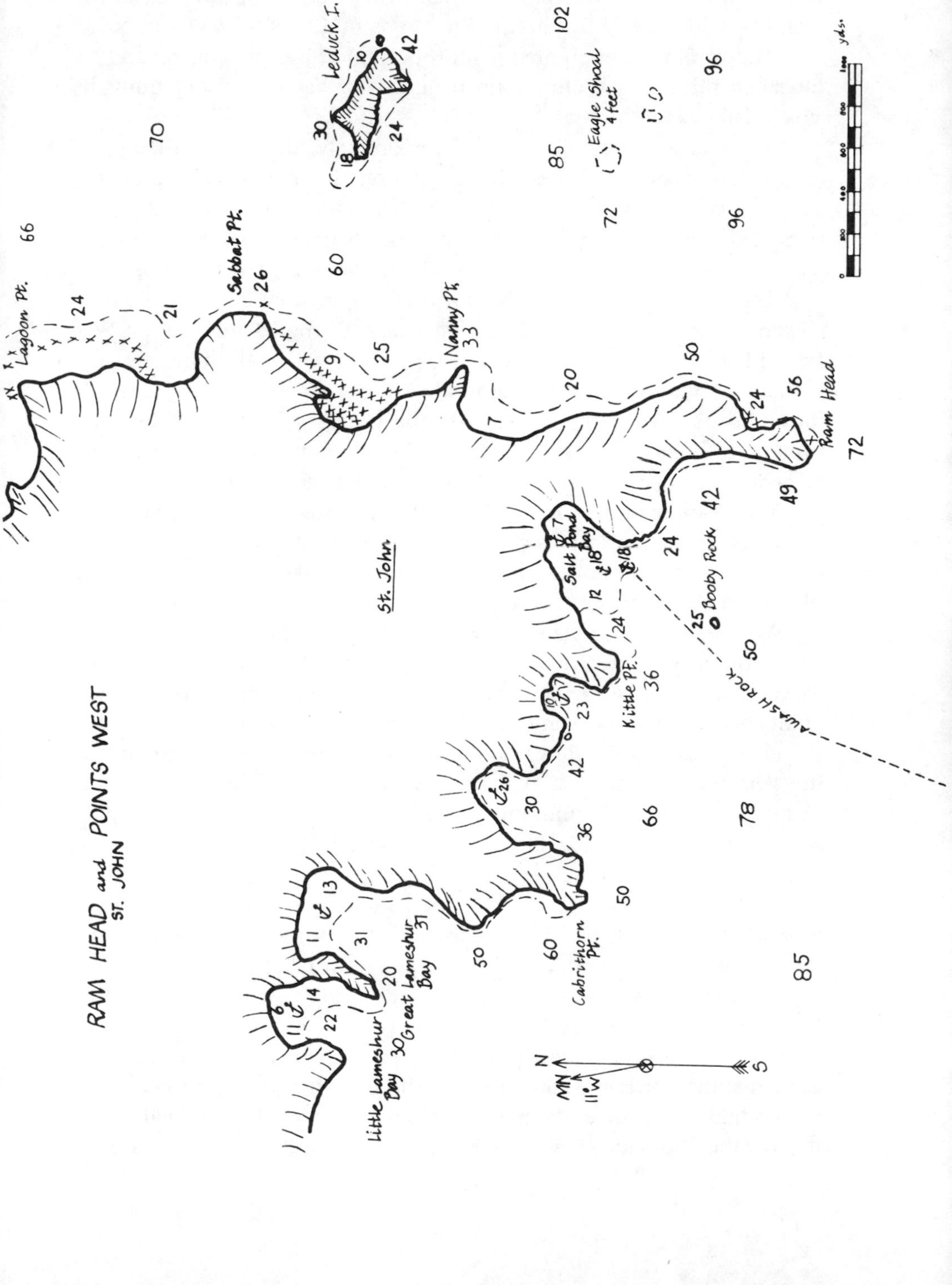

RAM HEAD and POINTS WEST
ST. JOHN

St. John

Keduck I.

Eagle Shoal
4 feet

Lagoon Pt.

Sabbat Pt.

Nanny Pt.

Ram Head

Salt Pond Bay

Booby Rock

AWASH ROCK

Kittle Pt.

Cabrithorn Pt.

Great Lameshur Bay

Little Lameshur Bay

N
MN
11°W
S

yds.

good reasons. The charts, especially those of Anguilla/St. Martins/St. Barts, are inaccurate in the extreme. Further they are such small scale as to be almost useless for exploring small coves; i.e., B.A. 2038 scale is 1 in 174,000, while the U.S. Chart OS 25241 is in a scale of 1 in 145,000.

And until the Dutch dredged through into Simsons Lagoon and established marinas, absolutely no facilities for yachts existed from the Virgin Islands to Antigua.

Anguilla is a low, flat island approximately fifteen miles long and very sparsely populated. It supports itself mainly by fishing, smuggling, cargo carrying (Anguilla had the last of the all-sail commercial schooners), and boat building. Tourism is practically nonexistent so Anguilla is a good island to visit to see what the islands were like twenty years ago.

The off-lying islands to the north of Anguilla (Fig. 1) that extend eleven miles from West Cay off Dog Island to the eastern end of Seal Island Reefs, are wonderful spots to explore. Given good conditions, that is, not too much wind and no ground sea, numerous anchorages can be found in this area. Diving is superb; the waters are not yet fished out; numerous wrecks lure the skin diver—exactly how many no one knows as no accurate list of wrecks has been compiled.

Because the north coast of Anguilla is exposed to the ground sea almost all winter, this coast is good in the summer but not in winter. However, the south coast coves are always excellent unless the wind begins to blow hard out of the southeast.

Westward of Anguilla Point are two superb anchorages in the northeast corners of Rendezvous and Coal Bay. For both bays, anchor as close as you can to shore in the northeast corner; be careful of the eastern points because the rocks and shoals extend further southwestward than the chart shows. Keep your lead line and/or fathometer going when feeling your way in, as the water is so crystal clear you will think you are about ready to run aground. But you will discover you are in twelve to fifteen feet of water. Mile after mile of beautiful deserted white sand beaches stretch off to the westward.

St. Martins, five miles south of Anguilla, has been invaded by tourism and probably will, in the not-too-distant future, go the same commercial way as St. Thomas and the U.S. Virgin Islands.

However, the charts don't show, and people do not realize, that Orient Bay in the northeast corner of St. Martins is completely inaccessible by road. It is only visited by a few fishermen who live in the area. The islands at the north and south ends of the Bay offer perfect protection in all conditions and an anchorage that almost guarantees there will be few if any other human beings in sight during the entire time you are an-

Fig. 1.

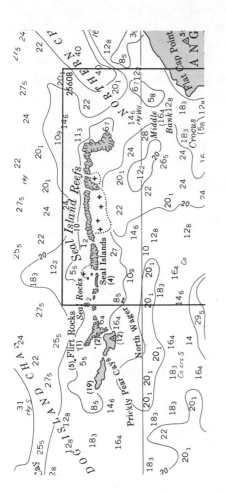

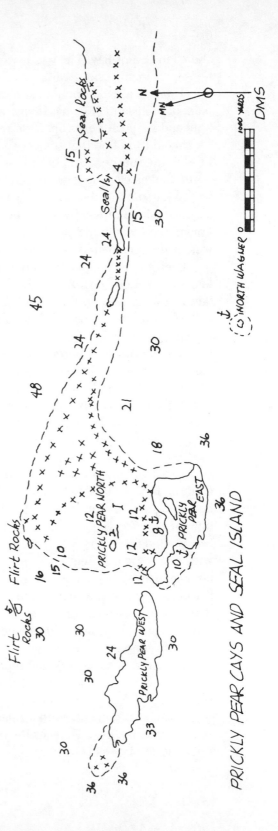

PRICKLY PEAR CAYS AND SEAL ISLAND

chored in Orient Bay. The wind sweeping unobstructed across the Atlantic is built-in air conditioning.

There is a good anchorage behind Islet Pinel west of the southern point of the island (Fig. 2). If you come in from the southeast with good light and keep your eyes open, you will have no problems.

Should you find that someone is already anchored behind Islet Pinel, head to the southern end of Orient Bay approaching Cay Verte from the north. Sail as close to leeward of Cay Verte as water permits; work your way as far south as the depth of water will allow; round up and anchor. A deserted island to windward is there for the exploring. Good snorkeling among the reefs to the south, cow pastures and deserted beaches to the west: what more could one ask?

Each time I approach St. Barts, I feel that I will be disappointed. I fear that modern civilization and tourism with its problems must certainly have arrived on the island since my last visit. Time cannot stand still. However, in St. Barts, although time has not stood still, the clock is running very slowly.

The chart for St. Barts is almost completely wrong as the main harbor is no longer as charted. Gustavia (Fig. 3) has, for the second time in ten years, been dredged. This time the dredging went all the way to the head of the harbor thus producing twelve feet of water almost to the bulkhead. Anchor anywhere.

The best system is to anchor fairly close to shore and run a stern line ashore as the wind boxes the compass at night. The harbor is none too clean, so if you like an early morning swim, anchor north of the harbor in Curasol Bay or Publiken Bay. Both of these have clean white sand beaches and pleasant swimming. The northern bay has a good small restaurant ashore.

Barbuda is a very attractive island that should be visited by yachts with much greater frequency than it is. It is a diver's delight with mile after mile of reefs plus approximately 300 wrecks. Conditions for spear fishing and snorkeling are superb. There are miles of deserted beaches as there are only two hotels and a very small population. The archaeologist can find Arawak artifacts; the sheller will be in heaven; this is apparently the ideal island.

However, it has a very bad reputation since none of the anchorages are really secure. Anchorage off the west coast of the island is excellent in summer, but almost impossible in winter with ground swell.

The charts don't show that Spanish Point and its off-lying reefs give protection to the east; Palaster Reef gives protection to the west breaking up the ground swell (Fig. 4).

Fig. 2.

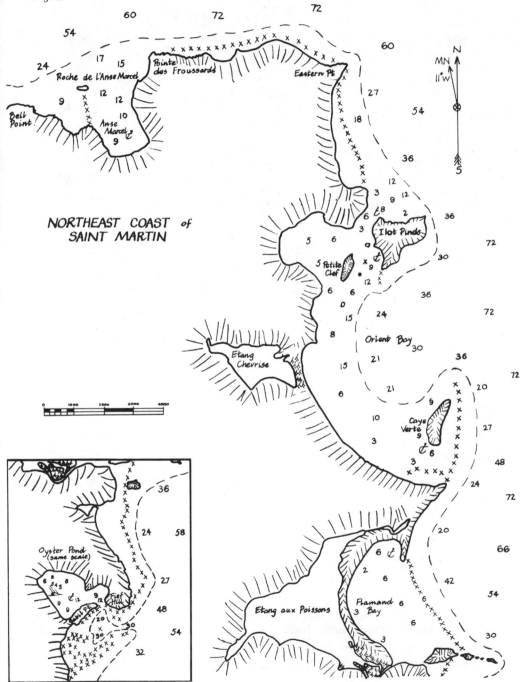

NORTHEAST COAST of
SAINT MARTIN

Fig. 3.

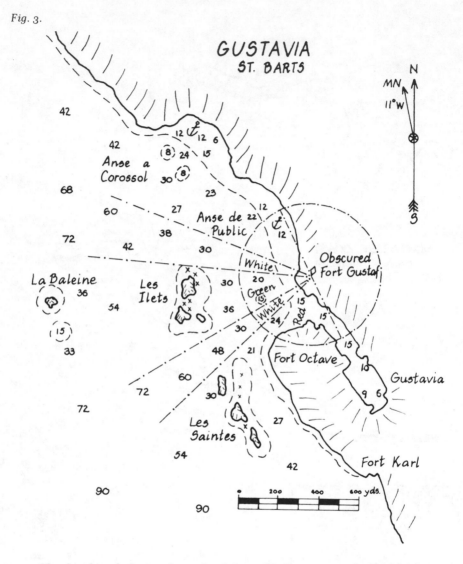

GUSTAVIA
ST. BARTS

The land and the reef south of Spanish Point completely block out the Atlantic swell while the trades sweep in from Africa, thus making this an excellent anchorage with ten to twelve feet of water good in all weathers.

The anchorage can be approached from the west from Coco Point by threading your way through the reefs. Care must be exerted as it is a zig-zag course because of the need to dodge the isolated coral heads. Spanish Point anchorage may also be approached from the south to windward of

Fig. 4.

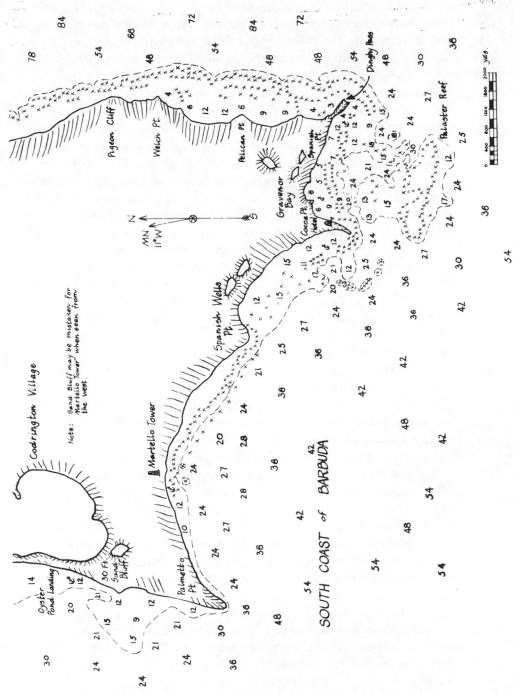

Palaster Reef. Here you must be really careful as the eastern end of Palaster Reef is hard to spot.

Once north of Palaster Reef, head for the breakers south of Spanish
Point; pass to leeward of the reef; then round up slowly and work your
way in as close to the shore as your draft will permit. Upon anchoring,
you are greeted with perfect beaches, a small thatched-roof shelter which
gives shade for a picnic, splendid diving, fishing, snorkeling, et al.

The chart does not show that in settled conditions you can work your
way inside Palaster Reef and explore the reef to your heart's content. In
settled conditions you may remain for the night inside the reef.

Although Antigua is well known to yachtsmen, few people realize
what Antigua has to offer. To most sailors, Antigua is English Harbour,
good air communications to the United States, an expensive taxi drive
from English Harbour either to town or the airport. They fail to realize
that Antigua has innumerable, wonderful little coves, good beaches, and
good snorkeling. Many of the island's coves are completely inaccessible
by road, thus you are almost guaranteed to be undisturbed.

The charts are relatively accurate, but it is best to use the U.S.
Charts. When the British reprinted their charts on Antigua, they discon-
tinued all the old ranges which are most useful in sailing around the
island. Detailed charts are necessary, as in many cases errors in the detailed chart have been corrected, but the general chart for the island
has not been overhauled.

A full week's cruise can be taken in Antigua with a different anchorage every night, many of them shared with few, if any, boats.

It is only a short beat from English Harbour to Nonsuch Bay, which
has so many anchorages that it is almost always possible to find an anchorage completely to yourself.

Again a short beat, followed by a reach and run, leads into the great
sheltered area of Parham Sound with its numerous islands, reefs, and
sand beaches. This is a delightful area where entirely deserted anchorages can be found. But one is reminded of the existence of civilization by
the roar of jets as they pass overhead after taking off from the airfield.

A short downwind run will bring you to Dickenson Bay with its miles
of white sand beaches, hotels, steel bands, et al. It is a short reach to al-
most-deserted Deep Bay, whose only inhabitant, the wreck of an old,
three-masted sailing vessel, has broken-off steel masts that are usually
inhabited by huge lobsters.

Another short reach brings you to Five Islands Harbor (maximum
draft seven feet), which is truly completely deserted: no roads, houses or
sign of habitation. The breeze which sweeps across the low land means it
is always cool.

A glorious smooth-water reach to the southwest corner of Antigua leads to a hard beat back to English Harbour. But this beat can be broken up by stopping at Carlisle Bay, a beautiful, sheltered anchorage, palm groves, an old-fashioned, relatively unspoiled West Indian village, and a very pleasant spot.

Then back to English Harbour and civilization.

Detailed sailing directions and descriptions of the harbors of Antigua are a book in themselves and cannot be covered in full in this chapter, but with the aid of the American General Chart plus the detailed chart 25202, 25203 Antigua can be explored at great length and in great detail. One can continually find deserted anchorages and mile after mile of beautiful white sand beaches completely uncluttered by hotels, guest houses, and the like.

The following charts are recommended as necessary for cruising in the waters between Anguilla and Antigua:

New No.	Old No.	USA
25201	1004	Antigua
25202	0366	St. John's Harbor and Deep Bay, and English Harbour
25203	5725	Parham Sound
25241	1834	Saba, Sombrero, Anguilla, St. Maarten, St. Barts, Statia
25242	0371	A detail chart showing harbors on Anguilla, St. Maarten, St. Barts
25161	1011	Statia to Montserrat, with inserts showing the harbors in detail
25204	1484	Barbuda

Guadeloupe to the Grenadines

From Guadeloupe south the Lesser Antilles take on a great change. Whereas the northern and western islands are windswept and dry, most of the southern islands are high, lush, and green. Fresh produce that is expensive and difficult to find farther north is easily obtained and relatively cheap.

Guadeloupe and Martinique give the islands a touch of France with superb cooking, chic women, open-air cafes where men of all ages sit sipping *Punch Blanc* or *Punch Vieu,* while their eyes follow the scenery passing by.

Dominica is scarcely ten miles wide, yet rises 5,000 feet into the sky. The mountains stop the rain clouds which pour into the island. As a result, Dominica is the farmer's delight and the sailor's nightmare. Rain is great for scrubbing teak decks but makes varnishing and painting difficult, if not impossible. Moreover, trying to anchor on the bold coast of Dominica is like throwing an anchor against a wall.

St. Lucia has a tourist boom, hotels being built, real estate selling rapidly, a new yacht harbor dredged by the village of Gros Islet, and a causeway to Pigeon Island that produces a large sheltered yacht anchorage.

St. Vincent remains generally the same as it has been for many years, basically an agricultural island with tourism slowly becoming an important part of the economy. The tourist development, however, is all centered around Kingston on the southern coast of the island and the remainder of the island remains largely undeveloped.

The Grenadines have changed completely. The uninhabited island and deserted anchorage are almost places of the past. However, the sailing is glorious and the people charming, completely different from one island to the next although the islands in many cases are only separated by channels a few miles wide.

Grenada to many sailors is St. George's with the Grenada Yacht Services and Yacht Club in the lagoon, the rocky and rolly anchorage off beautiful Grand Anse beach, and nearby the south coast anchorage of Lance Aux Epines (once less elegantly named Prickly Bay) with the Spice Island Boatyard. Few sailors realize they can easily spend a week or ten days exploring the south coast of Grenada, have anchorages completely to themselves, and never spend two nights in the same spot.

Like the northern islands, the Windward Islands have much of interest that is not covered by the charts.

Martinique and Guadeloupe are certainly worth visiting but do not explore unless you have the excellent French detailed charts.

One thing to remember when buying charts in the Lesser Antilles is that in Guadeloupe they are likely to be short of Guadeloupe charts but have plenty of Martinique charts; in Martinique the reverse is true.

Guadeloupe is in the midst of a yachting boom and has a number of large projects under way in an effort to establish it as the sailing center of the Caribbean. The island is in such a state of change that the best thing to do is to go to the old molasses pier in the southeast corner of Point-à-Pitre harbor. The pier has now been converted to a good marina and there one can find out the latest local information.

One of the most attractive little-known anchorages in the Lesser Antilles is found south of Francois between the islands of Petite Terres (Fig. 1). On Terre de Bas is the oldest lighthouse continuously operating in the Western Hemisphere, built in 1835 and in as good shape as the day it was built.

The charts of Petite Terres are on such a small scale that it is almost impossible to see any details. Even a magnifying glass merely shows the chart is wrong. There is no opening at the eastern end of the passage be-

Fig. 1.

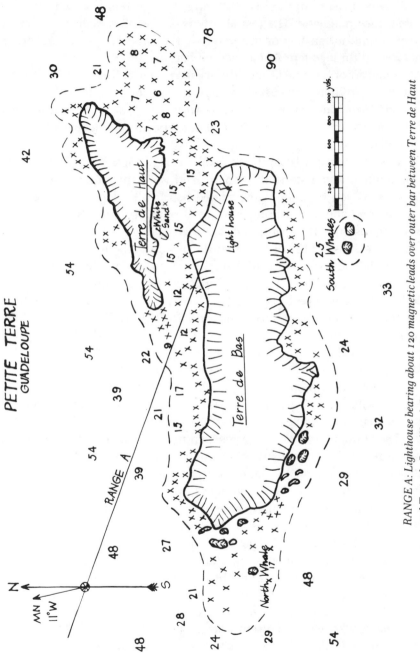

RANGE A: *Lighthouse bearing about 120 magnetic leads over outer bar between Terre de Haut and Terre de Bas. Watch for coral heads.*

tween the islands as the charts might suggest. The opening is completely blocked by reefs so that there is not even a dinghy passage.

To enter between the islands, bring the lighthouse to bear approximately 120° magnetic. The rest is strictly a case of eyeball navigation as there is nine to ten feet of water across the sand bar with coral heads sticking up three to four feet above the bottom.

Stand in on port tack until the western end of Terre de Haut bears approximately north by east then tack to the northwards and favor the Terre de Haut side of the channel. As you work your way eastwards, the northern side of the passage is free of coral heads and deepens to fifteen to eighteen feet.

Proceed eastwards until you spot a sand beach on Terre de Haut. Drop anchor, run a stern line ashore, and warp the stern in as close as you dare. If you have an old-fashioned boat with a long stern overhang you can probably jump from the fantail onto dry land. Snorkeling between the islands is superb; and if you wish to go spear fishing, a path leads from the sand beach to the northern side of the island.

The islands are now completely deserted as this light is untended and cannot be climbed. This is unfortunate as the view from the top of the lighthouse is superb. Terre de Bas was once a large estate. The foundation ruins of many houses can be seen and the old French chart shows a road leading to the west. Do not stay ashore on Terre de Bas at night as the insects will drive you crazy, but on Terre de Haut there is no active-insect problem.

French fishermen from Desirade and Francois visit the islands frequently for a day's fishing. To visit Desirade, charter one of the fast fishing boats which make the run in thirty-five minutes.

The anchorage at Petite Terres is in my estimation one of the best in the entire Caribbean, still unspoiled and usually deserted. The lighthouse keepers who manned the light in 1970 stated that we were the first "foreign" yacht to visit the anchorage. Few have visited since.

While it is very difficult to anchor in Dominica, the usual routine of dragging anchor at Roseau is no longer true. Carl Armour and his wife have opened a small hotel, The Anchorage, one mile south of town, and they have placed a number of permanent moorings available to visiting sailors. They will arrange tours through the islands and will also purchase vegetables and provisions. Having been born in the island, Carl knows it like his backyard and can be useful to visiting sailors.

One way he was most useful was to clarify the mystery of the rock off Scott's Head. Both U.S. and British charts show a rock uncovering seven feet approximately 200 yards off Scott's Head. Sailors have been continually spotting a rock very close on Scott's Head, have mistaken it for the rock shown on the chart, and as a result they hit the rock that is supposed to be above water.

There are actually three separate rocks with approximately six feet of water over them 300 yards off shore. Moreover, the rocks directly north of Scott's Head extend offshore farther than are shown on the chart. Thus, when passing Scott's Head, stay well off shore or you are likely to come to a very sudden stop.

Martinique like Grenada and Antigua is often underrated by yachtsmen. They are only familiar with Fort-de-France, Anse Mitan (called Anse de Cocoties on the chart), and the two harbors to the south of Fort-de-France, Anses d'Aslet.

However, the south and east coast of Martinique is lined with harbors, so many that one could spend two or three weeks cruising around the island of Martinique (Fig. 2). To do this it is absolutely essential that you purchase all the French charts as they are excellent, detailed charts done by French Navy personnel blockaded in Martinique during World War II by the U.S. Navy.

You should encounter no difficulty in cruising the east coast of Martinique provided you are equipped with the French charts and a boat that can go to windward. Some people who have tried to cruise this east coast have been stopped by the fact that their boats went to windward so poorly they could not work their way out to the east coast. The trip may be done in easy stages. Work your way southeast to Sainte Anne; spend the night there; then leave early in the morning to beat around the southeastern point of Martinique.

Eric Hiscock has often said that a sailboat is only seaworthy if it has the ability to work its way off a lee shore under sail without using its engine. Boats which do not fulfill this definition of seaworthiness should not go exploring the east coast of Martinique.

The one thing to keep in mind about Martinique is that vast areas of the chart show no soundings. This does not mean that there is no water, but just that the water is six feet deep or less interspersed with numerous coral heads. It is perfectly possible to take boats drawing three to four feet into many areas of the east coast of Martinique where no soundings are shown.

The Cul-de-Sac Anglais area is described as Martinique's Tobago Cays, a superb place for exploring in shoal-draft (five feet or less) boats. Cul-de-Sac Fregate is another attractive anchorage but make sure of your bearings before running in. There is deep water in the channel but breaking reefs and coral heads on both sides.

Fig. 2.

EAST COAST of MARTINIQUE

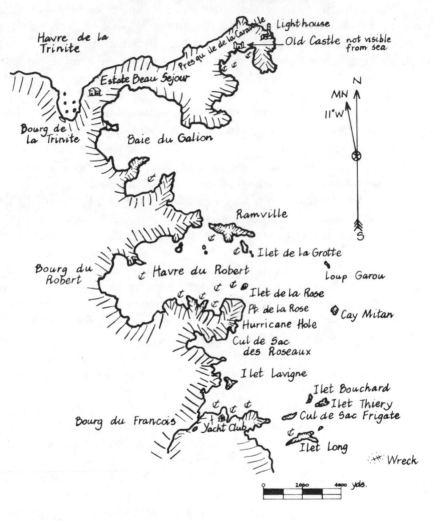

Mouillage de Francois provides numerous excellent anchorages, a chance for a delicious meal and shower at the yacht club. The town of Francois can be visited either by dinghy or taxi. This area should only be entered via the northern entrance, Passe du Francois; the eastern entrance is just too dangerous.

Finally, Cul-de-Sac Tartane, locally referred to as Treasure Cove or Treasure Harbor, is superb. Reputedly, in years gone by it was a sheltered pirate harbor complete with a small castle or fort. It has excellent fishing and is a fascinating place to explore in a dinghy.

Pigeon Island at the northwest side of St. Lucia is now joined to the island by a causeway which has destroyed the wonderful seclusion of Pigeon Island but has made a superb anchorage between Pigeon Island and the mainland (Fig. 3). The area has been dredged to a little more than three fathoms and has a sand bottom with good holding.

Where the chart shows a stream south of Gros Islet there is now a twelve-foot channel dredged into a lagoon approximately eight feet deep.

Fig. 3.

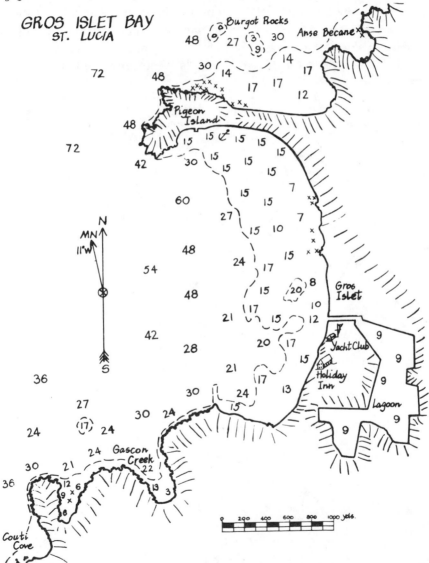

GROS ISLET BAY
ST. LUCIA

In years to come undoubtedly a large marina will spring up in this lagoon. Unfortunately they did not dredge to more than eight feet, so many of the large deep-draft boats, of course, will be unable to enter the lagoon.

When sailing south down the coast of St. Lucia, give Grand Calle Point a very wide berth as the rocks extend out from shore farther than the chart shows. Many yachts have come to a sudden stop, some with considerable damage by running on this reef.

One harbor that is shown on the chart but seldom visited is Labourie, a most intriguing anchorage (Fig. 4). This harbor should only be entered under ideal conditions with the sun high. The man who made the English Admiralty chart appears never to have seen the harbor. The reef on the eastern side of the entrance to Labourie Harbor is not as indicated on the chart but extends at least 150 yards westwards from the eastern point.

Fig. 4. RANGE A: The western end of the village brought to bear roughly north magnetic. When reef is abeam to starboard, head up into anchorage.

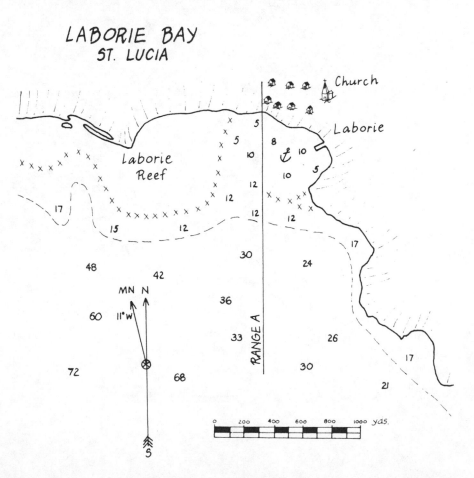

To enter, place the houses on the western side of town on a bearing of north by east and keep a good lookout to starboard. Once the reef is abeam to starboard, head northeast toward the church, round up and anchor wherever it is convenient. There is about nine feet of water in the harbor.

Mike Smith of *Phryna* has warned that an eye must be kept on the rain clouds when considering going to Labourie. If there are heavy rainfalls in the area, the stream that empties into the harbor spews out so much mud that it is impossible to find one's way in and out of the harbor. Thus it might be wise to avoid this harbor during the summer rainy season.

On the large island of St. Vincent, Cumberland Bay, popular with yachtsmen in former years, has lost much of its appeal. The locals have become too aggressive at selling their produce and services and all too adept at stealing dinghies. The better anchorage is Wallilabou Bay, the next harbor to the south (Fig. 5). The charts for this area are wrong; the conspicuous radio pylon is not as shown on the British and U.S. charts but rather it is on the hill forming the south side of Wallilabou Bay.

Here the Stevensons have a handicraft shop. They are former yachtsmen who are trying to swallow the anchor and are most friendly to visiting boats. They have a few moorings out, but if they are occupied, drop anchor and throw ashore a stern line which someone will tie to a palm tree. On the North side of Wallilabou Bay you may see traces of a dry dock which was begun in 1973 but as yet is still unfinished. Instead, they continue to haul boats the hard way at the Villa, the anchorage inside Young Island.

Wallilabou Bay is normally a secure anchorage but when there is a heavy ground swell running continue southwards to Bequia or Young Island.

The Grenadines are to many sailors the finest sailing area of the Lesser Antilles. They stretch approximately eighty miles from St. Vincent to Grenada. As might be expected, the charts are none too accurate, having basically been made in the last century.

This is an area of eyeball navigation. Stay alert, sail only when the sun is high, and you should have little trouble. Two important landmarks that might cause confusion are the two sand islands marking the south entrance to the Tobago Cays. They have presently disappeared but could reappear on very short notice.

The axis of the Grenadines runs northeast and southwest. Thus though usually it is a hard beat from Grenada to Carriacou (exception 1973 when there was so much southeast wind that frequently boats laid Carriacou in one tack), the rest of the cruise north from Carriacou to St.

Fig. 5.

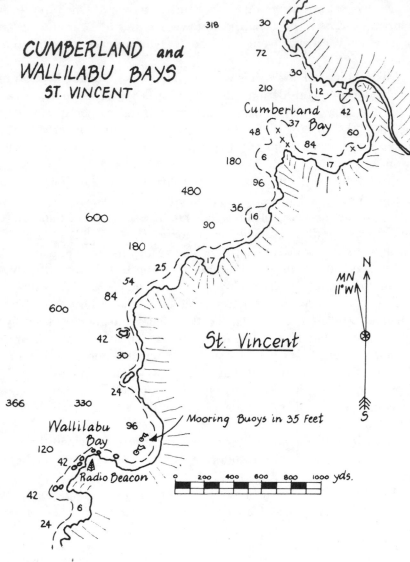

CUMBERLAND and
WALLILABU BAYS
ST. VINCENT

Cumberland Bay

St. Vincent

Mooring Buoys in 35 Feet

Wallilabu
Bay

Radio Beacon

N
MN
11°W
S

Vincent is a close fetch on starboard tack. South from St. Vincent to
Grenada it is usually an easy downwind slide.

Two seldom-visited small coves can be found on the west side of Cannouan. L'Anse Goyeau and Corbay are both small, deserted anchorages
with room for at the most two boats (Fig. 6). You will enjoy good swimming and snorkeling, and these anchorages are fine in normal weather
but either uncomfortable or unsafe if the ground swell begins to run in.
These harbors are convenient in that they break up the long haul from

Fig. 6.

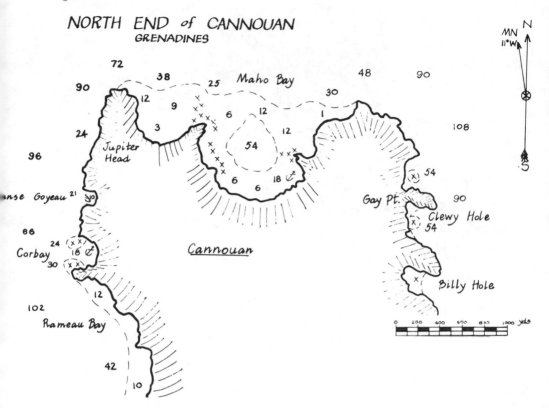

NORTH END of CANNOUAN
GRENADINES

Bequia to the Tobago Cays.

On the south and southeast coast of Grenada are a series of harbors
that provide excellent exploring with swimming, spear fishing, snorkeling, shelling, beaches, and anchorages (Fig. 7). It is a superb area often
overlooked by skippers sailing north to the better-known harbors.

The reefs and sand bars on the south coast have changed considerably since the Admiralty chart was made.

The most important change is in Mt. Hardman Bay. The chart shows
an exposed sandbar 500 yards south of Mt. Hardman Point and numerous shoals further south. In the last ten years this sand bank does not
even bare at low water, but the reef 1000 yards south of Mt. Hardman
Point has now become an island six feet high made up of star coral piled
up by the action of the wind and waves. The locals have named it Tara,
and it is worth exploring in a dinghy as it is alive with sea life. Care must
be taken as the current sweeps around it. Wear sneakers or rubber boots
while landing.

An excellent anchorage can be found under the lee of Mt. Hardman

Fig. 7.

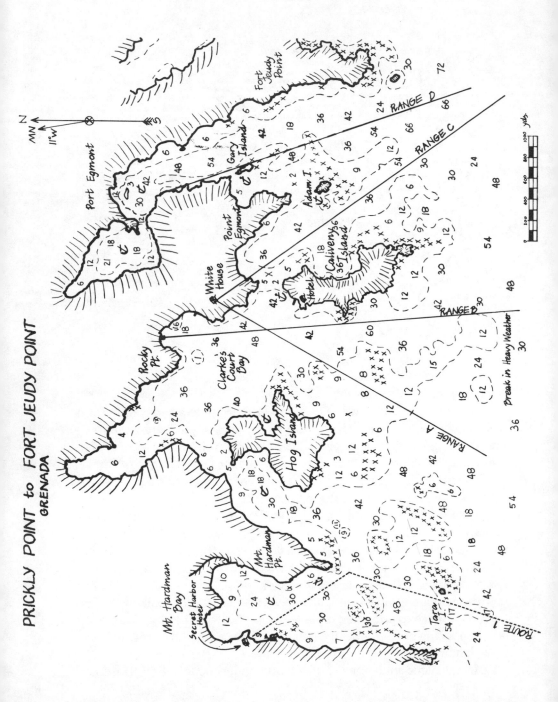

PRICKLY POINT to FORT JEUDY POINT
GRENADA

Point. Anchor due west of the saddle on the southern end of the point. From here a dinghy or shoal draft (four feet maximum) boat can be taken behind the islands and reefs as far east as Adam Island off Point Egmond. Good anchorages can be found behind Hog, Calivigny, and Adam Islands as well as in the harbors of Clark's Court, Port Egmont, and Calivigny, to mention only a few.

The Lesser Antilles are a fabulous cruising area. The average cruising yachtsman from another area should have little difficulty once he becomes accustomed to the fact that aids to navigation are few and for the most part the charts are based on largely uncorrected surveys of one hundred or more years ago. Talk to the local yachtsmen and fishermen, buy the latest cruising guide, be careful, and enjoy the finest in both sailing and anchorages.

⑥ ❊ Chartering

IF YOU ARE LOOKING for a sailing vacation in a warm area of guaranteed weather, the Lesser Antilles are hard to beat.

This island chain screens the Atlantic Ocean as it sweeps into the Caribbean Sea, and stretches in a 600-mile arc from St. Thomas in the Virgin Islands to Grenada in the Grenadines, with a rare variety of wind, sea, and subtropical scenery. For the seaman, the sailing is superb and varied. East, the only land is Africa, 2,500 miles to windward, and the trades blow in with great ocean swells. With no really large islands to block the wind in the Virgins and in the Grenadines, the breeze is strong and constant. The lay of the islands provides plenty of windward work going east in the Virgins and north in the Grenadines but gives beautiful sleigh rides sailing in the opposite directions. Among the larger islands of the Lesser Antilles, it is light airs or flat calms in the lee, and rail-down reaches on passages between. The boisterous wind and rolling sea make it some of the most glorious sailing a man could hope for.

Winter is, of course, the most popular season. But spring and early summer are just as nice and, in some ways, even better. The winds don't blow as hard in spring as in winter, the temperature is the same, the rates are lower, and the anchorages are less crowded.

The islands themselves provide enough variety to keep the non-sailors in a charter group happy. The eastern Virgins and the Grenadines are sparsely inhabited, dry, windswept, and surrounded by reefs where there is excellent snorkeling and spearfishing. Anegada, Barbuda, and Anguilla are absolutely flat, girdled by mile after mile of offshore reefs that have been the grave of hundreds of ships, making the area a diver's delight. Wrecks may vary from the remains of Spanish galleons through 17th- and 18th-century sailing ships, early 20th-century steamers, and modern yachts.

Most of the remaining islands in the Antilles are high, lush, and wet, with scenery of surpassing beauty. Gardeners and botanists will be enthralled by the spectacular flora, while historians will find of absorbing interest the fortifications and battle sites that date back to the days when these islands were frequently fought over as valuable pieces of colonial real estate.

The crew will have a field day shopping. The American Virgin Islands of St. Thomas and St. Croix are booming with shops of all kinds because they are free ports, and a special concession in the U.S. Customs law allows each tourist to bring in from these ports one gallon of liquor and $200 worth of goods, as opposed to one quart and $100 from elsewhere in the world.

The French islands of Guadeloupe and Martinique provide perfume and other French goods at reasonable prices, but if you're looking for a bikini, the selection is poor in the winter. The stocks come from France and no one swims in France during the winter; besides, most of the islanders say it is too cold to swim in winter! In spring and summer, the bikini stocks are up.

If you like to eat, the French islands are heaven—a bit of France set in the Caribbean. The food is so far superior to anything else in the Caribbean there just is no comparison.

All the islands have stores that sell local products, and the crew can't go beyond limits on shopping sprees, since not too much money can be spent. The native fresh food markets are especially interesting, but the one in Martinique is by far the best, and a must for anyone visiting the islands.

Getting to the Antilles is not as much of a project or as expensive as many people think. The regular New York–Grenada fare was around $550 in early 1979; excursion fares as low as $385; a flight from New York–St. Thomas can cost as little as $131. Pan American, British West Indian Airways, Carib Air, and Leeward Islands Air Transport all have island-hopping flights. It is possible to fly direct from New York to Antigua, Martinique, or Barbados by PAA, Air France, or BWIA and transfer to an island-hopping flight to reach the smaller islands. Sometimes it is impossible to reach the smaller islands without overnighting on Antigua or Barbados.

A word of warning about airlines in the area: They excel at losing baggage and at not honoring confirmed reservations. Make sure your baggage is clearly marked, and carry with you on the plane clothes for two days, so that if your bags are lost you won't be wandering around the tropics in a tweed suit. Also, be sure to reconfirm reservations—and be

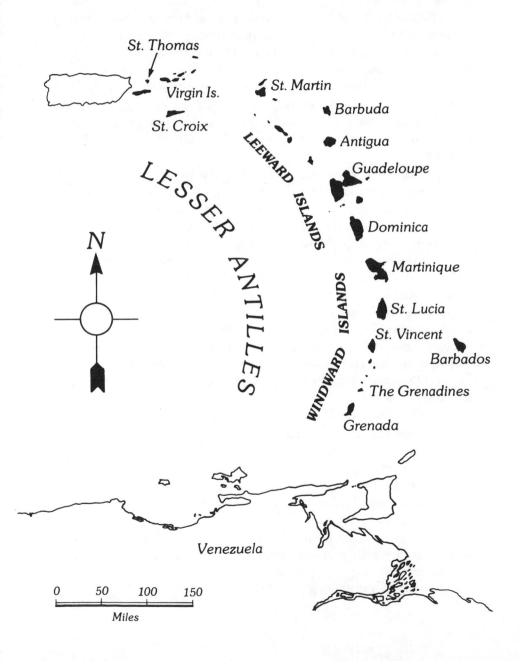

sure the schedule has not been changed. The lines are famous for revising schedules and failing to notify ticket holders—or failing to change their reservations to the new flight.

Air charter services are available from many of the islands, and a shorter hop for a party of three or four is frequently not too expensive. It sometimes results in a saving if it avoids the necessity of overnighting in a hotel.

Passports are not needed in the Lesser Antilles; the only papers required are proof of citizenship, birth certificate, driver's license, or the like, and a valid vaccination certificate. Once you join a charter boat, few if any papers have to be filled out; the captain takes care of the details. It is quite a project, because each island is independent of the other and has its own customs and immigration service, and the yacht must enter and clear each time. One of the greatest advantages of visiting the islands by charter boat is the fact that you don't have to fill out immigration forms yourself.

A great variety of charter boats is available in the islands, including a 40′ racing catamaran, a converted 12-Meter, fast cruising boats, and comfortable floating palaces that have all the windward qualities of a sand barge. Everyone should be able to find a boat to suit his taste—if the brokers do their job—which, all too frequently, they do not.

Charter boats are usually owner-operated, frequently by husband and wife, often by a man and his girl and sometimes by a skipper and West Indian crew. The boats vary from 35′ in length up to 116′, from the most crude to the most palatial, with uniformed crew, white-coated steward, hot and cold running water, air conditioning, and taped music piped to every cabin. But often the simple boat in which the charter party lends a hand is the boat that provides the most fun. Palatial yachts with trained crews are somewhat like cruise ships; you have little or no chance to sail the boat yourself.

Relatively few of the boats are really good sailers. Many described as auxiliary sailboats are in actuality less than 50–50 motorsailers and use their motors more or less continuously. Powerboats, except for out-and-out sportfishermen, are noticeable by their absence.

Bare-boat charters are now available, but the prospective charterer should think twice before contemplating this. The boats are generally small—thirty-five feet or less—and the wind blows hard, a steady fifteen to eighteen knots. It will frequently pipe up twenty to twenty-five and stay there for weeks, and sometimes it will blow a steady thirty knots for days on end.

Navigation and piloting provide little difficulty. With the aid of a good cruising guide, charts, and care—no night or twilight sailing near the islands, and no entering or leaving tricky harbors except when the sun is high—there should not be too much of a problem. But in this area, retribution is swift and often absolute. If you make a mistake and end up on the beach, it is frequently the end. The coral is hard, and the ocean swell will pound a boat to bits in no time. There is little tide rise to float you off, and in most of the area you are out of the range and jurisdiction of the U.S. Coast Guard.

Another disadvantage of bare-boat chartering is that by not having a local guide on board you may miss many of the best coves, fishing spots, restaurants, hotels, and guest houses. Still another most important disadvantage is that you must do your own cooking and dishwashing, something vacationers generally don't appreciate. And if you need a final consideration, bare-boat chartering is not so much cheaper than chartering with a crew.

On the other side of the coin, it is nice to have a boat completely to yourself with no strangers around. You can do what you want to do when you want to do it, not when the skipper wants to do it. Then there is a certain thrill to entering a harbor the first time, chart and navigation tools spread before you, wondering exactly how it's going to look as you round the point. The thrill of successfully completing a tricky piece of piloting is hard to beat.

One of the greatest difficulties for people planning charters is lack of comprehension of the distances involved in sailing between islands. Superimpose a chart of the Lesser Antilles on a chart of the East Coast of the United States and Canada, and the islands spread from New York to Nova Scotia. Brokers are continually tearing their hair because of letters like this:

"We would like to cruise the Windward and Leeward islands, and perhaps a few of the Bahamas with no night passages and sightseeing on shore every day. We have ten days at our disposal."

What with picking up the anchor, securing the dinghy, and beating into harbors, a boat is lucky to average five knots. As a result, if you wish to stop every night, swim, walk ashore, etc., forty miles a day is a good sail. Don't get overambitious; it will ruin your vacation. With twenty-two years of island cruising experience behind me, I'd list five cruises in the following order, based on wind, currents, and the availability of air transportation:

Virgins—One week is good, two better, especially if you want to visit St. Croix and Gorda Sound.

Grenadines—One week from St. Vincent to Grenada, but ten days if you are going in the reverse direction, because it is almost all to windward—not dead to windward, but a long starboard tack and a short port tack.

Martinique to Grenada or reverse—Two weeks. Best charter in the Caribbean. Easiest sailing if charter is booked from Martinique south.

Antigua to St. Thomas—Ten days. An excellent downwind cruise visiting the northern islands, some of which—Anguilla, Barbuda, Saba, and St. Barts—are seldom visited by yachts.

St. Thomas to Antigua—A wonderful sail—for those who want to get in shape for the Bermuda or Fastnet Race, or test the boat and gear. Two hundred and ten miles dead to windward against the current.

It's impossible for a broker to do a good job for you if you don't describe yourself and your party to him in advance. The vast majority of charterers have little or no sailing experience. To them, one boat is much like another. But skippers and boats do vary, and do have personalities that often can be matched to the charter party.

On the other hand, people who are good sailors often have definite ideas about the type of boat they'd like to charter. A good matching job can make life pleasant for all concerned. Once, on *Iolaire,* I was told by a broker that he had booked a charter consisting of four complete non-sailors. I thought it was going to be a miserable charter until he showed me the letter they had written. They stated that their hobbies were mountain climbing, skiing, and white-water canoeing, and that they wanted to learn to sail. We had a wonderful time.

The world's worst mismatch happened when one broker put a man and wife and three small children on a 12-Meter. Not only were they non-sailors from Des Moines, Iowa, who had never seen the sea, but they were seasick as soon as the anchor came up and panic-stricken when the boat heeled. They had a miserable time. Unfortunately there was nothing the charter boat skipper could do to improve the situation; they should have been on one of the floating hotels that doesn't sail very well, but also doesn't heel!

So, as a first order of business in chartering, it's important to write the broker a long, detailed letter giving this information: size and composition of the party, their ages, previous sailing experience, hobbies, interests, previous areas the party has chartered in, areas and dates desired, first and second choice, and how much party is able or willing to pay.

In regard to cost, it depends on the size of the boat and extras offered. A party of four may pay anywhere from $35 to $150 per person per day. A party of two will pay more, simply because they must pay the basic boat price rather than split it with another couple. Thus their bill will be at least $50 per person per day.

However, a number of what in the trade are referred to as "head boats" sail out of St. Thomas. They're on a schedule and an individual buys one bunk space on a boat that carries about a dozen guests. A word of warning: Some of these head boats are awful, while others are first-class operations—good boats with reliable captains and crews. Check carefully before you make any bookings. A *good* boat will be able to supply you with references from satisfied customers.

Time is an important consideration. The season basically runs from January 15 through April 15, with the Christmas and New Year holiday period also popular. February 1 to March 12 is the most popular, and must be booked in August or September of the previous year. Air reservations for the peak period are hard to get, too, so both boat and plane arrangements should be confirmed well ahead. These are additional considerations in favor of off-season chartering.

Whether to deal with brokers or directly with the skippers of the charter boats is an oft-debated question. By writing to a broker you will receive a list of boats and their available dates—a cross-section of what is available, all in reply to one letter. But it must be remembered that some of the best and most experienced charter boat captains do their own bookings exclusively.

Recently, some writers have been warning against rag-tag, unkempt, charter boat captains whose badge of authority is the costume of a beachcomber and the grooming of a tramp. Their usual advice is to deal only through a broker, since he'll know what the situation is. Some of the brokers sing this same tune, one firm going so far as to announce themselves as self-appointed "public watchdogs," and giving the impression that charter boat operators are a bunch of shiftless characters whom the brokers must fight to keep in line. In actuality, the majority of charter boat operators are hard-working individuals trying to make a living at a highly seasonal occupation. If the skipper doesn't look all spit and polish, remember that he is engineer, chief boatswain, able seaman, deck hand, and captain of the head all at once. If his boat doesn't look like a craft on the New York Yacht Club cruise, remember that he sails anywhere from fifteen to twenty-five weeks a year, and puts more miles on his boat in one season than most yachts do in five. The simple and foolproof check is to ask for references from people who have sailed with the skipper the previous year. Call them on the phone; or better, if possible, arrange to see them. Then you'll know exactly what to expect.

Brokers themselves are not all knights in shining armor. The biggest and most expensive advertisement does not necessarily indicate the best broker. Some brokers view sailing in the islands through rose-colored glasses and describe the cruising in terms of gentle breezes, calm seas, glassy calm anchorages, sundowners served under the awnings by white-coated stewards, clear nights, and on-deck sleeping under the stars. The truth is, it usually blows like hell between the islands, and there are occasional hard rain squalls—usually at 2 A.M.—that can leave you, your blankets, and your mattress a sodden mess. Many anchorages have a slight roll, and some a bad roll; few are absolutely calm. And the white-coated steward is often a figment of the broker's imagination. In some cases the advertisements are misleading, in others downright fraudulent. Unscrupulous brokers have been known to book anything that will float once they have run short of boats at the height of the season.

The answer here, as in dealing with the boats direct, is to write to a number of brokers and ask for references—names of people in your area who have previously chartered through that broker. You'll soon learn what kind of operation you are dealing with. There are bad skippers, bad boats, and bad brokers. Personal references will tell the story much better than advertising literature.

Nine out of ten people who arrive in the islands for charter have twice as many clothes as they need. It's hard to believe, but I have seen women arrive with spike heels, fur coats, hat boxes, and suitcases so large they wouldn't even fit down hatches, much less be stowable anywhere below. Few boats have any space at all for hard suitcases. Everything should be packed in duffel bags, though dresses and suits can be packed in collapsible hang-up bags. The square PVC waterproof duffels with nylon zippers are the most expensive, but are by far the best, because they're easier to pack than the round ones. And clothes themselves should be packed in plastic bags—to be safe from any deck leaks.

There are relatively few places to dress up in the islands. The main things to bring are shorts, shirts, slacks, one or two dresses for the women, and bathing suits. You will spend more time in a bathing suit than anything else. But the Lesser Antilles are much farther south than the Bahamas or Miami and the sun is stronger. During the first few days it is absolutely essential to wear long-sleeved shirts, slacks, and a hat to keep from getting sunburned. The coolest and most practical costume is long-sleeved cotton pajamas worn over a bathing suit. You won't win any fashion contests with this costume but you will avoid getting burned, and sunburn can ruin the best of vacations.

On the other end of the spectrum, it does get chilly at night. A light sweater is necessary, and sometimes a heavy one is comfortable. A foul-weather jacket is handy, but don't bother with the trousers and boots. Non-slip deck shoes and socks are essential, lest your feet and ankles get burned. And if the boat has a tiller, you'll want to cover your hands with socks or fingerless gloves, to keep the backs from being painfully burned.

For skin diving, most charter skippers provide face masks, fins, and snorkels. However, if you have extra-large or small feet, it is best to bring your own, though fins can be bought in the islands. Bring an extra duffel bag. Despite the best intentions, everyone buys more than he expects and then has no way to carry it. Traveler's checks are acceptable almost everywhere. Incidentally, the normal routine in chartering is to pay a fifty percent deposit on booking, and the balance ten days before you board the boat.

If you really want to make the skipper happy, write and tell him what you like in the way of liquor and soft drinks, and inform him of any dietary problems. Don't tell him what you like to eat; just tell him what you don't like and won't eat. At the same time, ask if there is anything you can bring with you for him. Often, in the middle of the season, a boat needs an odd piece of gear that can't be bought in the islands, and you may save him the months it takes to get things from the States through normal channels.

So if you're lured by the prospect of wonderful sailing through tropic isles, remember three things above all: Plan early, write letters with plenty of information, and demand references. By following this routine, you should be able to set up the vacation of a lifetime.

7 ❈ Gunkholing

IN 1962 WHEN I first visited Grenada the lagoon channel had just been dredged, the yacht club barely completed, Grenada Yacht Services was a figment of Ken Gooding's imagination, and perhaps five yachts were at anchor. The Carenage was crowded with large cargo schooners and small, sloop-rigged rum smugglers. When we cruised north to Martinique we only saw one or two yachts on the entire trip. The anchorage at the Savanne in Fort de France was empty, and only a few yachts were at Anse Mitan. Pigeon Island, the popular charter boat anchorage, was shared with one other boat.

Those not-so-distant days are gone forever, already. There are usually upwards of sixty boats in the lagoon at St. George's, Grenada, and more boats on the south coast. Popular anchorages like Tobago Cays will have twenty or more boats a night in them, and at times it gets too crowded for easy anchorage. The evening is frequently disturbed by the pop-pop-pop of generators.

Most charter boat skippers tend to stick to a fairly set routine, visiting the same popular harbors every trip. This tendency is reinforced by publicity on the area. The writers are usually on charter boats, and their view of the islands is greatly influenced by their skipper's habits. Many people who have visited the islands once or twice do not come back for a third trip, since they feel that in two trips from Martinique to Grenada they have seen all the good anchorages.

Nothing can be further from the truth. For the adventurous there is always the south and east coast of Martinique. Seldom visited by yachtsmen, it has mile after mile of beautiful harbors, and a full week can be spent exploring this coast. It is on the windward side of the island, and entrance and exit from the harbors is not always the easiest, but if you like to sail and explore, this area is hard to beat.

South of Fort de France, en route to Castries, St. Lucia, there are two small harbors worth visiting. They are only a few hours sail from Fort de France, and they make a pleasant break in the first long sail to St. Lucia. Grand Anse d'Arlet is a beautiful open bay, with white sand bottom and miles of perfect beach. A typical small fishing village is in the southeast corner of the bay, picturesque, but none too clean and very poor. The northeast corner of the bay is in sharp contrast, with summer cottages and beautiful gardens.

If there are other yachts in Grand Anse, a short sail south presents another anchorage: Petit Anse d'Arlet. It is best not to anchor off the town, but rather south of it by the small beach nestled between cliffs, where other yachts are seldom found, and the only habitations are a few farmers' cottages high on the hill. Town may be visited by dinghy, but I prefer to sit, look, and listen. The sound of church bells across the water is wonderful. If you forget to put on your bathing suit for an early morning dip, no one is around to know the difference.

Pigeon Island, Castries, and Marigot in St. Lucia have been described often and need no further build-up. South of them lies the incomparably beautiful anchorage between the Pitons. The water is so deep that it is almost impossible to anchor. It is best to sail on in, drop a stern anchor, and tie the bow line to a palm tree. On the starboard quarter, a mile away, Gros Piton rises 2,600 feet, while on the port beam Petit Piton, a mere 300 yards off, is 2,461 feet. As the moon comes up, the tall palms cast fantastic shadows. In the moonlight, Petit Piton seems about to fall over and crush the boat, while strong gusts blast down from the peaks, small swells rattle on the shingle beach, and anchor lines creak and groan. Dawn shows a nearby copra plantation in full swing. Formerly we always had the anchorage to ourselves but now very often there are other boats. The anchorage is so spectacular that it is still worth visiting.

Bequia with its cargo schooners, whaling boats, and small fishing boats is one of our favorite islands. A cruise in the lower Antillies was not complete without a stop here and a drive to Ross Lolley's shop on the hill, plus an afternoon drink at Friendship Bay while watching the whaling boats come in.

Why Ross Lolley ever came to Bequia no one knows, and why he should have built his house and shop specializing in fishing and skin diving gear halfway up the mountainside in the days when the island had no roads, is completely beyond comprehension, but build a better mousetrap and the world will beat a path to your door. Ross sold fishing tackle, lines, hooks, etc. at such a good price that everyone beat a path to his door. He not only had a good store, but also had a fabulous view and sold the coldest beer on the island.

A trip to Friendship Bay late in the afternoon is a must. Between three and four, the whalers return, and seeing them strike their sails, beach their boats, unload "de rock stone ballast," and skid their thirty-foot boats up the beach is a sight to behold. They are skidded up and chocked in a matter of minutes at a speed that makes some of our yacht yards look rather slow. A walk along the beach to Friendship Bay Hotel usually reveals a schooner or sloop being built, and a drink on the terrace of the hotel is a fitting close to a day here.

If it is not blowing too hard, and the sea is not running, a sail to Baliceau is rewarding. Here the fishing colony can be seen at work. They are not residents of the island, but sail over from Bequia and camp on the beach for a week or so at a time, catching and salting fish to sell in St. Vincent. Bring binoculars, for a climb to the top of the hill presents an incomparable view of the neighboring islands. The ruins of the sugar estate on Battowia can be seen. How they ever grew sugar on its almost vertical slopes is beyond me. They must have been superb seamen, since there is no harbor and everything had to be loaded ashore through the surf. There is no doubt that sugar was raised there, because the wind-powered sugar mill is still clearly visible.

South of Baliceau and Battowia is another of our favorite islands, Mustique, which means mosquito. After sunset, there are some on shore, but during the day and out on the boat we have never been bothered. The island, two-and-a-half miles long, was for many years owned by the Hazel family of St. Vincent. Recently, however, they sold the entire island. For the next few years it should be a charter boat skipper's delight. The new owners have spent a fortune building a dock, roads, and workers' cottages, importing farm equipment, and bringing much of the island under cultivation of sea island cotton. The cattle herds on the island have been expanded and improved.

Now the island has been developed as a resort for the very rich from Europe and Venezuela. Princess Margaret has a house here. The island is really worth visiting because of Cotton House—an expensive restaurant which was formerly a cotton warehouse. It is one of the most magnificently restored buildings in the area.

In the past seine boats could often be watched spreading their nets in the evening twilight. The perfect unison of their six pairs of oars was a sight seldom seen outside of a crew race, and very pleasant to watch. The traffic to and from Bequia is in the little double-ended Bequia boats, the descendants of whaleboats, always pleasant to watch. Often we have spent two or three days at anchor here in perfect isolation.

South of Mustique lies Savan Island, again a small fishing colony. Despite the small size of the island, its lack of arable land, total lack of water, and lack of an all-weather harbor, there are a few people who live on the island permanently. The fishing in this area is so good that the fishermen live here despite the disadvantages. In calm weather an anchorage can be made here, and in rough weather it is worthwhile to sail between Savan Island and Savan Rock, as the surf on the rocks is spectacular. Photographers can get a wonderful shot of the hole right through Savan Rock.

The Tobago Cays, Petit St. Vincent, and Prune Island have often been described and are no longer uninhabited. In the Cays there is a semi-permanent fishing camp. Former charter skipper and circumnavigator John Caldwell has built a cottage colony and hotel on Prune (now called Palm) Island, and there is another fine hotel on Petit St. Vincent; but there still remain one or two uninhabited islands that can be visited (ideal for marooning a mutinous crew or charter parties that have gotten out of hand!). To the west of Petit St. Vincent are two small uninhabited cays with the names of Pinese and Mopion, which might sound attractive until literally translated; they mean Bedbug and Crab-louse. In calm weather a tolerable lunchtime anchorage can be had in the lee of these islands.

The anchorage behind Frigate Island provides another place of refuge. The swimming is good, and the frigate birds nesting on the island and soaring on air currents provide a pleasant diversion. The wide, shallow bay to the northeast of the anchorage provides a perfect place to sail a dinghy, and the broad barrier reef and shoal water will keep the apprentice diver and shell enthusiast happy for many hours. The small town of Ashton is far enough away on the other side of the bay to provide the desired privacy.

On the west coast of Union is seldom-visited Chatham Bay, almost completely deserted and unspoiled, with fine beach, good swimming, and excellent fishing off the northwest point of the bay. There is always a breeze, and sometimes a veritable hurricane seems to funnel down from the hills.

Carriacou's main harbors of Hillsborough and Tyrell Bay which have received a lot of publicity, are attractive; but one is seldom alone there. For something different, visit the windward side of the island, where the anchorages are sheltered by a barrier reef with entrances at its north and south ends. A sail behind this reef is spectacular, with plenty of wind, calm water, and white sand bottom only a few feet under the keel. Absolutely crystal-clear water makes it easy to dodge the scattered coral heads, and anchoring behind one of them will provide excellent snorkeling from the boat; no need to use the dinghy.

The anchorage at the town of Windward Side is interesting in that it is the home port of many schooners and sloops. As it is on the opposite side of the island from Hillsborough, it is well removed from the prying eyes of officials. Smuggling is a major industry, and inspection of a sloop can usually reveal whether she is a rum smuggler. If she is truly a fishing sloop, the rail cap will be badly scored where the lines are hauled in over the rail, while a smuggler's rail cap will be unscored.

Saline Island south of Carriacou provides yet another good anchorage. If your boat draws six feet or less, it is possible to anchor out of the tide in the shoal water of the island's cove. The uninhabited island has ruins of an old lime kiln to explore, good shelling along the shore, and excellent snorkeling on the western shore. Here the bottom drops from ankle-deep at the shore to forty feet in an almost vertical slope. The tide runs through the channel like a mill race making the rocks and reefs on the north side inaccessible except at slack water. Birds soaring around the vertical cliffs of White Island to the west, Carriacou's hills to the north, brilliant water colors and a complete absence of people make a perfect setting.

Grenada's harbors and anchorages are frequently underrated. For a leisurely cruise, it is possible to sail for a week without leaving Grenada and spend each night at a different location. In the summer when there is no ground swell, Sandy Island on the northeast tip of Grenada provides a lovely anchorage with a high hill spilling down to palm groves, perfect white sand beaches, reefs for the fisherman, a deserted house, shells galore. Grenada close to the south, and the Grenadines to the north. From here, Grenville on the east coast provides an excellent next stop, though entrance is a bit hairy dead downwind running a range, with a sudden luff through the aptly named "luffing channel" to round up and anchor behind the reef. The town of Grenville with its commercial schooners is under the stern. Fishermen in their little inboard-powered double-enders provide color as they pass to and fro, and the town has a number of beautiful old buildings, a nutmeg factory, and shops selling fresh spices.

Beating dead to windward from here out the narrow channel, which is not well marked, is a case for eyeball navigation. It may put a few gray hairs on the skipper's head, like the time when we couldn't find the buoys or marks and were told "De marks fall down, de buoys sink, and we is negotiating for de replacement."

The south coast of Grenada has five separate harbors with numerous good anchorages within each harbor. You may have complete seclusion, or anchor off Spice Island Boatyard at Prickly Bay (locally referred to as L'Anse aux Pines). The whole area abounds with white sand beaches, shoals, reefs, mangroves, and high cliffs. Decide what you want and you will find it here, in an area only five miles across.

Uninhabited islands and the deserted anchorages are rapidly disappearing and will soon be a thing of the past, but you can still get away from it all in the southern islands with a little thought and imagination, and a little of the spirit of adventure. All cruises in the Antilles are good, but some are really great.

 8 ❀ Bare-boating

THE CHARTER BUSINESS in the Lesser Antilles has boomed in recent years. In the early 1950s, there were only five or ten boats chartering as a sideline. Now it is a major business—in all the islands there are probably 900 boats available for charter. Originally, all chartering was done with boats that had a skipper and crew on board. One good reason for this was that in years gone by there were few, if any facilities in the islands—no cruising guides, few navigation lights, no buoys, and no places to purchase charts. Sailing in the islands was difficult for a stranger.

Boating, September 1969.

This situation has now changed. In recent years many buoys have been established and shore facilities have been built. It is now possible for any competent, careful sailor to bare-boat charter safely in the Virgins or in the Grenadines. A few years ago, there were a few individuals chartering a few miscellaneous boats—now there are many organizations operating whole fleets of boats for bare-boat charter.

The advantages of a bare-boat charter are obvious: You are completely your own boss—there is no professional skipper to tell you what to do or where to go. There is also a sense of adventure that is missing in chartering a boat with a skipper giving the orders.

There are, of course, some disadvantages. Since you are new to the area you may miss some of the more interesting harbors or the best snorkeling reefs or the best restaurants. But the biggest disadvantage is that when you bare-boat charter, the responsibility for the safety of boat and crew rests entirely on you. There can be no blaming of someone else for trouble when you are the skipper.

If you are considering bare-boat charter the best thing to do is consult the ads in the boating magazines and write the various organizations that offer bare-boat charters. You'll discover they come in various sizes and shapes, ranging from small 24- to 26-footers up to gold-plated ocean racing machines. When the brokers or operators have sent you information on the various boats available, you can then sit down and select one that fits your tastes and capabilities. If you are used to fast racing machines you may not be happy on a small, tubby motorsailer. And if you are used to relaxed cruising you probably won't be happy with a hot racing machine.

There are many organizations in the bare-boat charter business that are doing a fine job. Others are not too good, and some are downright incompetent. The only way to find out which is which, is to ask the organization you are dealing with to supply you with references: the names and addresses of people who have chartered from them the previous season, and, if possible, on the boat you plan to sail.

Then write to or talk with each—it's well worth the price of a lunch to discover an incompetent before you charter from him.

Different organizations supply different amounts of equipment on board the boat. With some, all you have to do is to buy your cigarettes and liquor, step on board with your sea bag, and you are ready to go. In other cases you'll have to provision the boat fully, bring along your own binoculars, and possibly even your own tool kit. Thus it's important when booking a bare-boat charter to have the operator of the boat send you a complete inventory of equipment to be found on board.

Check this inventory against what you'd put on board your own boat for cruising in the area you've chosen. If the necessary equipment is not there, either request that it be placed on board or, if the equipment list appears to be very scanty, switch to another organization. It must be remembered, of course, that there is no fog and little continued bad weather in these parts of the Caribbean, so navigational equipment that is necessary up north—barometers, for example, and accurate taffrail logs—is not necessary in these islands. The only navigational gear really needed is charts, parallel rules, dividers, pencils, a good compass, and, of course, a good supply of common sense.

When selecting a boat, don't be too impressed by a long list of luxuries—hot and cold showers, pressure water systems, air conditioning, electrical or mechanical refrigeration, and some of the other fancy gear that is today installed on a boat. Most of these things are difficult to keep working even on a privately maintained yacht which is used only a few weeks or months a year. But this type of equipment installed on a charter yacht that will be sailing twenty or twenty-five weeks a year under different skippers is extremely difficult to maintain. Try to charter a boat that has a minimum amount of fancy equipment.

Many owners of bare-boat charter yachts have taken out their original engines and installed hand-starting diesels just to make sure the engine can be started even when the battery is dead. The presence of such an engine usually indicates an operator who is experienced in his business.

In bare-boat chartering there is a very definite and serious dual responsibility—of the charterer to the operator, and the operator to the charterer. In the first case the charterer must be truly competent to handle the boat he desires to charter. This does not necessarily mean you have to be an ocean-racing or ocean-passage specialist, but it does mean that you must have had adequate experience in the type and size of boat you plan to charter. Sailing dinghy experience is not enough to qualify you for a forty-foot cruising boat.

There is also the requirement of carefulness with someone else's boat, a requirement frequently forgotten by some of the most competent sailors who undertake bare-boat charters. If you feel like taking a risk with your own boat by sailing doubtful waters at night in spite of the hazard of running aground, that may be your affair—but when you're using someone else's boat you must be much more careful. You also have a real responsibility to the next charterer. If you damage the boat and it takes time to put her back into commission, the next charterer, who has made his plans and has flown a great distance for this sailing vacation, finds himself without a boat. This is grossly unfair to both the operator, who loses his money, and the charterer, who has had his vacation ruined.

One of the major complaints that operators of charter boats have is that charter parties often leave the boats like pig sties. This too is unfair to the operator—although he is responsible for getting the boat ready for the next crew, he shouldn't have to deal with a mess.

The operator has a very definite and important responsibility to the charterer, in addition to providing a seaworthy boat. He must check the competence of the charterer as to general boat handling ability. There is a further problem: If boats are damaged, insurance rates go up. Every accident makes it more difficult to obtain a good rate on renewal.

The wise charter boat owner will not only check the competence of the charterer, but he'll also go over the charts with him and give him a cruising manual for the area. He'll warn the charterer about the pitfalls of the area in which the boat will be sailing. And, most important, he will give the charterer a complete manual covering the operation of the boat and all its equipment. Perfectly good boats all too often get into trouble because the charterers are unfamiliar with the individual boat and when something goes wrong they do not have tools, equipment, or manual to rectify the problem.

In this, the bare-boat charterer's position is like that of the delivery skipper. A complete stranger when he steps on board, he must in a short time familiarize himself with the boat and all her equipment. This can be very difficult in anything but the simplest of boats, especially if a really good manual is not provided. And with the manual, an equipment list showing the exact location of all items should be furnished.

The operator of the boat also owes it to the charterer to make sure that the boat is absolutely reliable—few things are more irritating than to fly 2,000 miles to discover that two days must be wasted while equipment is fixed and parts are flown in from the States.

Many bare-boat fleets are made up of different boats all operating under the same management. For such fleets, there should be a small yard in which the management does all the maintenance. Otherwise when a boat breaks down it must be taken to the nearest boatyard to be repaired. But the outside yard may not be able to do emergency repairs immediately and thus the charterer is disappointed. It is really necessary for a bare-boat charter organization to have its own yard and, perhaps more important, a fleet of identical boats, if they intend to operate efficiently. An identical fleet means that a complete set of spare parts— even down to complete spare engines—can be maintained. Spare engines, spare spars, sails, stoves—the works. Thus if there is any breakdown the replacement parts are immediately available right in the area.

This, unfortunately, is not true with most fleets. It is possible to set up a really accurate maintenance schedule only if all the boats are the same, and all parts interchangeable. Fleets of non-identical boats have two strikes against them before they start—obtaining replacement parts on short notice is difficult at best—and it's frequently impossible.

The bare-boat charter business has now become so large that boats are specifically designed for the service. They should be simple and rugged with a minimum amount of electrical equipment on board and a good bilge pumping system, and they should be compartmented to make them virtually unsinkable. The sloop rig with a roller furling jib provides simplicity, and if it is possible to have a midship cockpit with separate accommodations fore and aft, complete with separate heads, it is well worth the effort. Midship cockpits tend to be wet, but a well-fitted watertight dodger can make the cockpit comfortable in even the worst weather. All cockpits should be at least 6′ 6″ long so you can stretch out and sleep under the stars.

The ballast keel should be bolted outside the hull. No matter how carefully charter parties are screened, the boat will touch bottom at least every other charter—with outside ballast the fiberglass shell will not usually be damaged.

Many boats have been adapted to this service—in some cases very well, in some cases poorly. Where most boats suffer in adaptation to bare-boat charter in the islands, is lack of ventilation. It is hot in the tropics. There should be many hatches and they should be reversible, opening fore or aft. There must also be numerous ventilators, at least four inches in diameter and eighteen inches high. Many boats in the tropics have windsails—tubes or funnels made of canvas, which conduct fresh air below. They can't always be set up under way, but they're invaluable at anchor.

To sum it up, a person who wants to charter a bare-boat should first evaluate his own competence, then contact several firms that offer boats suitable to his taste and experience. Then he should check each boat carefully from the information sent, and request references from the firms managing the boats. He should discuss with people who have already chartered the boat the suitability of the boat and the efficiency of the firm managing the boat.

He should investigate what the supporting facilities are for the fleet he is dealing with. If you are going to the expense of flying to the islands, make sure that your boat will be ready and in good condition at the time you desire. Similarly it is ridiculous to waste one or two days of your valuable vacation time provisioning the boat. This should be done by the operator—he knows the boat, the area, and the type of stores available.

When all decisions have been made, all that remains is to pack your seabag with the right clothing and personal gear (see chapter 2 of this section) and take off for a great vacation cruise in one of the world's best cruising grounds. It's worth doing it right.

III

The Lighter Side

⑨ ❊ Crazy Capers of the Charter Fleet

YACHT CHARTERING in the West Indies has become "big business." Anyone who wants to cruise the Caribbean has only to contact a yacht broker or agent, hop a jet and make a half-day switch from anywhere in North America to his privately chartered vessel. Upon arrival, he can be reasonably sure that the boat will be well found and professionally operated in a reliable manner.

All this has developed in the past twenty-five years. Before then, you had to be on your own to cruise the area after sailing or shipping your own boat there, and it was such a rare feat that you usually wrote a book about it and everyone envied you.

In the early 1950's however, various factors began to combine to bring about the situation we have today. Yacht chartering started in a modest way, and the beginnings were pretty colorful. Some of the early adventures have become a part of the modern legends of the Caribbean, and, even though today's operators are mainly reliable businessmen, they aren't exactly the gray-flannel-suit-and-Homburg type yet. Local color is far from dead.

The first of the factors that started the development of the charter business was the advent of Commander V.E.B. Nicholson and family. Retired from the Royal Navy after World War II, he purchased the venerable schooner *Mollihawk* and was on his way around the world with his wife and two sons when they casually happened into English Harbour, the abandoned Royal Navy Dockyard at Antigua, planning to do some work on *Mollihawk*.

One thing led to another, and the Nicholsons ended up in the charter business while helping to launch the "Friends of English Harbour," an organization which has to a large extent renovated and restored the old

Dockyard. They now have a travel agency, are agents for a large fleet of charter boats, and operate a marine store, radio station, and hotel. This can happen if you are a charming Irishman with two strong, charming Irish sons.

The second factor could be found northwest of Antigua at St. Thomas in the Virgin Islands, with its incomparable harbor and good air connections. Until about 1950 or so there were no charter yachts there, but circumstances conspired to change this situation. At that time St. Thomas was a divorce mill. There was nothing to do on the island and no way to get to St. John, or to the other Lesser Antilles. Air communication was then minimal and the island was overloaded with wealthy, bored would-be divorcees with nothing to do and no place to go.

This was the situation when the first of the post-war escapists began to wander down into the Caribbean in sailboats. With few exceptions the owner-skippers of these first yachts to cruise the islands in the late forties and early fifties were young, adventurous, single, often good-looking, and always broke. What to do to raise money? The most obvious solution was to take the rich, bored ladies of St. Thomas out for a sail to St. John's wonderful, deserted beaches.

From such informal beginnings, the combination of adventurous young men who needed a buck and a retired Commander RN who wanted to repair his yacht has created a business that has done much to raise the standard of living in the islands, and to add to the tourist explosion that is now occurring.

Today the charter business is most often entered into by a married couple that has chucked life in the States, sold everything, and is trying to make a go of it in the islands. In some cases owners send their yacht down with a skipper and charter her out when they aren't using her, to minimize their expenses. This is all to the good for charter parties. Boats are better kept and crews more reliable, and amenities of life such as food in variety, fresh water, showers, ice in your drink, and engines that run, are there for the asking.

But to go back; as I said, it must be admitted that some of the pioneer characters were amusing and colorful in the extreme; for instance, Roger and Al, both very athletic and good-looking, excellent as raconteurs, and great on the bongo drums. Each evening after returning from charter they would go to the Virgin Isle Hotel to drum up trade and book the next day's customers, usually for a day trip to St. John.

First as they sailed out of the harbor, Roger or Al would entertain the onlookers by standing on the end of the bowsprit with the spinnaker halyard in his hands, swing off to leeward and come in over the stern pulpit. It was a great performance and the charterers loved it. Then, once clear of the harbor, it was off with all the clothes. "What, you have never been sailing before? Well, everyone takes their clothes off when sailing in the tropics." It was quite a sight, two men and six to ten women with not a stitch of clothes among them, and, wow, the sunburns.

Then there was Sandy, a character and a half. He was of undetermined age, but he did claim to have fought with Pancho Villa and in the various revolutions in Haiti and Santo Domingo into the '20s and '30s. He looked like Popeye the sailor: beard, round face, pipe, gigantic forearms covered with tattoos, striped shirt, and bell-bottom trousers. Sandy had a habit of finding some sweet young thing and inviting her for a moonlight cruise to St. Croix. He would row out to the boat and set all sail, saying to the sweet young thing, "Time to lay below for a grog. Don't worry, she will sail herself."

Whenever we awoke in the morning and found his boat tacking around her anchor with everything sheeted in flat we knew that Sandy had found a new girlfriend. There was always a surprised expression on the face of the girl when she poked her head out of the hatch to discover that she still was in St. Thomas.

In another case things did happen almost exactly as described in the best selling novel *Don't Stop the Carnival*. A woman did sell her hotel, did buy a big boat for her bartender-cum-lover, and he did indeed heave her overboard not too many months later. It has been said that *Don't Stop the Carnival* was good but overdone, but to those who lived in St. Thomas in those days it is thought to be underdone, and slightly embarrassing to those who can recognize themselves all too well.

All types have ended up as charter skippers. One gal got divorced in Germany and discovered that her husband had taken the stocks and bonds and left her with the boat. Being a tough-minded gal she shrugged, hoisted sail, crossed the Atlantic, and went into the charter business. It was quite a shock when salty characters from up north arrived to discover that they had a female as a skipper for their vacation.

In other cases, couples on extended cruises arrived broke in St. Thomas and found that chartering offered a way to recoup their finances. There was one who arrived in that state and discovered friends already in St. Thomas doing day charters. They started chartering in company, as the new arrivals did not have detailed charts of the area, and, as usual, the harbor office was out of them. One day they left Yacht Haven together to run dead downwind to leave through Town Cut at the lee end of the harbor. All was fine until the new skipper realized he was ahead of his "guide" and did not know where Town Cut was, nor could he spot it.

At the last minute, he found the cut and jibed over, and his mainsail blew out. He sailed on through under mizzen and headsails, and when the other boat caught up the skipper called over, "Don't worry, Jack, you can use my spare mizzen as a small main."

He did so for the next few months, and it blew so hard that winter that the mizzen did fine as a main, just like having a permanent double reef.

Apropos of windy winter weather, the harbor master's office has an interesting method of describing how much it blew during the winter. Often the small craft warning is up for weeks at a time, so long that they frequently wear out and have to be replaced. As a result the harbor master's office will report, "Yes, it was a windy winter. It was a six-flag winter, year before was only a two-flag winter, not much wind."

Trying to save money to get on with the next cruise causes much penny pinching, some of it unsuccessful. Jack and Ruthie decided to live on the native diet of dried salt cod, fungi, and rice, but they had to give it up, as the boat began to smell so bad that no one would come on board, much less pay for a charter.

The first crews hired by charter boats were really a wonderful bunch of boys. They were off the Anguilla and St. Barts schooners, and no matter how hard you worked them, they had their three square meals a day, a dry bunk, and less work than they had on the schooners. In those days, the schooners had no auxiliary engine, no donkey engine for handling cargo, and still set main topsails and fisherman staysails. They were good sailors and not afraid of work.

Some were truly amazing. The most famous, Just, from St. Barts, could not read or write, yet could take a diesel or gasoline engine to bits and pieces, reassemble it perfectly, and it would run. Someone had taught him how to read a leaf gauge and a micrometer, and he would find himself a literate friend to read the manual to him.

I had one boy from Montseratt who was somewhat of the local philosopher and humorist. When I came back from climbing a coconut tree with my legs scraped, Phil sat and laughed, "Boss, you is okay, you get up the tree, but boss, you climb dat tree like a white man; you got to learn to climb a tree like a black man." People would ask him when he was going to get married, to which he would reply, "I is one of 21 children. No one never saw fit to marry my mother, so I don't see fitten to marry someone else's daughter." Often people would ask me what Virgin Gorda (the name of an island in the Virgins) meant. I would reply that it meant fat virgin in Spanish, at which Phil would burst out laughing, "Boss, ain't no such thing as no virgin with a fat belly."

He was also a good sailor, but when jibing he would let the main-sheet run through his hands till they almost smoked. When warned about rope burns, he would reply, "Ah gots burn-proof hands." He did not mind the rain as long as he could keep his head dry. Each time a squall came by he would dive below, come up with an old wool navy watch cap on his head and wrap himself around the standing backstay, making quite a picture with rain rolling off him and his white teeth flashing as he roared with laughter at the rest of us huddled in foul-weather gear.

Some of the crews were young divorcees, signed on for other than their sailing ability. One skipper had a great crew: good-looking, excellent cook, never got seasick, worked like mad, but just could not stand wearing clothes. Many charter parties had all their inhibitions scared out of them when they were served an excellent breakfast by a beautiful girl whose total covering was the pot holder by which she was holding the frying pan.

This type of crew perhaps was scenic but not very stable, so one charter skipper decided he knew the solution. He placed an ad in *Yachting*'s Swap Chest: "Good-looking, adventurous young charter skipper owns own boat, looking for crew (female) wishing to share experiences and adventures; send photo and vital statistics." He was inundated with replies and finally selected one after checking facts and figures. She came down, was crew for a few years, and finally dragged him to the altar.

Some of the couples chartering were happily married, but others were not and were famous for their fights from St. Thomas to Trinidad. At times husbands have been shoved overboard, hysterical fits have been thrown, wives put ashore, and lessons in how to swear in several languages given to all for several miles to leeward. The charterers' reaction is varied. Some are so happy with couples that they will not charter unless a husband-and-wife team is aboard. Others, perhaps burned by the above type of thing, will not set foot on a boat that is run by a husband and wife.

The crews today are generally not nearly as picturesque. West Indian schooner hands have been replaced by bored college students looking for an adventurous vacation, and the sexy cook by some career girl between jobs, who usually has no romantic attachment to the skipper and eats too much of her own cooking. The female cooks all seem to have that well-padded look.

In the old days, the charter fleet came from local craft that had been hurriedly converted to charter boats. A two-burner primus sufficed for cooking. A small deck ice-box provided ice for three or four days, and after that you drank your rum neat and your beer warm. Water supply was meager. One boat had a pump so small, six strokes filled a water glass. There were no showers (except in a squall), minimal electric lighting and dinghies had oars only. It was a big event when you saw another yacht.

Things have now changed, boats are specifically built for chartering with huge water tanks, hot and cold running water, showers, and fancy stove, some even have air conditioning, huge generators, piped hi-fi, white-coated stewards, cordon bleu cooking with vintage wines and champagne, and large launches for water skiing. The deserted West Indian anchorage is pretty much a thing of the past. The luxury yachts have every comfort, but they are usually motorsailers more dependent on their engines than their sails. It is still possible, though, to find a boat that is plain, comfortable, and a good sailer, if specifically requested from charter brokers.

Today instead of deserted anchorages one almost always finds other yachts. This can be pleasant and sometimes congenial except for large generators. A really good charter skipper not only knows what boats have generators, but also knows which side of the boat it is mounted on, and he does his best to anchor on the opposite side from the generator exhaust. West Indian anchorages also even have water skiers now.

In years gone by many of the charter boats did not have engines, and others lost theirs in rather amusing ways. One lost her engine when the skipper told his crew to drain the oil in the engine and change it, which the boy did. Next time the engine was started, it ran for a few minutes, then seized up solid. It turned out the boy, straight from a native schooner, had filled the engine with the only oil he had ever seen, linseed oil.

My own boat, *Iolaire,* also lost her engine in a rather amusing fashion. Bob Crytser had purchased her shortly after her arrival in the islands from the Canaries. Her engine did not work and was rather ancient, so he sent her down to St. Lucia to have the engine overhauled. After much money had been spent, the engine was again working and they decided to go out for a trial run. The crew dropped the mooring and the engine was put into gear, but nothing happened; the shaft was turning but the boat was not moving. Deciding that the prop must be fouled by so much inaction a crewman put on a face mask and dived for a look. It is said that curse words were heard coming out of the air bubbles, and he came up to report that, after all that expense to fix the engine, the "trouble" was that both blades of the folding prop had fallen off while she was sailing across the Atlantic. Crytser was so frustrated that he ordered the engine dropped overboard and used as a mooring. For all I know it is still used that way in St. Lucia today.

When I purchased *Iolaire* she still had no engine, but she did have the world's noisiest generator, which resulted in another story. We were sailing back from St. John, the wind was light, it was getting late and one of the charter parties suggested that I start the engine. I decided that if they could not tell the difference between an engine and a generator I might be able to fool them. I went below, started the generator, fiddled with the carburetor until it was running its noisiest, and then went on deck and pointed out to everyone that since it was a very small engine we had better keep the sails up.

We spent the afternoon carefully trimming sails and catching every puff, finally reaching St. Thomas harbor just before sunset. As we rounded West Indian Company dock and came on the wind, we discovered that we had enough wind to sail quite nicely, so I suggested that we cut the engine, be sporting, and sail alongside the dock. As we secured everything and the charter party began to leave, they all thanked me for a pleasant day and one said, "It certainly was good that you had that engine, or we never would have made it back before dark." My charter skipper friends standing on the dock had very quizzical expressions on their faces, but no one let the cat out of the bag, and there were many laughs later.

Roger ended up with one of the strangest charters. Many years ago he was celebrating the end of a successful charter season and partaking in Carnival at the same time. A man approached him discussing a charter and waving a fistful of money. Roger quickly made a deal. "Go to the boat and load your gear aboard and I will be there Sunday night at 2400, the official end of Carnival." During the next couple of days Roger forgot the whole thing but his crew loaded the charter party aboard, bought the fuel, water, ice, and the like. Sunday evening the crew searched the town, retrieved the skipper, and at 2400 all was well. It was blowing half a gale out of the north for a course of southeast, and who passes up a fair breeze in a gaff-rigged schooner notorious for her inability to go windward?

They took off under power, set jib, staysail, and reefed main, shut down the engine, set the course, and Roger went below to sleep. Later he was awakened by a huge boxer dog licking his face. Roger decided that this must be a dream and rolled over but the boxer persisted. He opened his eyes; his head started to swim and his stomach to churn as the boxer continued to lick his face. It was all too much and he made a fast break for the hatch and a quick trip to the lee rail.

Sitting down and looking around he saw that the four lowers were set, trimmed in flat, and she was slamming hard into it. He also saw a motorcycle lashed to the lee rigging, and a huge canvas-covered crate lashed to the cabintop. Assorted other crates were lashed down in various places. As his head began to clear he asked questions. They had been chartered to take a couple and household goods from St. Thomas to Dominica. Household goods here meant grand piano (legs removed, lashed to cabin-top) motorcycle, (lee rigging) boxer dog (presently sitting on lap licking face) and other assorted bits and pieces that would not fit below. All this plus 200 miles to windward, plus a mansized hangover. Roger was ready to jump overboard, but then he looked to windward and on the port beam were the Saintes and dead ahead was Dominica.

He discovered that the wind had shifted back to east only a few hours previously; that he had been out cold for thirty hours; that the trip was al-most over and the money already earned. As he said later, "Best way to sleep off a Carnival I ever saw, and easiest money I ever earned," espe-cially considering that he took the charter at a flat rate and figured it would take five days to reach Dominica.

One skipper, Eric, had a subtle solution for charterers' persistent questions. It was so subtle that none of us realized it for many years. His boat should have been fast, but she was always the slowest one in the en-tire charter fleet. No one could ever quite figure out why, but after Eric sold the boat he confessed that if he traveled fast he would pass many points and each time that he passed a point he had more questions to an-swer. As a result the slower he sailed the fewer questions he had to an-swer.

There is an oft-quoted story on stupid questions that I know is true, as it happened on my own boat. I was recovering from hepatitis while chartering, so I had a very good native sailor on board who did just about everything for me. One day Robbie was sailing the boat back from St. John. I was half asleep on deck, we had just passed through Current Hole, and we were passing Cow and Calf, two rocks that rise out about forty feet of water. I overheard the following conversation.

"Robbie, what are those?"

"Why the Cow and the Calf," replies Robbie.

"Which is the Cow and which is the Calf?" asks the charterer.

"I'm afraid I don't know," replies Robbie.

"But how deep is the water?" asks another.

Robbie replies, "About forty feet."

"Do those rocks go all the way to the bottom?" asks the charterer.

With a perfectly straight face Robbie replies, "I haven't seen any rocks yet that float."

Sometimes the charter skipper can become an innocent victim. In one such case a charter schooner arrived in Bequia after having had a rough and slow trip up from Grenada. After a week of sailing, the wives all decided for a big dinner ashore and proceeded to get dressed as if they were going to the Ritz.

The skipper brought the dinghy alongside. The women climbed down the ladder and insisted on standing, as they did not want to get their frilly dresses mussed. The skipper cast off and started the Seagull, only to discover that the dinghy was leaking, in fact leaking so badly that they were ankle-deep in water before they went one hundred yards. He turned back to the yacht but the dinghy went glug, glug, glug while still twenty yards away. A line was thrown, everyone was rescued amid much hysterics, anger, and recrimination.

Needless to say, no one got ashore, and it was a rather cold and tense dinner on board. Next morning at first light, the dinghy was hauled up in the davits, and it was discovered that there were six small holes in the bottom. One hole still had a shoe in it, caught by its tall, spike heel.

10 ❖ On the Ways, West Indian Style

IN MY TWENTY-TWO YEARS in the Lesser Antilles I have hauled at most of the yards in the islands between St. Thomas and Grenada, and it has been a sometimes adventurous, often frustrating, and always amusing experience. The lack of equipment and spares has made for some amazing lash-ups, and the stories that go around the Caribbean as the people on the boats compare notes sound like a bunch of airline travelers trading their experiences getting in and out of Kennedy Airport in New York. What West Indian yards get along with would make Rube Goldberg's best concoction look streamlined.

Take Monsieur Grant's yard in Martinique for example. It has two drill presses that never cease to amaze when you watch them work. A small hand-powered one has a drill that turns with each revolution of a crank handle, forced down by an eccentric cam with a ratchet. It sounds crazy, but it works, and it's nothing to the boy-powered drill press in the back yard. This huge affair is worked by three little boys who climb into the rafters and spin the flywheel with their feet. The flywheel is geared to the drive shaft with eccentric cam and ratchet, and I have seen it make one-inch holes in heavy steel plate with no difficulty. When asked why he doesn't electrify it, Monsieur says that he can hire three little boys for ten years for the cost of wiring and installation, and in that area and that climate, little boys are easier to come by, more indestructible, and easier to replace than electric motors.

St. Lucia has a machine shop that has been "building" for fifteen years. It still looks as if it were under construction, and has for all that time, while its lathes, drill presses, and tools all stand semi-covered. When it rains, those ubiquitous West Indian small boys appear and wipe everything down with diesel oil, and it's all still in pretty good shape.

The mechanics, who are usually just grown-up "small West Indian boys," having started their careers hanging around yards, can pull off some neat tricks on occasion. The career of one ended when he reassembled a diesel engine with some loose nuts inside one of the cylinders. It made a very strange noise. Another was trying to remove the head of a small diesel. The nuts were frozen, so they were removed with a "West Indian wrench": hammer and cold chisel. He tried to pry off the head then, with no luck, so he rolled it over with the hand crank. Still no luck, so he started it with no stud nuts on and was just beginning to rev it up when the boss noticed what was happening and called a halt.

It is surprising what can be done with bits and pieces and a little ingenuity. When sale of a boat was contingent on her engine being in working order, which it wasn't at the time, the owner asked one of the better-known charter skippers, a whiz of a mechanic, to see what he could do about the problem. The engine was a Swedish Albin, and he looked it over, took some measurements, went to town and came back with a box full of American and English automotive parts. Then he completely rebuilt the engine, including American-made pistons and connecting rods. The engine ran, and the sale was made, but I often wondered what the reactions were of the next mechanic to work on it.

A bunch of us once discovered an old railway, and one of our gang started looking around in the bushes until he found parts of an old winch. Within a week he had the thing all assembled and only had to pour new bearings. Then he found an abandoned engine and got it working and before long we were hauling boats up to fifty-five feet with a winch and motor that cost less than $100 to put back in commission.

A sailor named Vladic, who got as far as Beef Island and gave up an effort to be the first Pole to sail around the world, opened a yard in that remote and inaccessible spot. Before the days of air strips it took two days to get to St. Thomas and back by various ferries and buses and it was a major project to work on a boat here. But perhaps it wasn't such a dumb spot after all, as there were two unmarked reefs within a mile of the yard. Very often a boat would leave, hit the reefs, and return for rehauling while the cradle was still in the water from her launching. Some even believed that they usually left the cradle in the water for a while after each launching, as they knew that the boat would probably be back.

Vladic had a long-standing argument with fellow-countryman Bob, a charter skipper, who told Vladic that he should have tied the tracks of his railway together, rather than just seating them in blocks of concrete, because every heavy boat would spread them and jam the ways. Vladic refused to listen, the predicted happened, and every time it did, for years, Bob would call him on the RT to say "I told you so."

Their feud reached a peak once when Bob's boat was on the ways for a bottom painting before heading to Martinique for a charter. This was usually a beat, but the wind came around to northeast during the night, and the boat's crew gave her a quick painting themselves at dawn, so they could take off with a reaching breeze. The captain woke Vladic up to ask him how much the charges would be for the job, got the figure, said "Fine, and here's an extra twenty" as he wrote the check, and said "Now put us back in."

Vladic was so mad that he wouldn't take the check at all, even though it would have meant an extra profit, and for years afterward, every time they met, Bob tried to pay him but only produced another explosion.

Sometimes Vladic would disappear for days while a boat was on his ways, and the crew would fuss and fume, wanting to get back afloat. The yard crew would not touch a boat without the boss there and tempers would stay short for days. Finally, one skipper couldn't take the delay any longer, so, after the yard crew had gone home, he lashed the cradle to the winch, disengaged the winch, paid out more than enough cable slack and climbed aboard. His crew then cut the lashing with an axe, and down she went with a roar. As they were rounding the point, who should they meet but Vladic on his way back after his long absence, and he almost had apoplexy at the sight of the boat leaving and the bits and pieces of cradle, blocks, and chocks floating around the harbor.

Often boats were stuck for days or weeks, half-in half-out of the water as frantic calls went out by radio for jacks, chain, blocks, etc. One seventy-five-foot ketch was stuck this way and seemed all set for a long period on the ways, so her crew took off spearfishing, leaving one non-sailor aboard polishing some brass, as he was completely useless at any other boat activity. Without telling anyone, two of the yard boys happened to notice that this was not the usual case of the tracks spreading, but just a jammed wheel, and they managed to free the wheel. With a hell of a roar the boat ran free and took off into the harbor with nothing but one idiot brass polisher aboard, while the yard boss came running from inside and the crew came screaming back from spearfishing to get the situation under control. The yard boys were pretty hurt and couldn't understand all the fuss, because they thought thcy had been very helpful.

Another yard was established on Tortola, which was a hopeful sign, but there were a few difficulties. A nice range marked the entrance, but if you followed it, you would go hard aground. They never kept schedule, and delays went on for days here, too. Help would show up after answering an ad in British trade journals, take one look, and leave, and you ended up doing all your own work. Although almost all customers were American, there was not a single American tap or die in the place, so everything ended up with British threading. Then you might haul in Martinique and get all metric stuff, and a subsequent owner would find he had a pretty interesting collection of stuff on his hands.

For years, cheapest hauling in the islands was the large dry dock in Martinique. Yachts would go in with a large freighter and the cost would be pro-rated by the ton—twenty-ton yacht against 5,000-ton freighter made a fairly good ratio—but there were problems here too. Sometimes what started as a quick paint job for the ship would turn into a prolonged replacement of bad plates, and whatever yachts were in would be stuck there for perhaps a month. This would dry them out badly, and they would need a power pump to keep them afloat when they finally went back in.

Monsieur Grant's yard was famous for years, and it was always an experience to work with him and his foreman, Gabriel, as they spoke no English. Whatever you said to Monsieur, his first answer would be "Non." After a while the "nons" would become a little less emphatic, and when you finally got a "peut-etre" out of him you were over the hump. They did good first-class yacht work, but the atmosphere was a bit steamy. The yard was at the mouth of a small river that was more like an open sewer, the mosquitos were ferocious, and, if you drew more than six feet, you had to winch your way for the last 200 yards through soft goo on the bottom.

The West Indian Co. in St. Thomas had a method of hauling yachts that left many a gray hair through the charter fleet. They had a floating crane dating to Danish days that sat on a steel barge. As it aged, it leaked more and more often, and each time it did they poured a little concrete in it. They never bothered to pump it, and there were some spectacular near-disasters as a result. When hauling a heavy boat and the crane would begin to take the strain, the other end would start to lift, and water would rush to the crane end. Stability would suddenly become minimal and the crane operator would let the boat back into the water with a tremendous splash.

If and when you made it out of the water to the concrete dock, you were set down directly onto it and shored up with old oil drums or something, which made it a bit hard to get at keel bolts. The company took a dim view of your chipping holes in their concrete, so the routine was to slip back there at night with sledge and chisel, cut a hole in the dock, remove keel bolts and cover the hole with boards. When the keel bolts had been replaced, you then liberated some concrete and sand from the West Indian Co. and filled in the hole under your boat.

At St. Lucia, to use the government slip, you had to hire a complete crew of diver, winch operator, boiler man, water man, etc., pay their charge to a different department of the government for each man, and bring the chits to the hauling boss, who would then go round up the crew. Then you had to hire a truck to bring the coal to fire the steam boiler that provided power for the steam driven winch. By the time you had done all this red tape, you sometimes decided it was really easier to sail on somewhere else.

Some of the best operations were run by the West Indians in their own way, such as the one at Bourgers Bay, Tortola, where a slip next to the dance hall could handle boats to sixty feet. The windlass was hand-powered, and if the boat was coming up too slowly, a quick trip to the dance hall for a bottle of rum always did wonders in speeding things up. A few cases of cold beer were the best guarantee of a clean bottom, and everyone was cheerful, prices were cheap and the work, while rough, was reliable and solid. Wide seams never bothered anyone. I've seen them caulking one you could put a finger through.

At Hassell Island, Creque's slipway had a strange method of securing a yacht in a big slipway intended to hold 1,500-tonners. One heavy post was secured off center in the middle of the cradle, the boat would be brought in until her mast was even with the post, she would be given a slight list toward the post, lashed there, mast to post, and then up she'd come. It looked strange but it worked, and there were no supports in the way while bottom painting.

The West Indians sometimes knew how to use manpower to solve what could be quite an engineering problem. The owner of a 40' x 18' catamaran of four-and-a-half tons displacement was all set to lay down skids, build a cradle, and get out all kinds of tackle to launch her, but a local friend in the construction business had a better idea—65 men and a case of rum. Using short lengths of line, they picked her up, carried her fifty feet, set her down, swigged the rum, and did it again. Three swigs and she was launched.

This system was used at Grenada Yacht Service when two eighty-foot masts from the yacht *Jacinta* had to be rebuilt. For a case of beer per mast to the mate of a banana ship in the harbor they had the masts lifted out and placed on deck. Then she was taken to the GYS yard and moored stern-to, and everyone available in the yard, probably forty people, was drafted. For two cases of beer per mast, the world's largest centipede carried them down the dock to the shop and reversed the process when they were repaired.

The Vallejo Brothers yard in Puerto Rico restored faith in human nature for a lot of people with Don Hogg's little steel sloop *Potlatch*. Through a series of emergencies the boat was tied up in the yard for over eighteen months while being sanded in preparation for fiberglassing, and even lost her stick through a yard mishap. When she was finally done, the yard refused any payment, even for materials.

But then there was the big schooner that needed hauling, and the yard boss said she was too big and too heavy. Finally the owner persuaded him that it would be a simple job—just one chock needed at the forward end of the keel where there was a little rise. Murder was almost committed when the boat emerged, as there was substantial rocker to the keel and the cradle was now beautifully bowed to the curvature of it.

A sense of humor helps if you ever have anything to do with hauling in the West Indies.

11 ❧ The World's Wackiest Wayfarers

IN THE WEST INDIES, one of the favorite diversions is watching the parade of yachts that stream into the islands from across the Atlantic. We don't have all the entertainment facilities like TV and the latest movies, but it is real fun and games to see what manages to get across the ocean from the other side.

In the years I have based in West Indian ports operating a charter yacht, I have seen innumerable voyagers reach the islands. The extremes have been extreme, from the ultimate in luxury such as the yacht *Half-O* (See *Yachting,* May 1961, and Feb. 1962), to the German who arrived in

Yachting, November 1965.

a folding kayak. It is said that anything watertight cast adrift off the coast of Portugal will eventually end up in the West Indies, such as the glass fishnet floats that drift in, and some of the vessels that arrive would seem to have less chance (and are much less watertight), and even less speed potential, then the glass floats. On them, the people who have made the passage offer many extremes themselves, and the collection is one of the wackiest set of wayfarers that ever descended on an area. Not all of them are wacky, of course; many are sensible, forward-looking people who plan well and execute their voyages with fine seamanship, but one tends to remember the more oddball types. They make the best stories when Caribbean sailors gather in a cockpit for a session of yarning and reminiscing.

Half-O's was the ultimate in the sensible, well-planned voyages. She was a brand-new North Sea trawler type of hull with all the latest equipment. The owner wanted to cruise in comfort and safety with cost no particular object, and she had radar, loran, RDF, auto-pilot, ship-to-shore, roll dampers, and the whole list. Creature comforts were attended to by deep freeze, hot and cold water (tons of it), a galley that would make a hotel chef drool, and the supplies to go with it. I never saw a more comfortable, relaxed lot.

At the other end of the scale was the bearded German doctor who arrived in the kayak amid much fanfare and eventual publicity my first winter in St. Thomas, V.I. Now this was a truly amazing performance! He was some seventy-odd days at sea in the tropics yet was not badly sunburned, nor did he have a very good crop of salt-water boils. He also had the world's best varnish and chrome. The varnished spars, paddles, and cockpit coaming were in good shape, and the chrome was unpitted.

The vast majority of arrivals fall between these extremes. For some, it is the result of a lifelong dream; to others it is just another pond to cross. There are a few who have lost track of the number of crossings they have made, so often have they done it.

Amid all the extremes, some averages have developed. The boats 45′ and up average about 21 days from the Cape Verde or Canaries and 25–28 is the average for smaller boats. Then there are the 40–70 day crowd who have fitted out with twin staysails that are much too small. They have read stories of thirty-knot trades and they rig their skimpy sails for self-steering, sit back, and come across like a lead balloon, even becalmed some of the time.

Much better times are usually turned in by boats that keep normal fore and aft rigs and have helmsman watches, and the boats that have two big gennies wung-out have done best of all. It is interesting that most of the best runs have been made by boats relying entirely on sail, rather than those that switch the power off and on, and to the best of my knowledge, no multi-hull has made a truly fast passage. (In 1968 Eric Tabarly beat the previous Los Angeles-to-Honolulu record by twenty-four hours in his multihulled *Pen Duick IV,* but such success has been rare.)

How do they navigate? How many stars are there in the sky? you might well ask. The methods have been varied, interesting, and in some cases, distinctly novel. Some really make a project of it with morning and evening stars, morning, noon, and afternoon sunlines and the whole routine. Others simply work with the sun, using H.O. 214 or 249.

Then there are the wacky ones. Sometimes they are so broke after outfitting that all they can afford is a "Nautical Almanac." Latitude is simple, and for longitude they get along by using equal altitudes before and after noon. Or, even more basically, one voyager with sextant but no watch, simply found the latitude of Barbados and ran it down until he hit the island. Of course his log was off and he spent an anxious two-and-a-half days looking at an empty horizon where he thought Barbados should be, but eventually it appeared. Another was so poor that he could not buy a sextant but had a watch and radio. He sailed south from the Canaries until he saw the Cape Verde Islands, then turned west and got his longitude by timing sunrise and sunset. He made it.

The most casual approach in the "sail west and you'll hit something" school was the guy who said "I can't miss the whole bloody string of islands if I head west, and I don't care which one I hit." But somehow he missed, passing between Trinidad and Grenada, the only spot where he could without sighting land, and fetched up on the Venezuelan coast. It was too tough to beat back against the trades, so he kept on going to Panama. I often wonder what finally happened to him.

There are some wonderfully varied reactions toward mechanical equipment. The patron saint of the no-power school is Peter Tangveld, who had little success with the engine in his *Dorothea* in the Mediterranean and was spied by a Scotch friend in Majorca trying to get the engine out. Scotty lent a helping hand and they finally got the engine unbolted and out on the hatch on deck, where Scotty assumed Peter was going to overhaul it. Instead, Peter merely put his foot against the side of the engine and shoved. As it disappeared into the harbor under a great splash, Scotty, an excitable sort and very Scottish in his tendencies, screamed, "Why did you do that?"

Peter calmly replied, "I don't want anything in the boat that I don't understand. I don't understand engines, and I don't understand heads, and now I'm going down to unbolt the head and throw that overboard too." This he proceeded to do, and he has since gone around the world minus engine and head, visiting Pacific ports that supposedly can't be entered without power.

Others swear by engines and give them complete overhauls while passaging. In one case a diesel was practically rebuilt on the trip across. Some have plenty of power but forget to use it until the batteries are so low that the engine can't be started. One delivery crew of the casual type found themselves in that fix on a slow boat, and, knowing they would have to keep sailing even though no one liked nightwatches, played bridge every evening with the dummy to steer.

There was a humorous incident on my own boat, *Iolaire,* after her fifth crossing. The engine hadn't seemed to work very well and was therefore not used much. She was sold immediately after the passage, and the new owner, hearing of the engine's unreliability, spent a fortune having it overhauled. When it was finally fixed, he dropped her off the mooring to test it. She was put into reverse. Nothing happened. She was put in forward. Nothing happened. Deciding the prop must be fouled, he went overboard to clear it, and the water almost became steam-heated at his reaction when he found that both blades had fallen off the folding prop during the crossing.

Water supply is always a big question, and it is met in a variety of ways. Some of the fancier boats carry tons of it, have condensers or stills running off their engines, and provide continuous showers for the crew. On others, more care is taken. The usual thing is to carry a reserve supply of some sort, but there is no real need to use more than a half gallon per day per man. This has been worked out as a standard, even in the tropics.

A small pump, so that you have to pump like hell to get results, and a small sink, are two good ways of conserving water. The ultimate in the difficult-pump approach is in a Folkboat in which a retired British naval officer commutes back and forth across the Atlantic. She is equipped with fiberglass tank with a rubber hose where the vent normally is and another hose where the pump suction would normally be. When you want water, you put the vent hose in your mouth and put the other hose in the teapot. Then you blow two tuba solos' worth, and about the time you turn purple you have managed to get enough water for two cups of tea. There is never any trouble with people using too much water on this boat.

Putting stores aboard for a transatlantic voyage is another major project, and here again the systems vary in the extreme. On the big yachts with freezers, there are fresh foods all the way, chilled wine with every meal and ice-cold beer in the afternoon. Without mechanical refrigeration, ice usually lasts for the first week at most, and then it is canned or dried foods and warm drinks, with an occasional flying fish picked off the deck for breakfast. (*This was true in the past but now with a properly designed icebox, a boat crossing the Atlantic should be able to keep ice for a minimum of two, if not three, weeks. It should be noted that* Iolaire's *icebox, which is not as efficient as it should be, still enabled us to have ice for thirteen-and-a-half days on an eighteen-and-a-half day transatlantic passage. It's said the reason we went so fast is that the skipper dislikes warm beer!*)

Everyone has gone through the banana routine. Excellent bananas can be bought cheaply in the Canaries, and everyone takes on a stalk or two. For the first week they are too green to eat; then they suddenly ripen all at once, and it is bananas for breakfast, lunch, and dinner and in between for the next couple of days.

Wine is cheap and good in Madeira, but the rum is the most foul-tasting stuff ever concocted. No matter how you disguise it it still tastes like damn poor turpentine.

Limes are a wonderful addition to ship's stores. They are cheap and last indefinitely. I took a kidding from Count Pehr Sparre crossing on his *Arabella* when I loaded a tremendous supply of limes, but I had the last laugh when the last two were used to mix drinks at the coming home party in Essex, Conn. Since we had gotten stuck, as everybody else does the first time there, with Madeira rum, doctoring with limes had been the only way you could even think of drinking the stuff.

For the budget voyagers—and there are always plenty of them—cheap food can be made to do. Rice, curry, dried fish, oatmeal, lentils, potatoes, onions, dried peas, and the ubiquitous banana fill the bill. The record in this department was set by a boat whose stores for a crew of two on an Antigua–England voyage came to $15. They made it in good health, if somewhat bored with their diet.

The crew question brings on some of the wackiest situations of all. Some boats arrive with crews that have been carefully selected over the years, after much planning, for their skills and compatability. Others have gotten together during fitting out and at least have some idea of each other's capabilities. At the opposite end, and surprisingly frequent, are the pierhead jumpers. They leap aboard at Lisbon or Gibraltar just as the lines are being cast off, usually taking advantage of some last-minute emergency that has left the skipper short, often with hardly a toothbrush to their name.

A famous yachtsman had crew trouble in Lisbon, got rid of his crew and advertised in the London *Times*. Two young Irishmen answered, supposedly small-boat sailors, and each thinking the other knew more than he did. The skipper discovered as they set sail that neither knew anything, but they received the first of many sailing lessons from him going down the Tagus, and his determination paid off. They were adaptable and good-natured, and everything worked out fine.

In another case, a boat taking on stores in Gibraltar for a crossing was visited by a young, good-looking, athletic Englishman. He made friends with the crew in the pub, and, after a few evenings, decided he would like to go along on a share-expenses basis. His ignorance was very evident, and the crew decided to have some fun. They told him, since he was so obviously a good athlete, that it would be his job to climb the masts and tie the head of the sails to the masthead after they were hoisted, and that he had better get in some practice before they set sail. Every day he went faithfully up and down the masts several times, and they let it go on for almost a week before admitting the hoax.

Even women get into the act. One fairly large boat picked up two adventurous ones who had hitchhiked all the way from South Africa to Morocco and were anxious to go across. They signed on as cooks, but their cooking was so atrocious that the males soon took it over again, relegating the women to dish washing and below-decks cleaning. There have been cases of lonely single-handers taking women on at the last minute "to improve the scenery," and their availability never ceases to amaze. It isn't only men who are adventurous.

On the seamy side are the operators who pick up a crew in the Med on a share-expense basis, use the crew's money to buy stores, then manage to get rid of the crew by intimidation or simply sailing off and leaving them, picking up another crew (and more expense money) before they finally leave. It's a wonder some of these characters are still alive—they won't be if the jettisoned crews ever catch up with them.

Another variation of this theme is to say that money is waiting in Barbados, hire a crew on promise to pay after the passage, and then, on arrival, say that there must be some mistake and the money has failed to come through. It is illegal to strand a crew in a foreign port, but there are characters who have gotten away with this more than once.

The boats themselves vary, of course, from little more than glass floats to luxury yachts. New boats come across after hardly a shakedown. Old, beautifully kept ones become familiar over the years on repeated visits, and usually have fewer difficulties than the new boats. Every so often one of the well-publicized circumnavigators stops by.

A number of the boats are actually ancient. A young Englishman named Paul Johnson made it to Martinique on Christmas Eve in a sixteen-foot ketch built as a fishing dory in 1894 from Scottish larch taken from a wreck. Her planks therefore were an unknown number of years older than that. She is still in good, solid shape. There are others, much younger, that make you wonder how they float.

Perhaps the oldest of all was the *City Of Biddeford,* built in England in 1836, a true cod's-head and mackerel-tail hull with semi-circular bow. She was still sailing as a trading ketch as late as 1959 after crossing at the end of World War II.

Weather cloths and dodgers are a vital part of a passage boat's equipment, and the smaller the boat the larger the dodger, cloth, and lifelines loom, to the extent that it is impossible to move around on the decks.

The most amazing thing is how relatively few boats have been lost out of this strange armada. While the glass floats do make it, some boats haven't. Sadly, about a dozen have disappeared without trace after departure from Europe in recent years.

Considering what has made it, however, I don't think anyone in the islands will be truly surprised any more until someone, no doubt with a woman stowaway as crew, sails in on a bale of hay.

12 ❊ Racing in the Eastern Caribbean

THE OLD COMMERCIAL sail rule in the Lesser Antilles is "de biggest boat got de right o' way," and although this rule does not carry over to racing in the Lesser Antilles, it is worth remembering. Frequently when starting in an Eastern Caribbean regatta (especially in the cruising division) you discover one of the "big 'uns" such as *Antares,* a 90-foot gaff-rigged schooner, *Gitana IV,* the incomparably beautiful 90-foot yawl, *Mighty Ti* (*Ticonderoga*), the 72-foot ketch, or the 72-foot ketch *Eileen,* charging through the smaller boats on crowded starting lines like unguided missiles. They can't stop and are usually so hemmed in on all sides that they cannot turn. Time for us little guys to get out of the way!

This daredevil game is what racing in the Eastern Caribbean is all about, and seldom anywhere else will you see such a collection of hot ocean racers, cruising boats, and classic "big 'uns" all on or near the same starting line.

Sail, November 1977.

The islands in the Lesser Antilles chain stretch from the Virgins to Trinidad in a great crescent about 600 miles long, encompassing not only some of the finest cruising waters of the world, but also offering yachtsmen near-perfect racing conditions. From approximately mid-November through early August the daily weather report is 12-18-knot, east-northeast to east-southeast winds with higher gusts. (Seldom does it say how much higher in the gusts!) Tides are minimal, seldom more than eighteen inches, and although there can be strong currents, most of the Eastern Caribbean race courses are laid out to avoid major tide rips. Seldom does the racing sailor have to contend with currents of more than one-and-a-half knots. The temperature at sea during the day is in the mid-to-low eighties. The sun shines most of the time, and even during rain squalls you seldom need to put on anything more than a foul-weather jacket.

It's no wonder then that six major and around eight minor regattas are held during these "near-perfect" months. Eastern Caribbean regattas usually consist of day races 12–35 miles long. The major international regattas start in October with the three-day Rolex Cup Regatta in St. Thomas, U.S. Virgin Islands. This is followed by the Petit St. Vincent Regatta, another three-day affair, over Thanksgiving weekend at Petit St. Vincent in the Grenadines with feeder races from St. Vincent and Grenada. For many years one of the premier events in the Eastern Caribbean was the Grenada Round-the-Island Race, the first Sunday in January when the big turkeys, 80-90-footers, raced around the island of Grenada.

During the winter from January to mid-April there are no big regattas in the Caribbean; everyone is too busy killing himself trying to make some money in the short tourist season. But then Lulu Magras decided that St. Barts must have a regatta. Few notices were sent out, but the jungle telegraph picked up the news, and over forty boats assembled in St. Barts in mid-Feburary 1977, for a great party and a good race. In mid-April the tourist season eases off, and the British Virgin Islands hold their three-day spring regatta with good courses throughout those islands. Late April or early May is the high point of the entire racing program, Antigua Sailing Week, a series of five day-races and a good deal of hijinks ashore. Whit weekend (see your calendar for the exact date) is the very popular, 11-year-old Bequia Regatta, where boats race from St. Vincent to Bequia, Bequia to Mustique, and Mustique back to St. Vincent. A colorful workboat free-for-all rounds out the competition.

The exception to the day-race regattas is the three-year-old St. Maartens Tradewinds Race in May, in which multi- and monohulls sail a rhumb line of over 750 miles in three legs, which takes about a week. The season is rounded out by the Carriacou Regatta on August Monday (the

British bank holiday on the first Monday in August). This is basically a spectator's regatta, a cruising race from St. Vincent to Grenada with the fleet anchoring off the miles-long beach at Hillsborough Harbor to watch the largest collection of local boats racing in the Eastern Caribbean.

The scene in Eastern Caribbean racing is Antigua. The sight that greets the crew arriving from up North is absolutely mind-boggling! Each year old Admiral Nelson must roll over in his grave as though some-one had an electric drill tied to his feet. In place of the calm efficiency of the Royal Navy, today you find assembled (or perhaps it would be better to say crammed in with a shoehorn) in the midst of the restored 18-century Nelson's Dockyard a collection of over two hundred yachts of all sizes, shapes, and nationalities. Some have come to race; others to watch. Others come to drop their hooks while the crews disappear for a week on-board the various hot racing machines, many of which travel many miles for the regatta, sometimes arriving at the last minute.

Standing around the Antigua committee desk, you feel as though you are at a United Nations meeting with no interpreters. Looking at the attire (or lack of it) and the languages to match, you think of the Tower of Babel. Twenty-six nations were represented in 1977. You hear French, Spanish, German, Italian, Dutch, Finnish, Swedish, Norwegian, Afrikaans (and sometimes even Zulu), plus English and American, definitely two different languages.

Skippers' meetings in the Eastern Caribbean are necessary because there are often special local rules which at times have caused more than a little confusion and argument. Over frequent objections from competitors the chairman of the race committee usually replies, "All decisions are final; no appeals; we may not be right but we are damn well official. Case closed." Because of mail delays and failure to order them in time, the latest racing rules are frequently not available in the islands until a year or so after they go into effect. Thus, you might race under the 1973 rules in 1976, which can cause more than a little confusion when you file a protest quoting rule number and section.

The competitors and their boats are an interesting lot. No one can figure out how the Trinidadians and Puerto Ricans can race extremely hard and skillfully every day, party all night, stagger on board, and race again the next day. They try to prove who is the best sailor by day and the best drinker and partier by night. It is a close race in both cases.

Jol Byerley, the leading OWIH (Old West Indian Hand, a skipper who has raced in the Eastern Caribbean fifteen years or more and is considered native) is found with his *Morning Tide* at all the major regattas. Actually, *Tide* is syndicate-owned, but Byerley, being the hottest sailor, skippers. Despite her age, the ten-year-old Sparkman Stephens design is always the boat to beat. *Tide* was second overall and won her class at Antigua this year. Allegedly, Byerley moved out of his apartment in the officers' quarters at English Harbour because it was not big enough to hold all his trophies.

My own forty-four-foot *Iolaire,* the one-gun yawl, featuring a properly-mounted brass cannon, has had one of the longest racing careers in the Eastern Caribbean. At age seventy-four the "flying grandmother" is not winning races, but she was first raced in 1953 in St. Thomas, and she can still take off like a scalded cat once the sheets are eased.

Many top-notch skippers and crews arrive in Antigua expecting to clean house and are shocked to discover that they are hard pressed to get anywhere near the top. First, they are very surprised by the quality of the competition. Secondly, newcomers are working under a disadvantage as there are many distractions on the racecourse. In 1978, for example, George Sustendhal skippered *Southerly,* a fifty-two-foot ketch. He recruited an all-girl crew; all of them sailed topless, and some of them went bottomless too. Needless to say, this distracted the opposition and some of the very numerous collisions that occurred in the 1978 Antigua Week were blamed on the *Southerly*'s distractions and attractions. In other words, top-notch skippers sometimes do not do as well as they should because they are spending too much time watching tits and tails rather than sails.

One of the more famous foredeck bosses is Peter "Turkey Legs" Van der Sloot. Everyone in the Eastern Caribbean knows him as Turkey Legs, yet despite the fact that he has often raced Cowes Week, no one in Europe knows him other than by his proper name. When asked why, he replies, "Hell, in England it is cold, and I wear long pants."

When I have sailed with "Turkey Legs" and he was running the foredeck of various boats we did much better than we should have, not because we were faster or better sailors, but because "Turkey Legs" was a damn good reef pilot. We often took short cuts across the edges of reefs that others did not dare to. (Or perhaps they had more brains and common sense than we did). The fun ended a few years ago when they started buoying the edges of the reefs and making the buoys marks of the course.

This spirit of taking short cuts has manifested itself at various times when race committees were not exact in their course descriptions. For years the Round-St. Thomas Race started in St. Thomas, went up through Current Hole and down around St. Thomas and West Key, which is separated from St. Thomas by a very narrow, rock-infested channel. The first year *Iolaire* sailed in this race we were only doing moderately well approaching Current Hole. Our major competitors held high to go through the normal windward side of Current Hole but since the sailing directions only said, "Sail around the island of St. Thomas," we ducked through the shallow, narrow leeward passage saving four or five minutes and putting us back in the race. There were howls of protest at the finish. The following year, of course, everyone was planning to go through the leeward side of Current Hole and again the instructions read "around the island of St. Thomas," but at the last minute at the skippers' meeting the rules were amended to read "around St. Thomas and West Key." One of the members of the race committee had discovered that I had twice sailed *Iolaire* through the cut between West Key and St. Thomas, which I would have been able to do again under the wording of the instructions, saving at least thirty minutes.

Racing buoys in the islands have always been a problem. They drag out of position; lines chafe through; and buoys go adrift. Often the fishermen come by, haul them up, and liberate line and anchor for their fish pots. Result: no mark. This is a most discouraging situation when you are in the lead; the race is sewn up; and you find no marker. It is also discouraging when the mark drags but is still there. You round the mark, win the race, and someone protests that the mark was out of position. Then the race is thrown out! These events are now pretty much things of the past as at all the major regattas a stake boat now precedes the competitors and replaces missing buoys. I think some of the race committees have found it cheaper to pay off the fishermen before the regatta with line than to replace anchor, buoy, and line during the race.

One trick in Eastern Caribbean racing is to judge the "higher gusts" of the weather report. The wind always blows; sometimes it just blows harder. Going to windward, #2 genoa, and reefed main are *de rigueur* for the International Offshore Rule (IOR) boats. Sometimes it blows even harder. In the 1977 British Virgin Islands Regatta the first day it blew a steady 30, gusting to 40 and 45, occasionally easing off to a mere 25. The winning boat, Dick Doran's Swan 44 *Gitana,* was carrying a double-reefed main and #3 jib. The main split, so they triple-reefed the main and went more quickly. Despite the wind velocity, *Titon,* a chopped and cropped Cal 2/30, raced by a pack of mad Puerto Ricans, set a spinnaker on the short downwind leg and got away with it. With a double-reefed main and a well-chocked-down spinnaker, they planed right by a number of larger competitors who just stared in disbelief when the kite went up. The second day the wind moderated to a steady twenty-five, so most boats used spinnakers, producing some really wonderful downwind gyrations including a couple of roundhouse jibes. The third day was great, just a nice steady twenty with no squalls.

Although one of three legs in the St. Maartens Tradewinds Race is billed as a "close tack" from Tortola to Martinique, the race is beginning to attract most of the available multihulls in the area. The 1977 fleet was split almost equally between mono- and multi-hulls. There was no multi-hull division at Antigua Sailing Week that year because the multis were doing their thing at St. Maartens, which had been scheduled at the same time. In the Tradewinds Race the multi-hulls do have some long reaches where they can really pick up their skirts and fly, but then, as with any boat, they lose time in light airs under the islands and beating to windward. In 1977 the winning multi-hull, the 61-foot *Maho,* sailed the rhumb-line course of 760 miles in 94 hours, 21 minutes, averaging eight knots.

The leg that separates the men from the boys is the beat from Cade Reef to Holiday buoy along the south coast of Antigua. There is nothing between you and Africa to the east, so a big sea builds upwind, and the current is from the same direction. You must stay inshore and short-tack up the beach. By the time you have made your thirtieth tack, your crew is screaming for mercy. As you round Holiday buoy and set the spinnaker or wing the jib for the run home, the crew collapses on deck with beer in hand. They lie there congratulating themselves that the leg is over, that they are still alive, and thanking God that the Cade Reef/Holiday buoy leg is in only two races. If it were more than two, the bilge-boys' union would call a strike, especially in the cruising division.

Handicapping is done under the West Indian Yachting Association (WIYA) Rule, developed over the past seven years by measurer Alfred Rapier. It is a simple rule that works. A boat can be measured in the water and a rating calculated in a matter of hours, a point greatly appreciated by visiting yachtsmen. The rule handicaps a diversity of types quite well as was shown by the results of 1976 Antigua Sailing Week. The final outcome was so close that the winners could not be predicted until the fifth and final race. The leaders included *High Tension,* a hot new one-tonner from England; *Chubasco,* a 67-foot S&S yawl from the West Coast designed to the Cruising Club of America Rule; *Morning Tide,* Jol Byerley's ten-year-old S&S 34, designed to the original IOR; *Olinka,* a 57-foot S&S yawl designed over twenty years ago to the Baltic Cruiser Rule; *Joker,* the winner, a four-year-old, chopped and cropped, Ray Creekmore-designed three-quarter-tonner; and *Scarlet Shamrock,* a new Ron Holland half-tonner.

In all the regattas the difference between second and fifth after three or more hours of racing is frequently about a minute. You have only to make a slow tack, have one riding turn, and you have lost four places. This puts a premium on helmsmanship and sail handling rather than on the design with a low rating. Luckily, no one seems to be designing to the WIYA Rule or feeding it into a computer, as we might discover there are some holes in it you could drive a tank through.

There are various options open to the yachtsman from up north who wants to race in the Caribbean. He can bring his own boat down strictly for racing in the racing divisions, or cruise his boat and also race. If the boat is not hot enough for the racing division, he can enter the low-pressure cruising (no spinnaker) division. If she is a big, old gaff-rigged boat, the traditional division provides some *no*-pressure, fun racing.

If you cannot bring your own boat down, boats of all types are available for charter. There are big ones where the charterer, if experienced enough, can race the boat with the skipper just keeping an eye on things. In other cases the skipper races the boat with the charterers trimming sheets. Bare-boats can also be chartered, bare-boats that vary from being competitive in the racing division to sand barges that even in the cruising division are only along for the ride. In the British Virgin Islands Regatta there is a separate division for bare-boats under charter and sometimes the same arrangement holds for the Bequia Whit Weekend Regatta.

For those who just want to watch, frequently the day before a regatta starts there is a feeder race from a nearby island—usually a reach. Watching the "big 'uns" storming across the finish line is a sight to see, especially in Antigua where the finish line is Fort Barclay at the entrance to the harbor, or between Pimese and Mopion (literal translation Bed-bug and Crab-louse) off Petit St. Vincent (PSV) at the end of the St. Vincent/PSV feeder race. They boom across the line at hull speed. In the 1976 Guadeloupe to Antigua race, "Big *Ti*" averaged 10.9 knots for 39 miles, even beating the multi-hulls. After crossing the line in Antigua the competitors had to round up and douse sail immediately before they clobbered a boat in the overcrowded harbor or piled up on the beach, either of which would have been quite easy to do.

There are many northern yachtsmen who return year after year to their favorite regatta in the Eastern Caribbean. Llwyd Ecclestone, owner of *Ricochet,* stated categorically that he had ". . . raced all over the world in all sorts of regattas, and there is absolutely no race week or series of regattas in the world that can compare with Antigua Sailing Week." This is certainly high praise from the man who has raced at Cowes, in the Southern Ocean Racing Conference, in the Canada's Cup competition—you name it. Unfortunately, he has not tried any of the other Caribbean regattas or he might become so spoiled with the near-perfect racing conditions that he might give up sailing elsewhere.

MAJOR EASTERN CARIBBEAN REGATTAS

Wooden Boat Regatta, Jost Van Dyke, BVI

Labor Day. For wooden boats only. Organized in 1974 after an evening of drinking in Foxy's Bar. Eighty boats crossed the line in 1976.

Rolex Cup Regatta, St. Thomas, USVI

October, three days. Hard-fought regatta in variable conditions. Most competitors from British and US Virgin Islands and Puerto Rico with a sprinkling from the lower Eastern Caribbean.

Petit St. Vincent Regatta, Petit St. Vincent, Grenadines

Thanksgiving weekend, three days. Feeder races from St. Vincent and Grenada. Close competition. Plenty of wind, not too much sea. One racing division, two non-spinnaker cruising divisions. Competitors primarily from lower end of Caribbean, Antigua south. Excellent racing, superb parties.

Round-Grenada Race, Grenada

First Sunday in January. Traditionally a big-boat race around the island with entire crews flying in from the US to charter and race the "big 'uns" in ideal conditions. Entries have dropped off recently.

St. Barts Race, St. Barts

Mid-February, one race. Started informally in 1977 by Lulu Magras with over forty boats. A good race and a good party. Will become annual.

British Virgin Island Regatta, BVI

Mid-April, three days. Plenty of wind, little sea, extremely good competition. New division in 1977 for bare-boat charters.

Antigua Sailing Week, Antigua

Late April/early May. Five-day races. Feeder race from Guadeloupe. Premier Eastern Caribbean regatta. Three racing classes (IOR), a non-spinnaker cruising class, and a traditional class. Good trade-wind conditions, two races in moderate-to-heavy seas off south coast of island. Good parties ashore.

Bequia Whit Weekend Regatta, Bequia

Seventh Saturday and Sunday after Easter. Course—St. Vincent to Bequia, Bequia to Mustique, Mustique to St. Vincent. Popular with visiting yachtsmen for the racing and the colorful workboat regatta in Bequia double-enders.

Carriacou Regatta, Hillsborough Bay, Carriacou

First Monday in August. Cruising race from St. Vincent to Carriacou anchoring in beautiful Hillsborough Harbor. Basically a spectators' regatta founded by late Linton Rigg. Largest collection of local boats racing in Eastern Caribbean—two days, three races, cash prizes.

Various Other Cruises

13 ❖ Puerto Rico and the Passage Islands

PUERTO RICO AND THE PASSAGE ISLANDS generally are neglected by cruising yachtsmen. All too many of them judge this area by San Juan, regarded by some as Miami with a Spanish accent, by San Juan's inhospitable commercial harbor, and by the rugged, rough, harborless north coast of Puerto Rico. The Passage Islands they consider the U.S. Navy's private shooting gallery.

As a result, most yachts heading for the Lesser Antilles coming from the United States go direct to St. Thomas. Similarly, when heading back to the United States, they tend to skip Puerto Rico and the Passage Islands. The only exception to this seems to be boats coming from the US via the Bahamas (see Route VI, "Home Free to St. Thomas," *Sail*, September 1974). These boats fight their way eastward along the harbor-shy north coast of Puerto Rico, usually stopping at San Juan. They are unimpressed with the city and its commercial harbor and depart nonstop to St. Thomas, 90 miles to the east.

Instead, boats coming from the Bahamas would be well advised to ease sheets, run down into Mona Passage, stop at Aguadilla or Mayaguez for rest, recreation, and resupply. If the ground swell is running in from the north, favor the latter harbor.

From either of these harbors a beginning of the shoreside exploration of Puerto Rico can be begun. Puerto Rico is a land of contrasts: the rain forest of El Yunque, the rolling sugar fields of the south coast, rugged mountains, open grazing lands, old forts such as the incomparable El Moro at San Juan, all demand an intensive tour.

The old Spanish city of San Juan is in great contrast to the new "Miami" San Juan. Small villages in the country are a relief from the U.S.-type urban sprawl of the areas surrounding the major cities. Spanish is

Sail, November 1974.

the language of the countryside, and is strictly a second language in the cities. The outlook on life is definitely Spanish; and if you wish to eat well, visit those restaurants whose menus are entirely in Spanish.

Once you have recovered from your passage from the Bahamas you are well advised to sail south around Cabo Rojo and work your way eastward visiting the anchorages on the south coast, which are close enough together to enable the average yacht to sail eastward in a series of short day sails. Admittedly, it is a beat all the way, but there is good anchorage every night.

Except for the area around Parguera, the whole of the Puerto Rican and Passage Island area is well charted in great detail and well buoyed. In the Parguera area, which is a *must* to visit on the south coast, one must use the standard West Indian eyeball navigation, as the general charts C&GS 901 and 902 are not really detailed charts.

Especially in the winter, when the wind is generally north of east, there is some shelter from the sea and from the full blast of the trades. As you work your way east, stay inshore on the shelf and play the wind shifts for all they are worth. The shelf will act to reduce somewhat the westerly set of the current. At night if they don't die out completely the trades frequently may shift to the north, giving you a reach along the coast early in the morning.

As the land heats up after sunrise, the wind veers to the east. In the summer months when the wind is east or southeast, the wind will usually die out at night and spring up from the east in the early morning, shifting gradually to the south as the day progresses. Keeping these variations in mind can save you a lot of windward work. You have numerous anchorages of varying types to choose from—deserted anchorages off La Parguera. Phosphorescent Bay is one of the best examples of phosphorescent waters in this hemisphere, second only to Santa Fe, in Venezuela. Other good anchorages are Punta Crillo, Isla Caja de Muertos (to be avoided on the weekends), Cay Berberia, Areecife Media Luna, to name just a few.

At Guanica you will find a sheltered anchorage, wonderful old fort, good shopping, while at Ponce is one of the most hospitable yacht clubs in the entire world, with thirty-ton travel lift, shopping, and a place from which to explore Puerto Rico further. One word of warning: the hospitality at Ponce is so overwhelming that you may be weeks recovering from the effects of it.

Puerto Ricans drink rum in various ways: neat, diluted with ice and soda, or in secret concoctions that sneak up on you. It goes down like an afternoon non-alcoholic fruit punch, but it has another kind of punch;

suddenly you can't stand up. The Puerto Ricans cannot understand how these gringos collapse in mid-afternoon before they (the Puerto Ricans) really have even started serious drinking.

While in the Fajardo area, a small side trip is well worthwhile for children (and for the many yachtsmen who are just boys at heart). It is the amusement park in Fajardo which has a genuine steam train on a narrow-gauge railway that takes you on a forty-five-minute train ride through cane fields in open coaches. The steam engine alone provides enough excitement, but the Puerto Ricans have gone one better—half-way through the ride, out of the woods gallop "banditos," who vault on board the open coaches and let off guns in all directions, scare the passengers, "kill" the conductors, and hold the train for ransom: true old-fashioned Wild West show in the tropics.

Once you smash your way eastward around the southeast corner of Puerto Rico, you must choose whether to stand to the eastward and anchor off the beaches on the western shore of Vieques and explore the area; or to head north eastward to Isleta Marina off Fajardo. The latter offers a full-scale stateside marina, with the advantage that if you want to be near but not in a marina you may anchor a few hundred yards south of it in glassy calm water behind the island. The island is only six feet high, thus breaks the sea but not the wind which makes this a great area for dinghy sailing. The shelling on the beaches and the shoal reefs is excellent. The skipper can use the facilities of the marina, the first mate can take the ten-minute ferry ride to Fajardo to visit the excellent supermarkets in the area, while the small-fry sail, row, swim, and shell in the shelter of the island.

It is a great place to have your radio tuned as there is a radio man at the marina. Since there are no high hills to block the signal, you can test the radio and make sure it is really putting out. This is practically the only spot in the Lesser Antilles where this can be done.

From Salinas eastwards to Vieques or Isleta Marina there is only one sheltered anchorage, Sea Pines Resort, north of Punta Guayanes. This is now open as a full-service marina. A warning though—if the wind is in the southeast and blowing hard, check with the Marina on VHF Channel 16 as to the sea conditions at the entrance to the harbor. Sea conditions are never really a problem for power-boats but could be a problem for those under sail. If you are in this area the fabulous vacation complex of Sea Pines is well worth a stop. As for other places to go into—there are none. It's just a question of putting your head down and working your way eastward.

The Passage Island area (Culebra to Vieques) is no longer the U.S.

Navy's private shooting range. All firing has stopped on Culebra, and now that the Vietnam war is over, the artillery on Vieques has been considerably reduced. From Isleta Marina one can work one's way eastward to the Virgins in easy stages, with numerous anchorages to visit. A word of warning, the anchorages at Icacos, Lobos, and Palominos are easily reached from Isleta Marina and the other marinas on the east coast of Puerto Rico. Thus they are usually inundated over the weekends and best avoided. Further, the highways and byways of Puerto Rico are to be avoided at all costs from Friday evening to Monday morning. The weekend in Puerto Rico is a good time for the cruising yachtsman to find himself an anchorage in the Culebra area if he wishes to have peace and quiet.

In the summer, there are numerous anchorages on the north coast of Culebra and Culebrita that are excellent with fabulous sand beaches. However these should be avoided in the winter as the beautiful white sand beaches are built and rebuilt each year by the northerly swell that makes the anchorages off these beaches vary from uncomfortable to downright dangerous. In the winter it is best to use the innumerable anchorages on the east coast of Culebra. If one is interested in snorkeling, and spear-fishing, the best areas will be the mile after mile of coral reef on the eastern side of Culebra and Culebrita.

Vieques is also worth exploring. Though the Navy still has the eastern end of Vieques, the western half of the island has numerous anchorages and beaches. Again, over weekends remember that Vieques is the vacation land of Puerto Rico and literally thousands of people visit the island and its beaches.

Also remember that many Puerto Ricans take their vacations in the summer. Over Christmas and New Year's there are so many holidays that many take the whole period off. And the same is true around Easter at which time the Passage Island area may be crowded. But the remainder of the year the area is empty. Few if any of the hundreds of bare-boats from the Virgins visit the area; so you should have your anchorages all to yourself.

Culebra is like the Virgin Islands were twenty years ago: dry, windswept, very sparsely populated, clean, totally deserted beaches, places where you can go skinny-dipping with no fear of intruders.

Boats leaving St. Thomas and heading back to the United States via the Bahamas in the spring can easily spend a week traversing the Passage Islands and the southern coast of Puerto Rico, enjoying varied, downwind cruising, taking departure from Mayaguez where food, fuel, ice, and water are available in quantity at a reasonable price.

14 ❋ Venezuela

As THE CARIBBEAN winter cruising and charter season winds down with a last big bang at Antigua Sailing Week, the old-time charter skipper and the experienced cruising yachtsman start thinking of the Venezuelan coast. It is an area easy to reach and is really south of the hurricane area. The booming winter trades that make winter sailing along this coast a real workout have largely died. The Lesser Antilles rainy season is avoided, and certainly Venezuela is a change of pace.

Although the language is Spanish, visiting the supermarkets in the cities reminds one of stateside shopping. The restaurants are plentiful and cheap with an unbelievable collection of fish and shellfish, oysters, shrimp, lobsters, squid, and octopus, plus the standard tropical fish, all served up in wonderful sauces. It is even the land of that wonderful pre-prohibition free lunch. Any good bar serves numerous and wonderful hors d'oeuvres with drinks. One can drink beer and have enough hors d'oeuvres to forget about time wasted ordering lunch.

The previous lack of interest in the Venezuelan coast can be ascribed to many different factors, a major one being the dubiousness of the reception a sailor was likely to receive. In years gone by, Castro frequently landed revolutionaries along the coast of Venezuela from small boats. As a result, Venezuelans were very suspicious of all strange boats and in more than one case shot first and asked questions later. This situation no longer exists and except for the occasional uncooperative, and sometimes downright obstructionist port captains, normally you probably will have few problems with Venezuelan officialdom. The individual Venezuelan is one of the most friendly and hospitable persons you are ever likely to meet.

A further reason why boats did not visit Venezuela is that few of us examined the charts and almost all of us believed the pilot charts. According to the pilot charts the wind blows continually from the east twelve months of the year at fifteen to twenty-five knots and the current runs to the west at a knot or more making it all but impossible to proceed eastwards without a really good iron genoa. Furthermore, to the vast majority, Venezuela was Caracas, 350 miles west-southwest of Grenada. The *Sail,* June 1975.

thought of the long trip down plus a beat back discouraged almost everyone.

Fairly regularly, a number of Venezuelan yachtsmen visit the lower end of the Lesser Antilles to cruise or to take part in some of our races. Finally, they convinced us that we had a complete misconception of cruising in Venezuela and encouraged a number of us to visit the area. All of us have been impressed.

First of all regarding entry, admittedly it is very variable, but the port captain at Porlamar in Isla de Margarita is helpful and friendly and the charge is reasonable. Entry fee is slightly more than $10 U.S. but this entitles you to a cruising permit good for all ports on the north coast of Venezuela. There are no other fees, no other entries; just carry the paper with you for a cruising area 400 miles to the westward, no further entering or clearing. This is a pleasant change from the Lesser Antilles where one must enter and clear practically every day.

Unfortunately, all other port captains are not necessarily so friendly. The Trinidadians never cruise on the west coast of the Gulf of Paria because the Venezuelan port captain at Guiria has been so singularly uncooperative over the years that the average cruising yachtsman can just cross off that part of the Venezuelan coast.

Similarly, the port captain at Maracaibo is less than helpful. When we arrived aboard *Skua,* since he had not seen a foreign-registered yacht for the past ten years, he decided to treat us like a 100,000-ton tanker with the attendant troubles. If you just enter Venezuela through Porlamar you'll have no problems.

Getting to Venezuela is quite simple from either Trinidad or Grenada. It is a broad reach or dead run—distance 140 to 150 miles—a nice easy slide and with the current behind her the average yacht can easily do it in twenty to thirty hours.

Once in Margarita you will discover that the weather pattern is not as described in the pilot charts.

From Margarita to Cape Codera you are sheltered from the normal trade-wind sea; this is especially true from Margarita to Barcelona, a distance of seventy miles. Here you are completely protected from the ocean swell. Further, in this area the wind usually dies out during the night, springs up light out of the west-to-northwest in the morning, then works its way around, while increasing in velocity, to north, north-northeast, finally settling down in the east blowing fifteen to twenty by midafternoon.

The current does run strongly to the west between Margarita and the Peninsula de Araya; but westwards of the Peninsula de Araya, along the shore, there is frequently a strong easterly set to the current. During the day the temperatures are pretty much the same as elsewhere in the Lesser Antilles, but come sunset the cold air falls down off the 5,000-foot-high mountains that line the coast, giving you, in effect, built-in air conditioning. Further, for some reason that no one seems to be able to fathom, the water along the coast of Venezuela is a good five to seven degrees colder than elsewhere in the Lesser Antilles.

Westwards of Cape Codera one finds a large trade-wind sea rolling in from the east or northeast continually. There really is no such thing as a calm sea along the Venezuelan coast west of Cape Codera. However, the mountains are so high along this stretch of coast that the wind usually dies out at sunset. It then remains either flat calm or a light offshore breeze springs up which enables a boat to proceed due east under power. Five to ten miles offshore the normal trade will be blowing out of the east.

Close to the shore a strong counter-current frequently is running as much as one knot to one-and-a-half knots to the eastwards. For those

DONALD STREET

COURTESY OF CORPORACION DE TURISMO DE VENEZUELA

who doubt the existence of the current all I can suggest is to go to Venezuela and to try some racing in the Caracas area. You will quickly believe in the existence of this easterly counter-current.

Offshore are the attractive islands of Islas de Aves, Los Roques, La Orchilla, La Tortuga, Le Blanquilla, and Islas Los Testigos. These are out in the westerly south equatorial current and there is no shelter from wind and sea among the islands. This means that the ever-present trades keep them cool and bug-free. Sailing from one island to the other heading westwards is a glorious sleighride; heading eastwards against the current is almost an impossibility. Hug the coast when sailing east, taking advantage of nighttime calms and the counter-current.

Venezuelan cruising is incredibly varied. Los Testigos are a pile of rocks sticking up out of very deep water with numerous small sheltered anchorages between the rocks—a good spot for both smugglers and fishermen.

The north coast of Peninsula de Paria is a vertical cliff dropping into the water making it practically impossible to anchor. There are numerous small coves but no detailed charts, little information on the area, and what is available is confusing. In reality this is a place to be explored in a motor-sailer or power-boat. There are a few small ports that do provide good anchorages as long as the ground swells are not rolling in: Carupano and Morro Puerto Santos.

The Isla de Margarita area is totally different. Though dry and arid, it was settled originally in the early 1500s when it achieved great fame as a pearling area. Today one can still dive for and find pearls in this area. If you are not capable of diving for your pearls, the whole island of Margarita is a free port; pearls come in from all over. It is possibly the pearling capital of the world.

Ashore, Margarita provides fabulous shops and excellent exploring. Numerous forts were built to protect the island from pirates, the English, the French, and the Dutch. The island has beautiful beaches, excellent hotels, and huge fleets of fishing boats, yet there are numerous small secluded anchorages. It is not necessary to go all the way to Bonaire to see the pink flamingo since you can see them in Margarita. The islands of Cubagua and Coche are only a short day-sail from Margarita.

A beautiful reach southwards brings one to Araya and its huge fort built to protect the salt works. The Golfo de Cariaco, thirty-two miles long, two to eight miles wide, surrounded on all sides by mountains, provides a glorious cruising area with anchorages too numerous to mention, and sheltered water at all times. From Araya westwards to Barcelona is

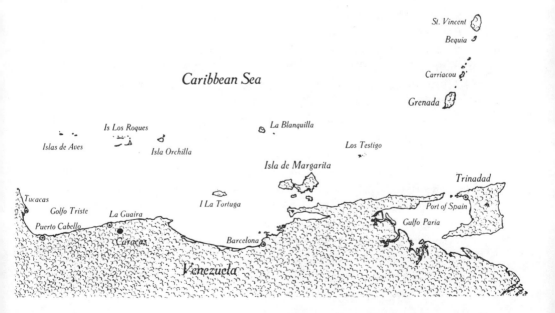

DONALD STREET

another unbelievable cruising area. Thirty miles of coast is completely indented with coves, harbors, isolated sand beaches and deep fjords reaching back into the mountains.

At Barcelona three miles east of Morro de Barcelona is the new hotel and yachting complex being built by prominent Venezuelan yachtsmen including Dr. Daniel Camejo, well-known Star sailor and owner of the McCurdy & Rhodes motor-sailer *Caribana*. This will provide a spot in eastern Venezuela with facilities for yachts.

Because of the strong tides and counter-current from the Isla de Margarita to Barcelona area the water is not particularly clear. In the Isla de Margarita area the sand has been stirred up so much that the charts made by the U.S. Navy in 1940 are singularly inaccurate since there have been extensive shifts in the sandbanks. Also earthquakes along the coast have changed the profiles of the numerous islands, created some new reefs, and obliterated others.

To find good diving one must visit the offshore islands. However if you do go to the offshore islands, especially Isla de Aves and Los Roques, you will find what is probably the best diving in the entire Caribbean. Los

Roques stretch twenty-five miles from east to west. The vast majority of the area is completely uncharted; the chart just shows numerous coral heads. However, exploring charter skippers such as Gordon Stout of *Shango* and David Price of *Lincoln,* Richard Weinman of *Narania,* David Stone of *Margay* and Paul Squire of *Stranger,* who have had plenty of experience at picking their way through coral heads by putting a man in the rigging, have been able to thread through the area not marked on the chart by sounding. They anchor many miles away from the civilization on the easternmost part of Los Roques, and are able to go spearfishing without even bothering to put the dinghy overside.

When cruising the Venezuelan coast one must remember that, though yachting is beginning to boom in Venezuela, the Venezuelan population is concentrated in a few small areas. The yachting centers are at these populous places. There are no yachting facilities at all elsewhere in Venezuela.

In the Puerto de la Cruz–Barcelona area there now exists at El Moro what is probably one of the most magnificent marina complexes in the Western Hemisphere. There are two separate marinas, both with full services. The eastern of the two, Amerigo Vespucci Marina, has facilities for even the largest yachts; it is connected to the entire El Moro complex providing, in effect, unlimited dockage space. The El Moro Marina, on the western side, provides facilities for boats up to nine feet draft with complete facilities but limited berthing space for visiting yachtsmen. There are some small facilities in Carenero, ninety miles to the west. The next facilities are in the La Guiria area. The largest is the fabulous complex of the private club of Puerto Azul. There is a smaller but very well-sheltered marina at the Macuto Sheraton Hotel.

Westwards of the airport of Maiquetia is a small artificial port and yacht club at Playa Grande. Fifty miles westward of this area at Puerto Cabello is another small marina in the process of organization. Outside of these above-mentioned places there are no facilities for yachts in Venezuela.

This does not mean that it is impossible to get any repairs done; if you speak Spanish it is rather the contrary. The offshore islands of Venezuela are alive with diesel-powered fishing boats and diesel mechanics are readily available. Similarly, Venezuelans, like Americans, live in their cars; thus electricians and electrical repair men can be found. Electronics men, forget about. Sail repairs are nonexistent. As far as I can figure out, Venezuelan racing yachtsmen send their sails back to the United States to be repaired.

Regarding weather, Venezuelans are virtually universal in their opinion that the best months to sail there are July, August, September, October, and November. This area of Venezuela is basically south of the hurricane belt and during these months there are few, if any, storms. The winds are lighter and the sea is less. Come the winter, it really begins to blow.

Various two-week cruises can be made in this area aboard a charter boat. Good sailors may enjoy joining a boat in Grenada, take a 20-hour sleighride to Margarita, and spend the remaining time exploring the Golfo de Cariaco, and the area between Margarita and Barcelona. Others may prefer to join the boat at Barcelona or Margarita (fly to Caracas airport, transfer to shuttle flight), spend two weeks exploring, and then fly back. Others who don't mind windward work may want to sail back to Grenada or Trinidad with the boat, but if not, a dead-head fee can be arranged to get the boat back to its normal cruising area. And remember that if the boat has a series of charters in the area, the skipper probably will forget about the dead-head fee.

If you are interested in combining diving and fishing, your best bet is to join a boat in the Caracas area, sail out (on a beam reach) to Los Roques and Los Aves, spending ten days to two weeks in this area. Although these islands are quite exposed, since it is a beam reach out and back, it should be easy sailing.

The cruising yachtsman has a great advantage over the professional charter skipper from the Lesser Antilles. The professional charter skipper who cruises the Venezuelan waters one way or another must eventually work his way back eastwards to the Lesser Antilles. However, the cruising yachtsman who has sailed south in November has cruised down the length of the Lesser Antilles upon reaching Grenada and can sail westward. He will then be dead downwind or reaching the entire time, ending up in Los Roques or Los Aves. From Los Roques he can stand north to Mayaguez on the west coast of Puerto Rico, 380 miles away, a beautiful beam reach across the Caribbean.

At Mayaguez fuel, water, and ice are available. You can put food from the cheap Puerto Rican supermarkets on board and depart for the United States. From Mayaguez you can cruise either westward through the Bahamas to the Miami–Fort Lauderdale area or stand northward to Charleston or Morehead City.

One last point to remember: it is possible to leave a yacht in Venezuela for a few months and return to pick it up. However, those pick-up places are few and far between. Probably the new marina in the Puerto La Cruz area or one of the marinas in the La Guiria area would be best.

So consider Venezuela in the spring, summer, and fall next time you want to cruise where the livin' is easy—and inexpensive, too.

15 ❧ Eastward Across the Pond

MANY SAILORS speak of sailing to Europe as "crossing the Pond." They say this because describing a transatlantic trip as a transatlantic trip immediately scares people. It conjures up thoughts of a 3,300-mile voyage and twenty-five or thirty days at sea. However many of us who like to go to sea do not particularly like to go to sea for long periods. Courtesy of Uncle Sam I spent three long sessions continuously at sea, one of 39 days, and two of 21 days, all in a guppy snorkel submarine. This eliminated for me any and all desire to remain at sea for long periods. I love to take off to sea, but while 12 days is wonderful and 14 okay, once the time reaches more than about 16 or 17 it's time to get ashore.

If you are crossing the Pond eastwards you shouldn't have to spend long periods at sea. If you take the northern route, depending on whether you jump off from Halifax or St. John's, Newfoundland, the distance is 2,200 or 1,700 miles. If you take the southern route, via Bermuda and the Azores, the longest jump is still only just over 1,800 miles. In any reasonably sized cruising boat the longest unbroken hop across the Atlantic can still take less than sixteen days, an amount of time which is easy on the crew and easy on the person who is responsible for storing the boat for the trip. Although it is simple to store a boat for two or three weeks plus reserves, it is a difficult proposition to store a boat for five weeks plus reserves. Further, you can change crew at various points so that with only three weeks available, crew members can make a long open-water passage, yet still have time to sightsee and play tourist at both ends of the trip.

Aboard any yacht going offshore for an extended period, both the boat and the crew must be capable of withstanding a full gale at sea. However, if you pick the route carefully, and choose the time of year with intelligence, the chances of your encountering a gale will be substantially minimized. For crossing the North Atlantic the ideal months are May, June, and July. April is too early and the gale frequency even down on the Azores route is high enough to deter the conservative seaman. After July

Sail, December 1976.

the West Indian hurricanes which largely miss the continental mass of the United States go waltzing across the Atlantic, making August and September poor months to be wandering around the Atlantic Ocean.

If you plan to sail the northern route—i.e., Halifax or Newfoundland to Northern Europe—July is the best month. It is possible to run into an early season hurricane, but the frequency of July hurricanes is very low. Usually they pass south of the great circle track from Cape Race to Fastnet Rock or the Scilly Isles. If you leave in May and June, bad ice months, you may have to sail southeast from Halifax to clear the southeast corner of the ice-fields, considerably lengthening your trip and forcing you down into the steamer lanes; whereas in early July you will probably be able to sail the direct great circle route from Cape Race or St. John's.

There are several advantages of this very far northern route: you are well north of the North Atlantic steamer traffic lanes; and the shipping is minimal. One year we crossed the Atlantic right through the shipping lanes in heavy fog. Even though we had a radar reflector up we still had the living daylights scared out of us about a dozen times—it was like standing in the middle of a superhighway with cars going by in both directions. But in July 1975, on *Iolaire*'s 70th-birthday cruise, the ice was well to the north; we sailed the great circle course north of the steamer lanes, and only saw one ship until we were approaching the coast of Ireland.

The northern route also means that you can work up the East Coast of the United States in short weekend hops which gives both boat and crew a shakedown. Manchester, Massachusetts, is an excellent port of departure. Unlike Marblehead, the harbor is sheltered in all weathers. With luck you can lie alongside a dock for days on end, which makes putting stores on board easy, and two good yards are close at hand, Crocker's and Manchester Marine. Stores and supplies are readily available only a short drive away. Food is plentiful and relatively inexpensive along the entire East Coast: Boston, Halifax, and St. John's, Newfoundland. For those who are interested in marine biology the northern route provides more marine life than any other. On *Iolaire*'s 1975 transatlantic passage on the northern route I saw more marine life than I have seen in total in my previous twenty-five years at sea.

Also there is only one long jump—from Halifax or St. John's, 2,200 and 1,700 miles respectively—when you are sailing to northern Europe, whereas if you go via the Azores there are two long jumps—roughly 1,800 from Bermuda to the Azores, and another 1,140 miles from the Azores to Fastnet Rock.

There are disadvantages. It is cold, so make sure you have a really good cabin heating and drying system installed and tested *under sail on all points of sailing* before you leave the Boston area. And there is fog. If you insist on having bright sunshine at sea don't take the northern route. It was nine days after we left Halifax before we ever saw a dim glow you could call the sun; and as one of the crew claimed, it was five days before we ever saw the bowsprit.

The southern route also has its advantages and disadvantages. From Miami to Bermuda is roughly 950 miles but that can be considerably reduced if you sail up the coast with the Gulf Stream under your tail to Charleston or other East Coast ports south of Hatteras, and then jump off direct for Bermuda. From Bermuda to the Azores in May or June the gale frequency is close to zero and the gales which do occur are usually near Bermuda. Thus, if you wait in Bermuda and leave with a good weather report, the chances of your being caught in a gale between Bermuda and the Azores are minimal. Further, the Azores route appeals to many people coming up from the Lesser Antilles. From Antigua, St. Barts, or St. Thomas the distance is roughly 900 miles. Coming from the warm climate most people wish to delay their return to the cold as long as possible. If they stand north to Halifax, within three or four days of leaving Bermuda they are back in the cold foggy north, whereas if they follow the Azores route they will have warm weather till the Azores and beyond. With luck they might even carry the warm weather right back up to Fastnet and western approaches. On the Azores route about the only chance of your getting caught in a gale, given a decent weather report when you leave Bermuda, would be at the end of the voyage when you are approaching Fastnet Rock, the Spanish or Portuguese coasts, or Gibraltar.

There are disadvantages in the southern route—if anyone can figure out a more expensive place to store a boat than Antigua, St. Thomas, or Bermuda he's more clever than most of us. You should examine the chart, figuring where the trip is to begin and end, look at the weather charts and great circle charts, and examine the tables of distances and comments on the courses which follow this article, in order to be able to make an intelligent decision in the light of the available boat, the crew's capabilities, their likes and dislikes, and the time they are willing to take.

Bermuda and the Azores are intriguing to everyone. Bermuda is beautiful, clean, and charming, and probably one of the best run and best organized areas you will ever see. It has beautiful swimming, excellent snorkeling, hotels that can offer a good meal, and night life if you look for it. Golfers and tennis players will feel as though they're in heaven. Bermudians are among the most polite people in the world, but this is also one of the most expensive areas you will find. However Bermudians are so charming and so polite it doesn't even hurt when they relieve you of your money.

In contrast, the Azores are mountain peaks rising out of the sea, inhabited by a very friendly people, not particularly well organized but intriguing in an old-world fashion. The islands are lush and green, and excellent milk, butter, cheese, fresh fruit, vegetables, and fish are all available on every island from the local daily market, with prices that are a relief after St. Thomas and Bermuda. The Azores are easy to approach as there are a number of good RDF beacons. The islands stretch across 300 miles of ocean in the east/west direction, they rise so high out of the sea they are visible at great distances, and there are no offlying reefs. You can practically put the bowsprit ashore before you will run aground.

Corvo, the westernmost island, has no port. Flores has a very small port which is not normally a port of call, so if you wish to visit Flores it would probably be best to heave-to offshore and leave some of the crew on board. The port of Horta on the main island of Fayal is the calling port most yachts visit in the Azores. One of the things to do there is to take the short ferry ride to San Jorge on the nearby island of Pico. Spend at least a full day or stay overnight in one of the small hotels. Pico is famous as a whaling station from which whales are still hunted in boats similar to those used by Captain Ahab in *Moby Dick*. The boats are superbly constructed, slightly larger than the standard Beetle whale boat as they are shore boats rather than boats to be picked up in davits. The Azores men are not as pure whalers as the Bequia whalers since they have lookouts stationed in the hills who communicate to town by telephone. The boats are frequently towed to the whaling grounds by a fast launch which helps herd the whales and also tows the dead whales in. However the final approach and killing are executed in the same fashion as in Captain Ahab's day.

There is a big U.S. Navy base on Terceira and an exposed anchorage at Angra da Heroimo with a small yacht club, friendly people, excellent daily market, and direct air communications to Boston.

Check the weather before leaving the Azores, then jump off for Europe: north for Fastnet Rock; northeast for Spanish and Portuguese coasts and Gibraltar. See the following table for details.

Port of Departure	Destination	Distance	Courses	Sailing Direction and Comments
Miami	Bermuda	950	N then NE	Stand north with the Gulf Stream under the tail until clear of the Bahamas, then swing northeast toward Bermuda.

Port of Departure	Destination	Distance	Courses	Sailing Direction and Comments
East Coast US	Bermuda	various	various	Various courses and distances, from 400 miles Morehead City/Bermuda to 700 miles New York or Boston/Bermuda. Bermuda is easiest to reach from ports south of Hatteras. North of Hatteras you may end up hard on the wind on starboard tack most of the way.
St. Thomas, St. Barts, Antigua	Bermuda	870 to 900	N	Follow the North Star. Carry as much fuel as possible as you will certainly run into 100 or 150 miles of light airs, and some boats have run into 400 miles of almost flat calm. But it can be done without an engine—witness *Iolaire*'s three passages, two of 6½ and one of 7½ days.
Bermuda	Halifax	740	N by E	With luck should be a reach all the way, and warm until the last thirty-six hours, when you come out of the northern end of the Gulf Stream and may be greeted by cold and fog.
Bermuda	Fastnet	2,650	NE quadrant	Sail approximately the great circle course, but sail north at the beginning to pick up the Gulf Stream and try to stay in Stream all the way across for warmth and favorable current. At 150 miles per day, which with the aid of the current should not be hard to achieve, it would mean a 17½-day passage.
Bermuda	Fayal (Azores)	1,820	NE then E	Absolute great circle course usually cannot be sailed as it leads right through the Bermuda high, where the fleet in the 1972 Transatlantic Race to Spain was completely becalmed. Rather, check the location of the Bermuda high and stand north around it, working north as the barometer rises, and finally

Port of Departure	Destination	Distance	Courses	Sailing Direction and Comments
				swinging south at the last moment to head into Fayal.
Manchester	Halifax	350	E then NE	Sail rhumb line, but have detailed notes and Nova Scotia charts and be prepared for fog.
Halifax	Fayal	1,640	SE	Not a normal route except for Canadian boats who have seen enough of the cold cruel north and want to get south to warm water for their trip across.
Halifax	St. Pierre	360	E then NE	Be prepared for plenty of fog, but once you reach St. Pierre there are good French meals ashore. French wine, duty-free liquor, excellent cheese, and what is allegedly the best French bread in the Western Hemisphere.
St. Pierre via Cape Race	Fastnet	120 1,780 1,900	ENE	120 miles to Cape Race, then 1,780 to Fastnet Rock, total 1,900. At 150 miles a day = 12½ days; at 130 miles a day = 14½ days. *Warning:* check via radio with St. John's, Newfoundland, who will be able to obtain from the trawlers the latest ice reports. Skirt the southeast area of the growlers, then sail great circle course to Fastnet Rock. July best month.
St. John's Newfoundland	Fastnet	1,700	ENE	At 150 miles a day = 11 days, 8 hours; at 130 miles a day is only 13 days!
St. John's	Fayal	1,200	SE	Probably only to be taken by a boat which was originally intending to go the St. John's/Fastnet route but finally decided the cold and fog were too much. At 150 miles a day = 8 days; at 130 miles a day = 9 days, 6 hours.
Fayal	Fastnet	1,140	NNE	If wind is east or north of east stand north on starboard tack with eased sheets until prevail-

Port of Departure	Destination	Distance	Courses	Sailing Direction and Comments
				ing southwesterlies are reached. Then reach off on other tack to Fastnet or Land's End—8 to 9½ days.
Fayal	Lisbon & NW Spanish coast	1,100	E	1,000 miles rhumb-line distance, but you should stand well to the north and approach the Spanish/Portugese coast on the latitude of destination, as otherwise with the Portugese trades blowing out of the north and northeast you may end up beating to windward.
Fayal	Gibraltar	1,140	ESE	Sail roughly the rhumb-line course and cross your fingers and hope. Where one gets an English-language weather report covering the area south of Finisterre is beyond me.
				NOTE: Sailing St. John's, Fayal, Fastnet increases the sailing distance but even for a comparatively small boat reduces the longest time at sea to about 10 days—makes this route somewhat appealing to a small boat based northeast coast of US or Canada.

If you follow the northern route you will find a number of attractive areas to visit. If you want to take the time, or wish to switch crews, you can cruise the coast of Nova Scotia on up to the Bras d'Or lakes. These are fabulous in that you have Nova Scotia scenery with no fog. You can exit from the northern end of the Bras d'Or lakes, and then make a short jump to St. Pierre where you will find a French colony in North America complete with excellent wines, French cheeses, wonderful meals, and maybe the best French bread in the Western Hemisphere. Trawlers of all nationalities call at the port for R & R, a break from the fishing on the Grand Banks. From St. Pierre you can either sail direct for Fastnet Rock via Cape Race—1,900 miles—or make a sharp turn to port at Cape Race and run up to St. John's, Newfoundland, and thence to Fastnet Rock—1,700 miles.

As you sail across the Atlantic by the northern route you may wonder why I recommend Fastnet Rock as a landfall*—actually the landfall will probably be Cape Clear, so called because of the low incidence of fog in that area. On my last two transatlantic passages to northern Europe, in both cases the last two days were brilliant clear sunshine with unlimited visibility so that we picked up the mountains of Ireland fifty miles out. When you see this land, why should you continue a couple of days farther on to Land's End and the southwest coast of England? You might find it more interesting to make a quick left turn and duck into any one of the dozens of harbors that litter the southwest coast of Ireland. Between Crookhaven, the first cove directly in behind Cape Clear, and Cork, sixty miles to the west, there are a dozen good anchorages, all completely sheltered and with no more than the occasional other yacht to share the anchorage with you. There is always the village store where you can immediately pick up fresh bread and a couple of gallons of fresh milk with cream so thick on top of it you can't pour the milk out of the bottle. Fresh butter, meat, and vegetables are readily available and, of course, if there are more than three houses, the inevitable Irish pub with draught Guinness. Irish pubs have wonderful liberal drinking hours and there's not a pub in Ireland that would remain closed when a visiting yachtsman has just walked ashore from a transatlantic passage.

With all these splendid temptations rapidly approaching fine on the port bow, why would any sailor continue on another two days to England and Falmouth to discover warm, flat British beer, the pub probably closed (no one has ever figured out British pub hours) and everyone watching a cricket match which is incomprehensible to an American?

Irish customs and immigration clearance are simple in the extreme—you call customs and immigration at Bantry Bay, who will probably ask what pub you are calling from—and they'll come to see you in a day or so! The only trouble with stopping in Ireland is that you may never be able to pry your crew away again.

A trip across the Pond is certainly not to be lightly undertaken, but neither should you be scared off by the thought of tremendously long trips and a continuous succession of gales. Getting there is half the fun, and once on the other side of the Pond you can cruise, or lay a boat up infinitely cheaper than in the United States.

**Weather:* BBC Radio 2 (1500m or 200kc). Don't cross to England without a copy of Reed's Nautical Almanac. BBC shortwave Big Ben (last stroke of the bell) gives a time tick every hour readily receivable world-wide. It comes in clear when WWV fades out.

16 ❧ Gateway to Europe—Cruising in Southwest Ireland

WHERE IS IT so warm all year that palm trees grow, boats can be left in the water, even in January and February, breaks in the weather can produce a nice cruising weekend, and your neighbor at the bar will swing into a ballad at the drop of a hat, or perhaps I should say at the raise of a glass? The answer, of course, is southwest Ireland, gateway to Europe.

In Southwest Ireland in general and in southwest Cork in particular you hardly know that the rest of the world exists, much less do you become involved in its problems. People are so insular in southwest Cork that they regard Dubliners as foreigners. Southwest Ireland is undoubtedly one of the friendliest places in the world, and is perfectly located as a jumping-off point for the sailor who plans to cruise to other parts of Europe.

Claude Worth, one of the first truly offshore amateur yachtsmen—he sailed offshore without a professional captain—sang the praises of cruising this coast in his little plank-on-edge cutter *Foam* in the summer of 1888. When we cruised there in 1975 aboard my yawl *Iolaire* we found it little changed.

A detailed book of sailing directions, *South and West Coasts of Ireland,* is published annually by the Irish Cruising Club and is available from Mrs. J. Guinnes, Secretary, Irish Cruising Club Publications, Censure House, Baily, Co. Dublin. You can cruise in this part of the country for weeks for the ports are only a few hours apart, each port is intriguing, and none of them is crowded. The only places where you will find a congregation of yachts will be in Kinsale and Crosshaven and even here deep rivers wind up beyond the yacht anchorages so that you can always get off by yourself.

From Crookhaven to Cork is sixty miles, deeply indented with bays, coves and rivers. From Cork if you sail the fifty-five miles to Dunmore East you will find that the land is lower and flatter with the harbors farther apart, but large rivers go well up into the hinterland where you can gunkhole and visit the old towns, castles, and battlements with which

Sail, March 1977.

Ireland abounds. In summer—June, July, and August—there are only four to six hours of true darkness, sunset is after 8 o'clock and twilight lasts until 10.

If you have sailed your boat across the Atlantic and have run out of time to spend in Europe, all is not lost. You can arrange to leave your boat in yards in either Kinsale or Crosshaven for months or even for the whole winter. The climate in southwest Ireland, warmed by the Gulf Stream, is so mild that the temperature in the winter just barely dips below 50 degrees. You can afford to leave your boat in this area for the winter as, at the present rate of exchange, yard labor for skilled shipwrights, machinists, painters or riggers ranges between $5 and $6 an hour—a far cry from the hourly charges in yards on the East Coast of the United States. Boats can be left afloat on moorings, hauled and left outside, or hauled and stored inside. You have only to look at the condition of the yachts stored in Crosshaven and Kinsale, and note the quality of the yachts constructed by the Crosshaven Boatyard to realize that in southwest Ireland a yacht can be maintained superbly.

So you're in southern Ireland; finally and foolishly you decide you've seen enough; and you are thinking of other places to go.

From anywhere along the south coast of Ireland you have only to haul up the anchor, head southeast, and a beam reach before the prevailing southwesterlies will take you the 135 miles to the Scilly Islands where palm trees grow, as the Gulf Stream warms the sea.

If the weather is settled, the Scillies are well worth visiting, if only to see the weekend rowing races. The various villages have pilot gigs similar to, but larger than, our Whitehall boats. These date back to the days when pilots were rowed out from the islands and put aboard sailing vessels in the western approaches. Today these gigs are still in commission or have been rebuilt. They show up periodically for hard-fought races between villages, a sight worth seeing, although reputedly the parties afterwards are rather hard to survive.

Here in the Scillies you will have to make one of the great decisions in life: should you go westward from the Scilly Isles to Land's End and Falmouth? It is a mere short jump, a day's sail—remember that daylight in this area during summer is sixteen hours or more. If you do visit Falmouth be sure to spend a weekend there, as the local oyster smacks come out on Sundays to sail closely fought races in the same fashion as the yachtsmen. But with their typical fishermen's disregard for the niceties of the racing rules, the races are much more spectacular, for example, a twenty-four-foot boat might have a twelve-foot nosepole sticking out in front to spear the opposition with.

Southwest England is like southwest Ireland—quite cut off from the rest of the country. The villages are small and the people friendly, the accent is totally different from the rest of England, and again deepwater rivers extend up into the hinterland, rivers in which a sizable yacht drawing seven or eight feet can sail ten miles or more into the countryside. A good rowing or sailing dinghy is a real asset if you want to watch the wildlife and scenery go by in quiet and solitude. This exploring can keep the crew occupied for days on end without your having to move the mother ship. Frequently, you can anchor in an estuary where four or five rivers join, so that each day you can explore a different river. Sailing leisurely along this coastline you might troll a fishing line for mackerel rather than a log line for distances. With the currents going back and forth at considerable speed the log line is not necessarily indicative of how far you have traveled over the bottom.

A few miles to the southwest of Falmouth, and very protected from a westerly or southwesterly gale, is the beautiful Helford River, where the Shipwright's Arms sells one of the best Cornish pastries to be found. Among the harbors to the east of Falmouth which are to be recommended are Salcombe, Dartmouth, where the river winds many miles inland between wooded banks, and Weymouth (usually very crowded), a useful port of refuge after rounding the notorious Portland Bill. There are several sailing guides to this area, the best probably being the *Shell Guide to the South Coast* by K. Adlard Coles, and the *Pilot's Guide to the South Coast* published by Imray, Lorie, Norrie, and Wilson.

How far eastward you should go depends on time and inclination. Going eastward to the Solent is nice, easy and downhill, but you must remember that, like going down east to Nova Scotia, it will be dead to windward coming back. The farther east you go the more crowded the harbors become, the more civilized, and the more you will sink or swim in international yachting. Certainly at some time in a sailor's life, even if he does not race, he should visit Cowes Week for a few days or more during an Admiral's Cup year, when it seems that all of Europe and certainly all the top yachts from the world have assembled at Cowes. There is nothing else like it in the Western Hemisphere.

Instead of turning eastward to visit England when you leave the Scilly Isles you can stand south for about 150 miles, to the west of Ushant, and down to the South Brittany coast. Before you make this jump, check the weather report as you don't want to be caught in a southwesterly gale off Ushant. The weather forecast is broadcast on BBC Radio 2 on 1500 metres or 200kc; times are given in Reeds' *British Nautical Almanac,* and *don't cross the Pond to Northern Europe without a copy.*

BBC short-wave Big Ben gives a time tick every hour (last stroke of the bell) which can be received worldwide.

The Brittany coast from Ushant to La Rochelle is a superb cruising ground—mile after mile of white sand beaches contrasted in other areas

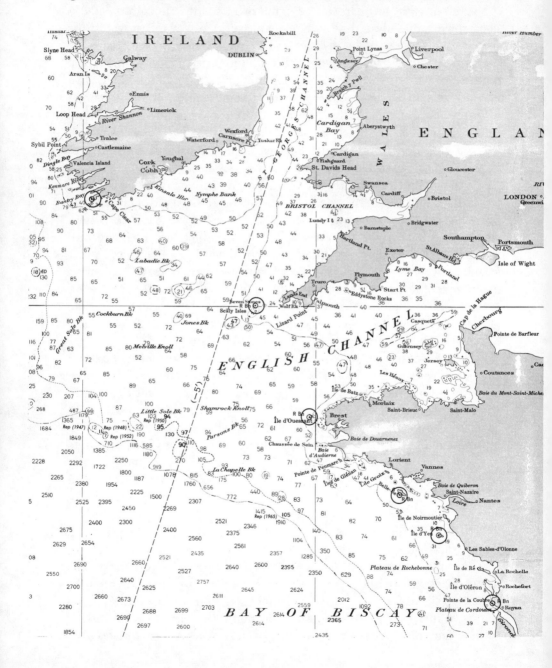

by miles of solid rock. Among the fascinating old towns is La Rochelle, an old Huguenot stronghold which held out in a long seige against the Roman Catholics in the late 17th century. Here the ancient watchtowers which guarded the entrance to the inner harbor are still standing, surrounded by the modern city of La Rochelle. Eating is such a popular sport in the area that when, after the La Rochelle Race, we went to one of the better-known restaurants to obtain reservations for lunch, we were told that all reservations were booked up for the next two weeks solid.

The ports along this coast are too numerous to mention by name. It is a case of taking out the guide, looking at the weather, scratching your head, feeling your stomach, and deciding where to go next. The best pilot book is probably the *South Brittany Pilot*.

La Trinite is an absolute *must* even though the new tourist town has completely swallowed up the old town. Everywhere you look the horizon is covered with groups of one- or two-dozen small boats, racing or being shepherded around by sailing instructors in high-powered rubber dinghies. There are many sailing schools operating out of La Trinite. As is true everywhere along this coast the food is superb.

Regarding eating, you will find no need to get your fresh stuff in the supermarket; every town has a "marché" certain days of the week. As soon as you arrive, inquire what day the village has its marché, be there early in the morning, load up with fresh fruit, vegetables, cheese, local pâté, fresh bread and hot croissants. Then row back to the boat for a light breakfast of coffee and croissants, and start preparing for a long leisurely French lunch, which should take at least an hour and a half to eat. Once you have eaten, instead of going to sea the only thing to do is to curl up and go to sleep.

North of La Trinite you find bay after bay, cove after cove, and the intriguing town of Benode where you can sail the river and anchor above the town. If you feel so inclined you can sail upriver on the tide to Quimper, enjoy the small provincial French town, and drop down the river on the tide in the afternoon or the next day. You can then continue back toward Ushant in long jumps or short hops depending on wind, weather, and your own mood.

Once you have cleared Ushant you can go back to the Scilly Isles or directly back to Ireland, or if the wind turns foul and blows hard from the west you can hop across to Falmouth and cruise in the Falmouth area while waiting for a break in the weather to jump back to Ireland. If, when you are returning to Ireland, the weather is good, Crosshaven makes an excellent landfall, but if the weather closes in with heavy fog, as it did with us, head for Kinsale as there is a powerful radio beacon on the Old

Head of Kinsale. You can home in with deep water right up to the beacon. When land appears, make a quick turn to starboard, then follow the coast around into Kinsale Harbor.

From southern Ireland there are other areas that you can visit. Those who are not afraid of weathering a gale in open sea, and who like to visit the wild and untamed areas of the world, can round Cape Clear and head north up the exposed western coast of Ireland with nothing between them and North America except 1,700 miles of gray ocean. The west coast abounds in beautiful, deserted, sheltered harbors, villages unchanged since the last century and where Gaelic is the native tongue, English the foreign language. The country is wild and wooly and so is the weather—beating to windward out of one of these harbors into the westerly winds and sea is strictly for the brave. Various Irish yachtsmen do this and claim it is a great and wonderful cruising area, but I'm afraid it is a little bit too wild and wooly for me.

On the other hand, if you sail east and north 160 miles to Dun Laoghair (pronounced *Dun Leary*), you find between the breakwaters the yachting capital of Ireland. It is the only really massive concentration of yachts in southern Ireland, with racing not only at weekends but also in the evenings.

The Dublin Bay 24s until 1964 not only sported long nosepoles but also double jack-yard topsails. In 1964 they switched to a modern bermudian rig, not only not so picturesque, but also under certain conditions not so fast. The clubs ashore—the Royal Irish, Royal St. George, Royal Alfred, and the National—among them possess what is without a doubt the largest concentration collection of brass cannon in the world—over thirty. Highly polished brass cannon are thickly clustered on the various balconies and aimed out into the harbor.

A short afternoon sail brings you to Howth, where the Howth Bay 17s still race, sporting jack-yard topsails as they rapidly approach their eightieth birthday. A stop in Howth is not complete without an evening in the Abbey Tavern—Ireland's most famous singing pub.

After Howth every sailor must make his pilgrimage to the yachtsman's Mecca—Scotland—to the home waters of Fife, Watson, Mylne, Glen-Coatts, and many of the other great yacht designers of the last century. Clydeside is still flanked with huge shipyards, and nearby you find wonderful yacht yards such as Robertsons, Fife, McGruer, and smaller yards of similar caliber. The Scottish highlands are an area of brilliant sunshine, howling black squalls rolling down off high mountains, long narrow lochs, and scattered population. Owners of great heavily built Scottish fishing trawlers will demonstrate their faith in their slow-turning

Kelvin engines by dropping a herring down through the air intake, and if the engine is running really well it hardly misses a beat as it fires the well-cooked herring out through the exhaust pipe. The supposedly dour Scotsmen become cheerful, talkative, and hospitable upon the arrival of foreign sailors, as it is a good excuse to demonstrate that a wee dram of good whisky from Scotland is infinitely better and more mild than all that specially brewed stuff that is shipped down to England and over to the United States.

Again, as in cruising down to Maine, you will have the problem of getting back to southwest Ireland. Watch your weather, and if a gale comes through, once the wind has switched to the north or east, get out and get south as fast as you can as otherwise you'll be wintering in Scotland.

We arrived across the Atlantic with a crew of six aboard *Iolaire* and, though I was happy to be in Glandore, as my wife was waiting for me there, the five young men in the crew looked at the little village of Glandore and thought, Where are the bright lights? What are we going to do? Seven days later everyone was sorry to have to leave and, after we spent the summer cruising and exploring throughout Europe on various boats and by other means of transportation, we wished that *Iolaire* had spent the entire summer doing nothing but cruising the southwest coast of Ireland.

The Art of Seamanship

[*Over the years, the author has written scores of articles on many aspects of seamanship for many boating magazines in the U.S. and abroad. There follows a selected dozen of these authoritative contributions to the seaman's art.—Ed.*]

17 ❖ Keeping Warm

AFTER 12,000 miles in seven months with no engine the crew of *Iolaire* came to some very definite conclusions about staying warm. Basically we realized that the survival experts really do know what they are talking about when discussing heat loss from the body. Further, the commercial fishermen of the northern countries are correct in sticking to wool clothing.

Survival experts, experienced in cold weather survival conditions, estimate that heat loss from the body is approximately 30 percent from head and neck, 20 percent from feet and ankles, 20 percent from hands and wrists, and 30 percent from the rest of the body. Thus to stay warm it is essential to keep your feet, head, hands, and, more particularly, your wrists warm. Do this, and the rest of the body will take care of itself. The main torso need not be protected and encumbered by layers of sweaters, sweatshirts and/or floatcoats, as the heat loss through the main torso is relatively minimal.

Our blood is just like the cooling liquid in an engine—blood temperature regulates body temperature. Where the blood comes closest to the surface, at head and neck, wrists, hands, feet, and ankles, it is most rapidly cooled, thereby cooling the entire body. To prove this point, on a hot day hold your hands and wrists in a bucket of cold water. Within minutes you will be cool. If they are kept there for ten or fifteen minutes you will actually begin to shiver.

Yachting, November 1976.

To keep the head warm, the old standby is the navy watch cap available at any surplus store, but better have your girlfriend or wife knit one out of unbleached water-repellent wool. The neck should be protected by a good wide woollen scarf—remember the jugular vein is right at the surface. As an illustration of how important it is to keep your head warm, remember our ancestors, who all wore night caps. They slept in unheated bedrooms, but keeping their heads warm kept them warm. Next time you feel cold at night put on a watch cap and you will probably wake up sweating, as did a member of the crew of *Iolaire* who tried this experiment. I survived in the unheated after cabin using only two wool blankets by just putting my watch cap on when I felt cold.

Hands and wrists need to be kept warm leaving fingers free to tie knots, open snap shackles, etc. This can be done by wearing wristlets—i.e., wool mittens with no fingers or thumb. By keeping the wrists warm the hands will still function comfortably in relatively cold weather, and I know, as my left hand was smashed at the age of twelve and circulation in it is poor. Without wristlets it won't work much below 55° F; with them it will work in almost freezing conditions. When working wear wristlets, when sitting on deck doing nothing or when steering (holding on to a metal steering wheel in cold weather is like holding on to a block of ice) wear a pair of waterproof mittens over the wristlets. In really cold weather wear a pair of wool mittens plus waterproof mittens over the wristlets, and take the outer two off for handling lines, etc.

Feet should be kept warm and comfortable by wearing boots that will permit two heavy pairs of wool socks inside without restricting circulation of the feet. The outer pair should be of unbleached water-repellent wool, the inner pair of normal wool. Change and wash the inner pair, but *don't* wash the outer pair. If boots are worn without shoes inside they should have felt inner soles, and spares should be carried so that when the soles become damp they can be changed. If expecting to do a lot of sailing in a really cold area get the type of boot that fits over sneakers or moccasins, which along with two pairs of socks will give really good insulation.

The remainder of the body is relatively easy to keep warm. A pair of good heavy iceman's trousers or British army surplus heavy wool trousers (I have a pair which cost me £1·10—the kind that practically stand up by themselves though it's best to aid them with braces), a light wool sweater topped by a tightly woven wool shirt—the old navy CPO shirt or its equivalent is unbeatable—will keep one warm with temperatures in the low fifties. Below that more insulation is needed: first wool long-johns (note *wool,* not cotton or synthetic), army or navy surplus are around 90p for a complete set. It should be remembered that long periods of time will be spent sitting down with the result that the tail gets cold. The solution is to take a pair of long-johns, cut the legs off and wear them under the wool trousers, giving an extra layer of wool where it is needed—or buy army surplus wool undershorts for 60p! Another solution is to sew an extra layer of wool on the seat of your trousers.

A good long, natural wool front-opening sweater on top of the CPO shirt will keep one warm and comfortable almost down to freezing point. Once temperatures get below freezing it's time to head to the nearest harbor. The sweater should be long so that one can sit on it, it keeps the tail warm, and will not pull up leaving a vast expanse of bare back when you bend over, and front-opening so that it is easy to get on and off. If you can persuade someone to knit one, have them knit it with a big heavy collar at least nine inches high, that will keep the back of the neck and head warm. Use natural water-repellent wool so that if you have leaky foul-weather gear it does not get really wet, only slightly damp. A natural wool sweater is best if never washed, but when the time finally comes to wash it—i.e. when your wife won't let it in the house—wash it, but on the final rinse add a few tablespoons of olive oil to the rinsing water which will restore the water-repellent property. One of our West Indian Irish-bred yachtsmen, John Bardon, swears it works!

It is hoped that the foul-weather gear you are wearing is keeping you relatively dry, but this is an aim that is all too often not achieved. Hence all this talk of natural wool, wool which has not had the natural oil removed from it and is therefore almost waterproof, certainly water-repellent. Many new synthetic insulating materials have come on the market in the last twenty years which are much lighter and warmer than wool when *dry,* but few are really effective once wet, and once wet they are all but impossible to dry while at sea. Wool on the other hand is still warm when wet and will easily be dried by body heat alone. If your clothes get soaked, go to bed all standing with your foul-weather gear on. By the time you have to go on watch again you'll be warm and only slightly damp. If your gear is only damp take off your foul-weather gear, roll up in a couple of wool blankets, and you will be dry next watch.

Wool blankets, in the opinion of many, beat sleeping bags on a boat. Sleeping bags once damp are miserable and virtually impossible to dry, while wool blankets will dry by body heat alone. Witness the fact that we took a wave down an open hatch right into the skipper's bunk. I swore, lifted up the blanket, and you could hear the water pour out onto the cabin sole. I rolled back in the blankets, which dried out in the next few hours so well that it was two months later on a sunny day in France that we bothered to dry them out on deck.

Having lived in the Tropics for twenty-two years it stands to reason that I don't like cold weather. Having to make regular early spring and late fall deliveries to the States from the Lesser Antilles or vice versa I have learned to keep warm on a minimum of clothing. Crossing the Atlantic well north of the Gulf Stream, as well as cruising and racing in English and Irish waters until November, we experienced our share of cold weather, yet this skinny (I weigh 125 pounds) tropical animal was continually wearing less gear than the majority of the crew. One of them dressed as described above, and being used to cold weather wore even less than I did.

With few exceptions my standard cold-weather gear was heavy socks, wool trousers, light sweater under CPO shirt, scarf, hat, wristlets, and foul-weather gear as needed. Cut-off long-johns were added in really cold weather, and a couple of times during the mid-watch an oiled wool sweater, but only when the temperature was in the low fifties.

[To check on his conclusions, Street asked Britain's Wool Secretariat to comment. Here is the interesting—if not entirely unbiased—reply.—Ed.]

A vast amount of research carried out by military authorities and a specific testing program initiated and supervised by Dr. Behmann at Kerkhoff Institute at Bad Nauheim, Germany, has conclusively proved that natural wool has all the synthetic fibres at a great disadvantage for heat insulation and protection from cold and damp extremes as often experienced by sailors. The chance of a wool garment becoming wet throughout is less than in the case of a man-made fiber garment and you can even sleep in wet wool clothing or blankets and wake up free from pneumonia because, due to a phenomenon known as heat of absorption, drying wool actually generates its own heat.

Wool can absorb 30 per cent of its own weight in moisture as against 7 per cent for polyester and surface water is absorbed by wool fibers and chemically bound without the fabric even *feeling* wet until the saturation value of 33 per cent is reached. Wool textiles show up well against man-made fibers with regard to relative heat loss and intensive research under cold and wet conditions similar to those experienced at sea have proved that under really cold climatic conditions wool has a higher thermal insulation factor than any other fiber. Wool fabric has a relatively rough surface composed of myriad tiny projecting fiber ends, and these prevent complete contact between garment and skin, forming a static insulating layer of air.

The body exudes moisture even when cold. This moisture must be removed or it will quickly carry away heat from the body at twenty times the rate of air it replaces. Wool fiber allows maximum diffusion of water vapor outward from the body for specified porosity or wind resistance. In addition, water vapor which does not pass through the fabric is readily absorbed.

In extreme cold conditions such as the Arctic where the insulation value of a fabric depends greatly upon the air trapped within it and on the surface, wool shows up to tremendous advantage. This is because wool fabrics are lofty and porous and because roughly 80 per cent of their total volume is air which is a very poor conductor of heat. It follows that the greater the percentage of air in the fabric volume, the greater its insulation value. This is particularly applicable in the cold, damp conditions experienced at sea.

The high absorption capacity of wool acts in three ways to increase body warmth:

1. It removes water which would accumulate in a fabric made of non-absorbent fibers;
2. With such water removed, it is not available to travel through the fabric for evaporation on the outer surface of the garment and so further accelerate the rate of heat loss;
3. As mentioned above, in the process of absorbing moisture (heat of absorption) wool actually creates its own heat.

Water repellency is a great factor of wool as a clothing for seamen because it gives reasonable rain and spray repellence without interfering with body ventilation. Three of wool's most important properties are a high capacity for water absorption, a natural repellence of the fiber surface for liquid water, and a resilience which provides an ideal fabric surface for shedding water and which also absorbs the energy of impinging rain.

The hairy characteristics of many wool fabrics resemble the surface of a bird's feathers and encourage the maintenance of rain in droplets or pearl-like globules. Therefore in a light shower rain tends to run off without wetting.

In a storm, however, falling drops of rain hit the fabric surface with considerable force. If the surface of the garment is hard and unyielding, all of the energy which has accumulated in the raindrop's fall can be utilized in pushing the drop into the fabric thus breaking the droplet form. On the other hand wool's soft compressible fabric surface can absorb the energy of falling droplets, taking up the energy which would otherwise be utilized in assisting the water to penetrate.

To sum up, wool has all the synthetic fibers beaten into the proverbial cocked hat for wear at sea. No wonder the late Sir Francis Chichester used woollen garments for his epic round-the-world trip.

 ❧ Keeping Dry

Foul-weather gear is supposed to keep you dry, and supplementary clothing should keep you warm and comfortable. But sailing always is a compromise and what you gain in one direction you loose in another. The dinghy sailor on a trapeze in cold weather has his mobility severely restricted if he wears foul-weather gear, sea boots, wool trousers, sweaters,

Sail, March 1975.

wool cap, etc. For him, a wet suit that keeps him warm and comfortable, and does not restrict his mobility is a good choice.

Some foredeck men on ocean racers also favor the wet suit. But for the average offshore sailor, a wet suit is uncomfortable, hard to get into, and can raise a really good crop of salt water boils in a relatively short time.

Heavy, thick foul-weather gear that will practically stand by itself is not necessary when sailing in the summer. In such conditions you can use the good lightweight gear that is available on the market. Remember, though, that foul-weather gear material is waterproof to a certain PSI (pounds per square inch). Light gear may be waterproof if you are standing in a rain squall or shower. But additional pressure compressed on the bottom of foul-weather gear when sitting, frequently causes leaking through the seat. Try it. Fill a shallow washtub with water six inches deep, put on your foul-weather trousers, and sit in the washtub with a good book and read for an hour. Then check the result.

If you really want to stay dry, the vast majority of offshore sailors, whether they be yachtsmen, professional delivery crews, or fishermen, are universal in their choice of a basic foul-weather-gear type of trousers held up by suspenders (braces to our British cousins) and a separate foul-weather jacket. The all-in-one foul-weather gear is popular primarily among dinghy sailors and inshore one-design racers.

I think it's essential for trousers to have a fly front. What is more discouraging than to be encased in foul-weather trousers, wool trousers, long winter woollies and suddenly you have to relieve yourself. Unless you have full-length hip boots under your foul-weather trousers (which allows relief between the boot and the foul-weather trousers) you simply must have a fly.

But the fly has to be waterproof. A straight zipper leaks like a sieve and must be protected by a waterproof flap that should be secured either by buttons, another zipper, or a Velcro flap.

Foul-weather trousers always should be roomy. A pair that may be plenty big enough for summer wear can become too small once long winter woollies, heavy trousers, and sweater are piled on. If you are going to buy a pair of pants, plan ahead by considering all the weather you will be sailing in.

Straps should be adjustable either by means of buckles (plastic, bronze, or stainless steel, not chrome-plated steel which is bound to corrode, jam, or rot the elastic). When purchasing foul-weather trousers carry a powerful pocket magnet and check the gear. Reject anything with magnetic metal components. All too often "solid brass" or stainless proves to be plated steel.

The legs of foul-weather trousers should have some way to secure the trousers tightly around sea boots. Otherwise, when you are working in the lee scuppers, water will drive up the leg of the trousers and fill your sea boots, which then will become cold, wet, and uncomfortable. Many sailors use heavy rubber bands (always carry spares) that are left wrapped around the sea boots. As the boot is pulled on, a rubber band is pulled up *over* the leg of the foul-weather trousers securely closing the gap. Other sailors prefer a light loop of shock cord secured to a button. The cord then can be wrapped around the leg and secured back on the button.

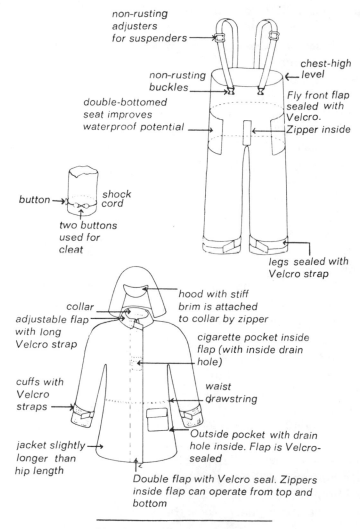

non-rusting
adjusters
for suspenders

chest-high
level

non-rusting
buckles

double-bottomed
seat improves
waterproof potential

Fly front flap
sealed with
Velcro.
Zipper inside

button

shock
cord

two buttons
used for
cleat

legs sealed with
Velcro strap

collar

adjustable flap
with long
Velcro strap

hood with stiff
brim is attached
to collar by zipper

cigarette pocket inside
flap (with inside drain
hole)

cuffs with
Velcro
straps

waist
drawstring

jacket slightly
longer than
hip length

Outside pocket with drain
hole inside. Flap is Velcro-
sealed

Double flap with Velcro seal. Zippers
inside flap can operate from top and
bottom

Ideal features for foul-weather gear

A third method is to secure shock cord to the trouser legs by looping it around one button; then sew two buttons two inches apart elsewhere on the other side of the leg. Take the shock cord around the leg and use the two buttons as a cleat. This way you will be able to adjust the tension to your liking even though the shock cord may stretch or you may use different diameters of sea boots.

Several types of foul-weather pants have a strap of Velcro material attached to the foul-weather trouser leg and the strap can be adjusted by means of a Velcro strip.

A good pair of trousers also should have some belt loops and an elastic retaining strap so a sheath knife and pliers can be slung on a sail stop, threaded through the loops, and the sheath held down by the elastic strap.

The right foul-weather jacket is always a matter of debate; should it be a pullover or front opening? Years ago, front-opening foul-weather jackets were closed by buttons or snaps and closure was a lot less than waterproof. This resulted in the popularity of over-the-head foul-weather jackets. These can be drier but their disadvantage is that they are hard to put on and take off. This is an especially important bad feature for someone like the navigator who may be going below decks frequently. If he dresses to be warm on deck, he will become hot and sweaty in short order if he can't shed his foul-weather gear and open his sweater.

For this reason, many good seamen feel a foul-weather jacket should be front-opening with zippers working from both top and bottom. The jacket should reach the hips and the zipper should be waterproof by being double-breasted with the zipper inside a flap that is secured either by buttons, a second zipper, or a Velcro seal.

A towel wedged around the neck helps keep you from getting soaked, but a good foul-weather jacket also should have a watertight and adjustable neck closure. Some systems use a flap with buttons (good but not infinitely adjustable) some use a lanyard (knots always seem to slip or jam), and others use a strip of Velcro secured to a flap; by far the best closure if the flap is long enough.

Not long ago during the fall I sailed south with a good foul-weather jacket secured with a Velcro strap. Great on the showroom floor but with a temperature of 36°, with a wool shirt, wool sweater, and scarf around my neck, the flap was too short to reach its strap. I did complain to the manufacturer and hope the flap now has been lengthened.

There are some who say you are not really driving a boat hard to windward until you are going so fast that, when you reach down into the lee scuppers to adjust a snatch block, the water drives up the sleeve, roars across your back and shoots down through the other sleeve! Priorities seem to have changed, though, and various methods are now used to prevent this from happening.

In addition to an outside wrist closure of a strap with buttons, or Velcro flap, there should be an inside wrist closure, a cone of material at the wrist sewn to the inside of the jacket, closed by light elastic, and adjustable with Velcro strap as Henri Lloyd does. (All Velcro straps should be at least two inches wide.) It should be waterproof but need not be the same cloth weight as the jacket material.

I feel an adjustable belt with drawstring should be located at approximately waist level. If the belt is at the bottom of the jacket, and the jacket is hip length, it is uncomfortable to sit down or climb out of the cockpit, and leg movement also is restricted. If there is no string at all, when you bend over with your back to the wind, the jacket blows up around your shoulders and spray drives in under the jacket, soaking the back and shoulders, just the thing you are trying to avoid.

The choice between a sou'wester hat or attached hood creates another debate. The sou'wester hat is excellent in that it has a stiff brim to keep rain out of the eyes when looking to windward. And when you turn your head, the sou'wester hat turns with you. Rain dripping off the edges of the hat does not run down over your nose and chin. However, the jacket must have a really good neck closure or spray will drive down the back of the neck.

Most modern sailors favor an attached hood but few fit really well, and none have an adequate brim to allow you to look to windward. When you are sitting in rain, very often water drips off the top of the hood, runs down your forehead, drips off the end of your nose and (if you have one) into your beard!

There is a solution. Put a long-billed swordfisherman's hat under the foul-weather gear hood. But unfortunately, this is just one more thing to look for at the last minute when putting on your foul-weather gear. A stiff bill or brim about six inches wide sewn into the front of the hood would completely solve this problem.

What would be the best of all possible worlds? A jacket with a big adjustable collar and a zipper inside the collar to which you can attach a policeman's type of hood with a long Velcro strap. This way a sou'wester hat can also be worn, and you would be able to wear any one of the three different types of headgear as circumstances required.

One problem in really heavy weather arises when all hands are called on deck in conditions needing safety harnesses, foul-weather gear, and life jackets. By the time the crew assembles all this gear on their persons, the emergency is nearly always over. One solution to this problem is the new Henri Lloyd jacket, which has buoyancy and a safety harness built into it.

Some of the boys who race around the world and on the maxi ocean racers will claim, with justification, that when the boat is traveling at fourteen knots a man going overboard with the harness as supplied by Henri Lloyd will probably end up with busted ribs or a broken back. This, admittedly, is true under racing conditions, but the average yachtsman is more likely to fall overboard while changing a headsail when the boat is semi hove-to doing three knots.

Old time professional sailors always used to wear a knee-length coat, sou'wester hat and hip boots—a costume seldom seen today. Knee-length boots have become popular and today you see many people wearing even calf-length boots. You can get away with them on a modern yacht because its high freeboard seldom puts anyone working in the lee scuppers in eighteen inches of water—as was the case in the forties, fifties, and into the mid-sixties with the low freeboard boats that then were common.

A serious sailor still should favor knee-length boots, and he should make sure they have a good non-skid sole. If you wear an over-the-sock boot, make sure you have removable inner soles and bring a spare pair in case the first sole gets wet.

Try your boots on with two pairs of heavy woolen socks to make sure they will be comfortable in cold weather. Always carry some plastic sandwich bags and rubber bands when you go sailing. Then, if the sea boot gets wet inside, on the next watch put the plastic bags on over your dry socks and pull them up with the rubber bands. Your dry socks will stay dry even in the damp sea boots.

Some people prefer an over-the-shoe sea boot. They are definitely bulkier and harder to walk in, but in cold weather this type of boot is definitely warmer, for the inner shoe provides an extra layer of insulation.

For really cold weather, it is possible to buy Norwegian wool (or sheepskin-lined) sea boots. They are really warm, but are only suitable for cold-weather sailing. Whatever boot you settle on, make sure you look at the sole. Some treads available do not always work very well on a modern fiberglass deck.

19 ❧ Shorthanded Watch Systems

A TIRED SAILOR is apt to make mistakes and therefore it is important to have some sort of watch system for any cruise that is going to last more than five or six hours. Admittedly, on an 18- or 24-hour sail, a watch system can be relatively simple; one- or two-hour helm watches with the helmsman calling on extra labor when it's needed. A twenty-four hour sail is rarely so exhausting that a few short naps won't be enough to keep everyone on his toes.

However, on longer trips, if the crew is to be well rested, well fed, and also enjoy themselves, it is essential that a routine be set up to maximize the balance of time for steering, ship's work, and sleeping. Even a single-hander needs to set up a watch system.

The single-hander invariably is accompanied by Charlie—a self-steering system that can take over the helm either continually, or for long periods of time. Charlie's helmsmanship is derived from a number of sources. It can come from the sails, from the wind vane, electronically, or hydraulically. Any of these variants on the self-steering device can take over the helmsman's duties, but none can take over the duties of either the skipper, navigator, cook, lookout, or crew. And this well-known fact gives the single-hander little time to get bored; it also gives him little time to sleep.

One of the dangers in single-handing is working continuously until the time comes when exhaustion, loss of judgement, or hallucination set in. To avoid this, a single-hander must set up a watch system that gives him a fixed time for work, and a set time to sleep. He should stick as closely to this schedule as he possibly can.

One of the great dangers of single-handing is being run down while asleep. It goes without saying that the danger is much greater at night than during the day. Thus the single-hander should try as best he can to reverse his watch schedule: sleep during the day and stay awake at night.

When two or more people are on board for a long passage, it is possible to set up a watch system so that someone is continually on duty. But the old routine of four on and four off wears a crew down in a hurry. The main reason is that four hours below just are not enough to catch up on

Sail, January 1975.

one's sleep. For this reason various watch systems have been developed. The most common hybrid is the so-called *Swedish watch system*, which was developed, I believe, in the 1920s.

This system runs as follows (Fig. 1): midnight to 0400, 0400 to 0800, 0800 to 1300, 1300 to 1900, 1900 to 2400. Because there are an uneven number of watches in a day, it is self-dogging and you do not stand the same watches on two successive days. Every other day one watch has a good six hours below where he really can catch up on sleep.

Fig. 1. Swedish watch system.

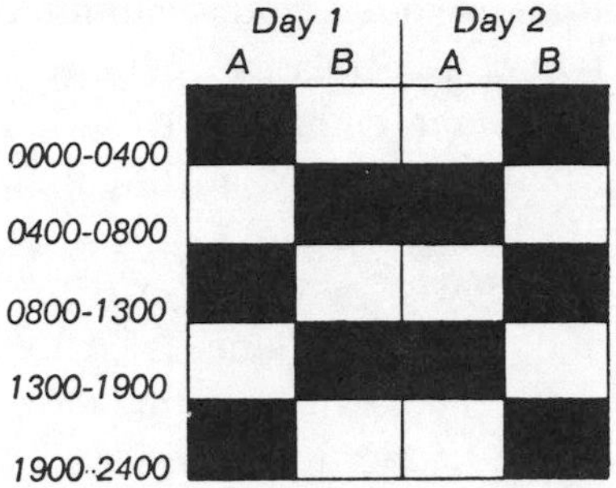

Day 1   Day 2
A   B   A   B

0000-0400

0400-0800

0800-1300

Watch section "A" spends 10 hours   1300-1900
on deck during day 1, 14 hours on
deck during day 2   1900-2400

The day a watch has a six-hour deck watch, he also has two five-hour watches below. The extra hour's sleep above the "normal" four makes a world of difference. Three to three-and-a-half hours' sleep is not enough; but four to four-and-a-half hour's undisturbed sleep is really revitalizing.

This system works very well with a four-man crew split into two sections. The watch on deck can alternate the helm one hour on, one off, and the lee helmsman can do any ship's work: cooking, washing up, navigating, and the like. Meals are served at 0745, 1245, and 1845 with the watch on deck doing the cooking and the oncoming watch doing the washing up.

However, if there is only a two-man crew and no self-steering, a straight six hours on the helm is too much for most people. You can do it but it could be so exhausting that it would take all the fun out of sailing. If the boat has no auto-pilot or vane-steering gear, and it cannot be made to track reliably by presetting the sails, then it is either time to find a third person or install self-steering gear.

If there are three people on board, most experienced sailors feel it is best to have one man on deck, two below, and make the length of watches dependent on the crew, the steering qualities of the boat, and weather conditions. If the boat steers easily and the crew is strong, four on and eight off does seem to work. If heavy weather develops, four hours on the helm is probably going to be too much, and the watches should be shortened to three hours, or in extreme cases, to two hours.

Remember that most doctors agree that the first hours of sleep are the most important. This means that if the watch on deck needs a hand, he should call the man *coming on watch* rather than the man who has just gone off.

A four on and eight off watch system does have one advantage on a long voyage: the crew settles into a routine for it has the same watch each day (Fig. 2). Some people like the four to eight, particularly the navigator. Standing the four to eight lets him take his morning and evening stars while on watch, gives him the midday to work them out, and he can throw in a sunline or two for even greater accuracy. While he does get eight hours' sleep at night (which other members of the crew may envy) he also is working for much, if not most, of the day.

Fig. 2. Three section non-rotating watch system.

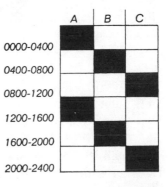

Watch section "B" should include skipper/navigator to get morning and evening stars

Other crew members tend to like the eight to twelve, for the forenoon watch usually has plenty of company on deck. The twelve to four in the morning *graveyard* watch is none too popular. One method of making it more palatable is to have the other watches stand one extra hour on alternate nights, thus shortening the mid-watch by an hour. One night the "mid" becomes midnight to three, another night it becomes 0100 to 0300. This usually will keep the mid-watch happy.

For crews that do not like the routine of having the same watch every night, a three-man crew can stand three-hour watches with three on and six off; it dogs itself automatically (Fig. 3).

When delivering boats, I frequently end up with a crew of three, plus a cook. The cook does not stand watches, but does do all the cooking. The off-watch crew member helps with the cleaning up. The three watch

standers use either the four on and eight off, or go to three on and six off.
It really depends on who is in the crew and the weather on a particular
trip.

Fig. 3. *Three section self-dogging watch system.*

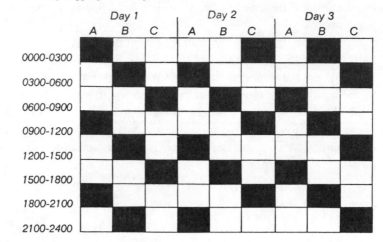

When cruising (as opposed to making a long-distance delivery) a
crew often can consist of a husband and wife plus some small children.
Here, a two-section watch system usually works best; the wife and the
oldest child (or best sailor—sometimes they are not synonymous) stand
one watch, and the husband and younger children stand the other watch.
Having the children stand a watch keeps them from becoming bored and
even the youngest can tail up a winch; all mine learned how to do it at age
three or less.

In moderate weather, an eight-year-old can learn how to steer for
short periods of time. Admittedly they can't do a full one-hour trick at the
helm but they can steer long enough for the husband or wife to duck
below to light the stove, check the chart, or what have you.

Of course self-steering gear does make life much easier. It has been
said that good self-steering gear is like having an extra hand. Actually
good self-steering gear is like having *two* helmsmen in that it can steer
for both watches. With good self-steering gear, a boat thirty-five feet or
under can be adequately and happily sailed by a couple for long periods of
time. Six on and six off with the watch on deck doing all the ship's work
gives plenty of time for sleep. The on-deck watch is doing a variety of jobs
so they do not get bored, and the below-deck watch is getting enough
sleep so that they do not mind being called on deck to help with the sails.

Though two good sailors are adequate for a small boat with self-steering gear, that will not be enough (unless they are Leslie Williams and Robin Knox-Johnson) for a big boat where the sails just get too large. With three crew on board a boat with self-steering gear, either a four on and eight off, or a three on and six off routine can be used depending on what suits them best.

A good alternate system is six on and six off for two of the crew with the third off for 24 hours, but he is the cook for that day. This, of course, means that every third day each crew member can devote his whole day to making three wonderful meals; and as a reward have a full 12 hours in the sack!

With four in the crew, and good self-steering gear, you really are getting out of the shorthanded class. However if you do end up in this very pleasant situation, try a three-section watch system with the fourth person the "duty cook" with the day off and a twelve-hour sleep as reward for a good day's cooking. Because there are three days for the cook to think about what he or she is to prepare, even a poor cook should be able to conjure up some appetizing meals.

These are just a few of the possibilities for shorthanded watch systems. There are an infinite number of other permutations and combinations that can be used, but flexibility is the key. A skipper never should be bound by a single watch system and he should be able to alter it as he sees fit in the light of the weather and navigational difficulties, and the capabilities of the crew. If one of the crew is a ninety-pound girl, or a small young teenager, they cannot, nor should they be expected to, stand the same long watch hours as an experienced seaman, especially in heavy weather.

More important, the skipper should apportion the watches so that he is able to obtain enough rest. The crew and the ship are his responsibility and it is no good to discover, at the onset of a gale, that the crew is rested but the skipper has run himself down to a point where he is tired and likely to make an error in judgment.

Years ago, when seamen stood watch-and-watch, they also put in an eight-hour work day during the forenoon and afternoon watches. One wonders when they slept. You must remember, though, that twelve- and fourteen-hour days were also common in the factories ashore. Of course when those men were on watch at night and were not actually trimming sails, steering, or standing lookout, it was perfectly acceptable to doze on watch.

It's often been said the sign of a good seaman is his ability to be able to curl up on the deck and go to sleep instantly. But he must sleep lightly enough so that a call from the watch captain will have him instantly awake and ready to go. It is an art that is learned over a long period of time at sea.

When you are doing ocean cruising on a long-distance basis, the most important thing to remember is that a good crew is a rested crew, and the tired crew is one that makes errors in judgment and gets into trouble.

Always set up a watch system that can produce the greatest amount of undisturbed sleep without conflicting with the safety and seamanlike handling of the vessel.

20 ❊ Organizing for the Voyage

WHEN A CRUISING BOAT makes port at the end of a long offshore passage, sometimes her entire crew is standing on deck, sea bags packed, ready to depart. They may be fighting mad; they may not be on speaking terms. And sometimes a boat comes in, secures, and the whole crew goes ashore to the nearest pub to celebrate their safe arrival and the great time they had.

What makes the difference? Basically, it is organization, tolerance, and the willingness of every person in the crew to do not just his share of the work but more than his share.

In most cases the organization is produced first by a good skipper. The crew feel their skipper can do any job in the boat better than anyone else on board. This gives everyone confidence in the skipper, the boat, and the likelihood of completing the trip with minimum difficulty.

But a good skipper is not enough. Everyone must know the ship's routine and what is expected of him or her. Organization is important and on the 70th-birthday cruise of my 45-foot yawl *Iolaire* across the Atlantic to England we tried to be as organized as we could. For example, the cooking chores were rotated on a regular basis through the crew (each member was cook for a day) though we still had one person who was, as we described him in the navy, Store King. He was in overall charge of purchasing and stowing food, and would help the cook find the food necessary for the meals to be served each day.

Another member of the crew was in charge of the electrical system;
Sail, January 1978.

another was "Chippy"—an English term for a ship's carpenter; another was the bosun, in charge of sails and rigging. Because *Iolaire* does not have an engine we did not need an engineer, as most boats would, but an important job was that of lamp trimmer—an old post going back to the days when a large sailing ship would have twenty or thirty lamps that would have to be filled, cleaned, trimmed, and generally tended to each day. With seven kerosene lamps onboard *Iolaire,* we discovered that the lamp trimmer was actually a full-time position, for cleaning, trimming, and filling the lamps each day required a fair amount of time.

Regarding the cleaning-up duties: everyone was responsible for his own gear, and the cook-for-the-day was responsible for trying to keep below-decks cleaned up. But on a long trip, no matter what you do to keep things shipshape, eventually the boat begins to get messier and messier and may come to resemble a pigsty. Our plan was to have a good old-fashioned navy field day every six days. Unfortunately, on this crossing we became rather slack in this rule enforcement. It would have been better had we made it an absolute rule, marked the dates on the calendar and stuck to them. But we didn't.

IOLAIRE'S SHIP'S ORDERS

Deck Watch

1. Helm—helm watches—one hour on, one hour off. At the end of each hour, retiring helmsman should leave cockpit and check decks for:
   A. sail trim
   B. coiled lines
   C. chafe, etc.
2. Enter *rough* log (small stenographer's notebook) every hour plus any change in course, with time of change, *and log reading.* When filling in course averaged, *be honest*
3. From 0830–1630 the helmsman should do jobs appropriate to his calling. *No reading* on watch 0830–1630. Check pages in back of work list for your department
4. Awaken oncoming watch 15 minutes early—make sure hot water, cocoa, and coffee are available for oncoming watch
5. Turn off compass light, all ship's lights at dawn
6. On-deck watch must have *knife, pliers,* and *light* (at night) before going on deck—safety harness as necessary
7. Answer up—repeat all orders so that the person giving them knows they are heard and understood

Ship's Routine

1. Stow all personal gear—at all times make sure foul-weather gear is hung up, and wet gear is hung from hooks and lanyards
2. Sleep in your own bunk
3. Turn off all electric lights not in use
4. Keep kerosene lights lit low in head, main cabin, and galley at night

5. Relieve watches on time, helmsman every hour
6. Check bilge every watch—when rail down, *pump* every watch
7. Every sixth day complete belowdecks clean-up, commencing 1300
8. Note in work log front pages any deficiencies in gear that should be put right—check back pages for your work list every day

Dangers

1. Vang chafe; vang must be rigged to cinch up on itself
2. Jib- and genoa-sheet chafe—switch to reaching sheets soon as possible
3. With wind on quarter or aft, preventer *must* be rigged
4. Chafe in general and all of the above should be checked by off-going helmsman every hour

Galley

1. Cook on duty from 0600–2000. Whenever galley and belowdecks are secured cook can sleep but is to be called on deck to help with sail changes rather than wake other watch
2. Cook must obtain location of food needed the day before his cooking duty
3. Cook must fix meals, clean up galley *completely;* sweep down belowdecks and *clean head* (after lunch). It is the cook's responsibility to keep belowdecks clean and neat
4. Galley routine:
   A. Oil knives when putting them away and sharpen if necessary
   B. Oil, do not scrub, frying pan
   C. Wash copper pot in *fresh* water
5. All items put into icebox *must* be in zip-lock or suitable watertight containers
6. Periodically, the cook must:
   A. Turn eggs every three days to prevent spoilage
   B. Pick out potatoes and onions (days two and five)
   C. Pick over fruit (days three and six)
7. Cook should begin preparing meals at 0600, 1100, 1630—meals served at 0730, 1230, 1830. Thermos bottles of coffee and cocoa should be made after dinner
8. Galley must be cleaned thoroughly—this includes:
   –removing and cleaning fiddles—pumping ice-box (three times daily)
   –scrubbing stove and baking pan (if used)
   –wiping under stove—wiping counters and all formica surfaces
   –spraying for bugs

We did keep a notebook on the chart table so that any deficiency in any department could be marked in the front of the book. Every morning the skipper, who stood the 0600–0800 watch, would check the notebook for the work that needed to be done. Then he would write down the individual jobs in sections in the back of the book: electrical, carpentry, sails, rigging, galley, etc. The person in charge of that department would be responsible for doing the job as soon as possible.

On a long voyage, tolerance on everyone's part is important—especially on the part of the skipper toward the crew. On *Iolaire* it happened that one member of the crew (one of the hardest working) would help out in the galley regularly, be happy to work extra hours on deck changing sails and retrimming with no complaint whatsoever. He worked hard and long at the chart table, learning navigation. But he hated to steer with a passion. He would do practically anything to avoid the helm, and we took this into account.

Another crew member was like a portable winch—six-feet five-inches tall, 210 pounds of muscle, and an ex-collegiate rower. Discomfort bothered him not at all; never a complaint about a sea boot full of water, a wave down the neck, or cold weather. In fact he was so unconscious of discomfort that he went for a week sleeping on top of the ice-box pump I was madly looking for. I had taken it apart to be worked on, and had carelessly put it in his bunk. He wasn't much of a helmsman and he could lose tools, flashlights, and shackles with unbelievable regularity, but we understood this and appreciated his own talents.

Such a diverse kind of crew not only teaches a skipper the importance of appreciating a willingness and ability, it requires that he be understanding and forgive some inabilities as well. He must instill in his crew the same idea, that is: "So who is perfect?"

Before any long trip starts, a skipper should sit the crew down and have a good discussion. Prior to this session, though, everyone should have read the ship's standing orders. Then any questions, objections, or desired changes should be brought up.

This session is perhaps a good time to explain one of my own beliefs: No reading should be allowed on watch. It is a hard rule to enforce but the reason for trying to enforce it is that if a watch on deck is reading, he is not really sailing the boat, trimming sails, checking for chafe, or keeping a lookout. If no reading is allowed, in periods of good weather when there is little to do other than steer, all the little jobs that are cropping up continuously will be done immediately.

Another rule of mine that sometimes is hard to enforce but I think is essential is the old navy routine of answering up and repeating orders. To some, answering up sounds silly but if it is faithfully done it eliminates a tremendous amount of confusion and misunderstanding.

The skipper always is responsible for the safety of the ship and for the care of the crew. All too often, inexperienced crews come onboard and the skipper does not bother to anticipate their mistakes by giving instructions to prevent their making them. A prime example of this is to allow a crew-member to come on deck without foul-weather gear when you are likely to have a wave on-board. What usually happens is that the crew gets soaking wet, then gets cold, tired, or seasick and then you have lost a crew-member. This is not the crew-member's fault but the skipper's for not sending him below immediately to get properly dressed.

Similarly, before leaving port the skipper should make sure all the crew has the proper gear. If one person has improper gear and is miserable, the feeling of misery can permeate the entire crew, which does not make for a happy trip. The skipper should watch his crew working on deck, sail handling, sheet trimming and steering. He must spot mistakes and correct them so that major foul-ups do not develop later because people are not doing their jobs properly.

Both skipper and crew must remember the saying: *different ships, different long splices*. There may be two or three perfectly good methods of doing the same operation. The crew should see which one the skipper uses, and do it his way.

But a good skipper must also keep an open mind and be willing to listen to suggestions from the crew (which never should be given in the middle of a tight situation). I have sailed with many skippers and have suggested different ways of doing things, suggestions that were accepted and appreciated. One of the broadening aspects of the yacht-delivery business is that you deal with all sorts of crew and all sorts of boats. Many crews come up with ideas or ways of doing things that never would have occurred to you because you have spent all your time sailing your own boat.

If a skipper is experienced, he may be able to keep the crew interested and happy by passing his knowledge on to those who are interested. For example, various members of *Iolaire*'s crew wanted to learn to wire splice, a skill I was happy to teach them. But I was not going to go up in the forepeak, drag out the wire, spike, and vise and get it all set up, then say, "Come, learn to splice." Rather, I told them anyone who was interested in learning to wire splice could go and find the wire, the necessary tools, set it all up in the splicing vise and I'd show him where to start making the tucks. We used up a fair amount of wire, but a couple of the crew got quite good at splicing wire.

Often, a boat does not have one skipper but is run by committee. This occurs frequently if the boat is owned by a number of people who run it in partnership. This situation is very difficult and my observation is that it seldom seems to work out on a long-term basis, though there are exceptions. Groups that do succeed in operating boats by committee usually succeed by doing the same things that hold a crew together under a single skipper.

If a boat is run by committee it is imperative that all the jobs be broken down by category and someone must be appointed, or volunteer, to take care of each job so the work load is evenly spread. It is best if people are doing what they like to do though there will be some nasty jobs like cleaning the bilges that must be passed through rotation for no one wants to be in charge of them.

As I mentioned earlier, it is important to keep a work book available so that when any member of the crew discovers something that needs to be done, he can put it down on the work list. Then the person in charge of that department can make good the deficiency.

Though a boat can be run by a committee, the decisions of seamanship really ought to be delegated to one person. If all the crew has the same abilities, one person may be more confident than the others and he or she should act as skipper. Whether this position will fall naturally to one person or whether the choice is made by vote depends on the individual situation.

On boats where there are two or three people of equal competence, sometimes it works out best if the position of skipper—perhaps it's better to describe it as *sailing master*—is held in rotation. For those going on a round-the-world trip, a skipper may hold the position for a month or so, or for one leg of the trip. Always remember that there is nothing more disastrous than trying to shorten sail in a squall with two people giving conflicting orders. So even on a boat run by committee it is essential that *only one person* be skipper at one time.

The crew that is organized, that is tolerant toward one another, and that has each member willing to do more than his share, is a crew that is happy and will sail together for a long time. But it is the skipper who, by example and explanation, can have a great influence in developing these qualities.

21 ❈ Your Boat Is on the Beach

As Dr. Bob Griffiths, skipper of the 53-foot cutter *Awahnee,* points out (with first-rate credentials): any seaman who spends a lifetime at sea stands a good chance of losing his vessel at least once somewhere sometime. The more you examine this statement and talk to experienced yachtsmen, the more reasonable it sounds. Griffiths lost *Awahnee* twice; the Hiscocks have twice come within a hairsbreadth of losing their 49-

foot ketch *Wanderer IV;* Hal Roth has lost (but salvaged) *Whisper;* I lost (but salvaged) my 45-foot wooden yawl *Iolaire;* Ahoto Walters almost lost his big ketch on Australia's Great Barrier Reef in the 1930s. Even Irving Johnson has had over the years a number of extremely narrow escapes from disaster. The law of averages catches up with the most experienced sailors. If you check back in your sailing career, you may be surprised when you tally up the number of narrow escapes you have had.

All too often the disaster takes the form of a grounding, resulting in serious damage to the boat. In many cases the boat is abandoned as a total loss when a bit of thought, energy, sometimes even brute force and a drop of natural animal cunning could have saved the day.

The basic rule in any salvage operation is: *Stay with the boat* as long as possible; at least one person either should stay on board the boat or should camp out on the beach. And remember that the forces involved in salvage work can be tremendous. With such loads, improper rigging of salvage gear can lead to serious injury.

Legally no one is allowed to go onboard the boat without the permission of the owners or the underwriters. However this rule is often honored in the breach rather than the observance. Worldwide, many fishermen regard any wreck as fair game and will strip it as clean as Mother Hubbard's cupboard in the blink of an eye.

Disasters take various forms. Sometimes a boat goes high and dry and is not holed in very shallow water—a relatively simple salvage operation. In other cases the boat is holed and sunk in a tidal area; this can mean that the boat is high and dry when the tide is out and is submerged at high tide. Or the boat can be awash or sometimes sunk completely out of sight in an area with a small rise and fall of tide. But as long as the boat is structurally sound and is holding its shape, it can usually be regarded as salvageable.

So sit down, breathe deeply, and take stock of the situation. Examine your resources and make a plan. Then, if possible, notify your insurance company; tell them what happened and what you plan to do next. Check out whether attempting a salvage operation comes within the limits of your policy. In other words, know what your alternatives are. And remember, the most essential thing in any salvage operation is to "keep the faith!" It is unbelievable the amount of work that can be done with little or no equipment given ingenuity, guts, and perseverance. Stay with the wreck; make sure a guard is posted at all times; establish a base camp; remove everything possible from the boat and stow it ashore under guard; and assemble all the gear and any people that might be useful.

While offloading the boat you cannot have too much help. But in the

When your anchor drags, your boat can be in the surf and on the beach before you can react.

early salvage planning stages too many people can be a liability as you end up with everyone trying to push his own ideas. So one or two people should become salvage masters. They should make a plan and then follow through the plan, recruiting extra labor as needed. Once the salvage operation commences it is practically impossible to have too much help. If excess labor is available, you should work in shifts so that the operation can go on 12, 16, or possibly 24 hours a day. The more quickly the boat is refloated and delivered to a cradle for rebuilding, the less the damage to the vessel.

If it is not possible to live on the boat when it is aground or semi-sunk, set up a good camp on shore—and I mean a good camp as salvage work is extremely hard. The salvors need hot food (even in the tropics) and shelter from sun, wind, and rain. Thus it is essential that one person (sometimes the duty is rotated each day) be placed in charge of making sure there is plenty of food and drink for the working crew!

Once the boat starts moving, i.e., by being dragged along the bottom or by being pumped out, should you lose the tide do not pack up and go home. If you are late coming back, you miss the first hours of the next tide or if something happens to the boat the whole situation can be lost. This is what happened to us on the thirty-six-foot ketch *Daru*. We almost had her afloat, went home for dinner, came back and she was half sunk. The pump would not start; she sank and rolled on her side; and we had to begin again. Once you really start making progress, work in shifts, camp on the beach, bringing in lights if necessary.

Make sure that everyone has plenty of warm clothing and foul-weather gear. Even in the tropics when you are working hip-deep in water, rain squalls can chill you to the bone as the rain is much colder than the water that you are working in. A change into warm dry clothes is essential.

When the salvage operation starts, assemble all the gear you possibly can: canvas, planks, blankets, roofing paper, caulking compounds, nails of all sizes and shapes, crowbars, wrecking bars (known as pig toe to West Indians), pumps (hand, gasoline, diesel), anchors, chain, tackles, everything you can lay your hands on.

If the boat is lying on the beach two essential things must be done immediately: first, plug all holes to the extent that the water is not washing back and forth through the boat; and second, keep sand out of the boat. The power of water sloshing around in a boat has to be seen to be believed. Water can break up the interior of the boat, can move bulkheads, can lift cabin tops off their carlins, or the deck off the hull. It does not matter if the temporary patches are not watertight as long as the surge is eliminated. If sand is swirling around, plugs must be placed so that the sand is not filling up the inside of the boat. If the boat fills with sand it will be absolutely impossible to move her.

When you make provisions for pumping, it doesn't matter if you use gasoline pumps, hand pumps, or buckets. Assemble all the equipment so that once the holes are plugged, the gear is standing by for hauling off and for pumping.

If the boat is lying on the beach or awash, as long as she is not holed the salvage operation should be easy. Tremendous line pull can be developed if a salvage vessel is available. A bridle can be put around the boat and she can be gently pulled back into deep water. When you are attempting to do this and are not using a regular salvage tug with a trained salvage crew, it is most important to remember that a propeller develops relatively little line pull in comparison to winches and anchors. The salvage vessel should anchor with a couple of anchors (see Fig. 1), run a tow line to the damaged vessel, then haul with both anchor windlass and engines. If the anchor windlass is not powerful enough, a tackle can be rigged to the anchor windlass and secured to the anchor chain by a chain stopper or a plain old-fashioned rolling hitch. The power of the anchor windlass can be increased by this method by anywhere from two to five times the normal line pull available (Fig. 2).

Even if no salvage vessel or big power vessel is available, if you have a big anchor or series of anchors and plenty of line, considerable line pull is possible using the boat's own winches.

The average anchor carried on yachts will come home rather than move the boat, no matter how good the holding ground is. It is a case of finding a really big anchor. Heavy anchors are not so hard to handle as you would think when salvaging.

When you are setting salvage anchors make sure they are properly set at the correct angles and buoyed so they can be retrieved after the salvage operation without enormous difficulties. This is where a good diver is a great asset as it is most discouraging to set an anchor, rig the tackle, and have the anchor come home rather than the boat go to the anchor.

Remember that large anchors can be handled with even a comparatively small boat. On one occasion we placed a 350-pound anchor with 120 feet of ⅝-inch chain using nothing but a small Boston Whaler. The anchor was loaded on planks on the Whaler, taken to a position we had previously marked with a buoy, and dumped overside. The Whaler then went back to pick up the chain, which was dropped overside, was shack-

led to the anchor, and then, using the outboard in reverse the chain was
streamed in the desired direction. Once the chain was streamed, line was
placed on it and the tackle was placed on the line. A diver swam along the
chain and lifted it over rocks to make sure it lay in an absolutely straight
line.

Smaller anchors were sent out in the surf. In this situation all you
need for equipment is a face mask, snorkel, and a good pair of sneakers.
As each wave rides in, you take a deep breath and hang onto the anchor

*Fig. 1. By incorporating blocks at optimum locations in the rodes the strain of the pull
from the boat is distributed evenly. Otherwise uneven strain can drag anchors or break
rode.* BRUCE BINGHAM

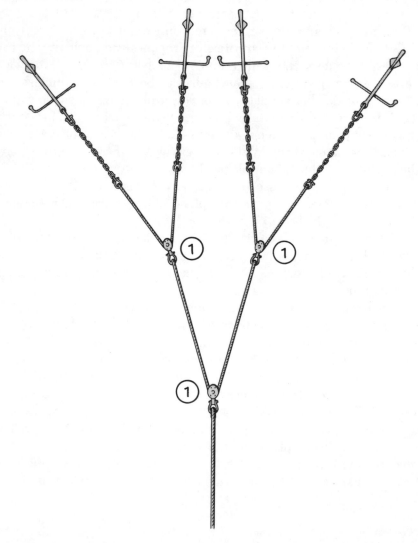

with it on the bottom. As the wave goes over your head, you stand up and drag the anchor as far as you can. Then you take another breath and dive under the next wave.

Other anchors had to be set in deep water beyond the surf. These were dropped with a length of chain secured to the anchors and the line was secured to really large fenders, three feet long. One person equipped with face mask, snorkel, and swim fins lay on top of the fender and swam right in through the surf. Once the line was in, a real strain was put on

Fig. 2. Block and tackle with rope fall led to rope drum on windlass gives additional purchase after chain has been hauled tight with wildcat and cat disengaged. BRUCE BINGHAM

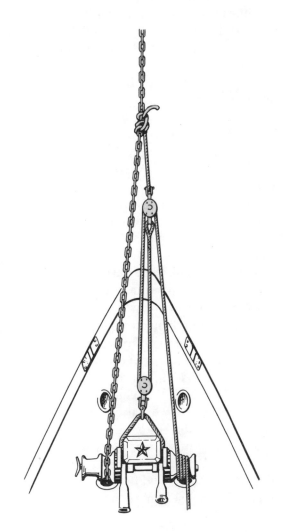

the line; then the diver had to haul himself back out through the surf unhooking the line from various coral heads, making sure there was a direct free pull. When you are working in surf or underwater you should wear a weight belt. The better the swimmer, the heavier the weight he will be able to wear and still semi-swim.

It should be remembered that except when actually swimming with swim fins it is essential to wear shoes as even the toughest feet become soft by immersion in water and rocks or coral will cut feet to ribbons.

If large anchors are not available the same effect can be achieved by setting a number of light anchors out in a bridle (Fig. 1) and running a heavy line to the boat. A bowline can be tied in the anchor line and individual lines can run from the bowline to the individual winches. If strain is taken on all the lines going to the winches, if the anchors are large and firmly dug in, the boat has to move.

If you are on a boat that is aground that does not have powerful winches available, all is not lost—provided you have manpower. Tremendous power can be developed with a block and tackle; a man can easily develop over fairly long periods of time as much as 100 pounds of line pull. Thus we once hauled a thirty-six-footer—drawing six feet six inches and aground in two feet of water—300 yards over the bottom and into deep water. We saved her by digging in a 250-pound CQR with 90 feet of chain secured to one-inch nylon. We secured a four-part tackle to the nylon with a rolling hitch. To the end of the four-part tackle, we secured another four-part tackle (see Fig. 3). Although this gave us a tackle advantage of 16, mark it down to 12 because of friction losses. We put six big men on the tackle. Thus on the hauling end of the tackle we were developing at least 600 pounds of line pull $\times$ 12:1 mechanical advantage = 7,200 pounds of line pull. It took three days of solid heaving but we slowly moved the boat 300 yards into deep water.

Both *Daru* and my own yawl *Iolaire* were holed when they were lying on the beach. Prior to hauling them off we first patched the hole and then pumped them out. In both cases, to repair the hole we had to jack the boat upright or partly upright to install the patch.

In *Iolaire*'s case, she was lying on her side so far over that we were unable to get jacks underneath the bilge. The frames were broken in a straight line to the extent that if we started jacking against the side of the boat we would have jacked the bottom half off the top half. We secured plenty of two-by-fours from an old construction project, knocked the interior out of the boat and X-framed across the inside of the boat to hold it all together (See Fig. 4). We then piled timber under her and slipped some flat, tapered, green heart wedges between the timber and the hull. These we drove in with ten-pound sledges. With only two of us driving wedges we were able to lift the twenty tons upright enough to slip screw ship-jacks at the turn of the bilge and jack her upright. Given patience and muscle anything can be lifted on wedges alone. And remember, big, old-fashioned ship-jacks (see Fig. 5) are infinitely more practical than the standard hydraulic jack.

Fig. 3. Without a windlass, additional power can be gained by hauling anchor rode tight and using one or more block-and-tackle rigs. BRUCE BINGHAM

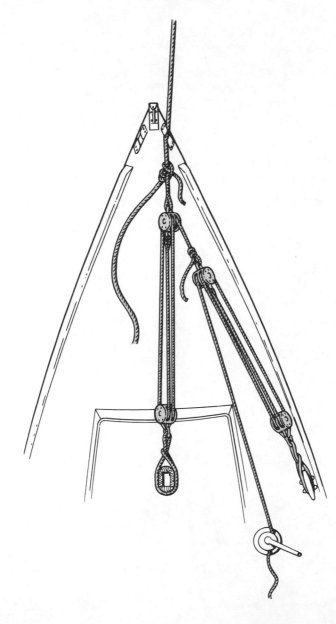

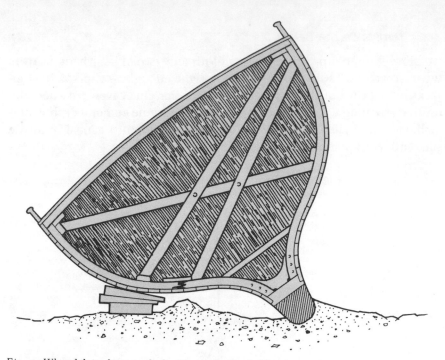

Fig. 4. When Iolaire *lay wrecked with six frames broken, temporary framing held hull in shape as wedges lifted boat upright.* BRUCE BINGHAM

Fig. 5. Heavy ship- or house-jacks can be more effective for salvage work than hydraulic jacks. BRUCE BINGHAM

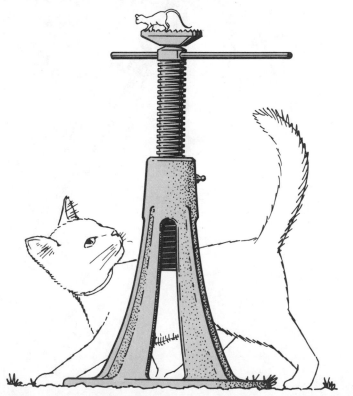

The hydraulic jack is much more powerful and easy to use but the throw on the hydraulic jack will probably only be eight to ten inches. As you try to jack the boat up, the hydraulic jack sinks into the sand, the result being that the hydraulic jack is at the extreme end of its throw and you have only lifted the boat an inch or so. However a good big old-fashioned ship screw-jack (also called house-jack) can settle down into the sand or rock and still provide a good foot of throw to lift the boat. Furthermore the ship-jack, a heavy mass of iron weighing the better part of a hundred pounds, is, because of its mass, not tossed hither and yon. Big ship-jacks usually are rated at ten to fifteen tons or more but you do not get that sort of capacity out of a jack unless it is extremely well greased and you have a large steel bar to use as a handle plus a couple of big men who are really willing to put their backsides into the bar.

As well as using jacks and wedges, a tackle to the mast can be extremely effective in forcing a boat upright. In the initial states when the boat is lying at forty-five degrees or so such a tackle cannot contribute to bringing the boat upright—the angle is too small. However as the boat becomes more and more upright tackles from the mast (or masts) can be extremely effective in lifting the boat upright.

In most cases it is inadvisable to use the normal halyard fittings as they are not designed to take a beam-on strain. Rather, pass a strap around the mast and above the lower spreaders, secure a block to it, and lead a line through it that has been secured to an anchor, deadman, or tree on shore. Take the tail to a halyard winch or tackle or both.

With a four-part tackle to an 8:1 winch, one man can easily exert a 2,000-pound line pull, which, in turn, will exert a considerable righting force on the vessel.

In the later stages of the *Daru* salvage we were pulling her upright by her halyards rather than by jacks. On split rigs remember to rig halyards to both masts.

For installing patches, roofing tar is usually readily available almost anywhere in the world and makes a good watertight seal. Also, underwater epoxy works perfectly well. It can be shoved into leaking seams or under patches and will solidify in the seams and stop the leak. The small cans of underwater patching compound are relatively useless in a salvage operation since when you are doing salvage work you have to buy it by the gallon and not by the half pint.

When you are putting patches on the boat, strips of light wood are much easier to use and are more effective than sheets of plywood because plywood will only bend in one direction and most boats are comprised completely of compound curves. Plywood is useful if you have a chine boat with no compound curves.

Once the boat is jacked upright or relatively upright you can install the patch. There are various methods of installing patches on wooden boats. On *Iolaire* we used layers of half-inch tongue-and-groove nailed to the planking; then roofing tar was laid in each of the grooves and underneath the new planking to form a watertight seal. We then spread canvas on top of the half-inch tongue-and-groove. This ended up making a completely watertight seal and was easy to do, as the half-inch tongue-and-groove was simple to handle. If additional strength is needed, additional layers of half-inch tongue-and-groove can be laid on to build up to the required thickness and strength.

We made a temporary patch on *Daru* with odd bits of wood and then strengthened the whole area by bolting a couple of 2 × 10s in place. This was an extremely difficult operation and bending the 2 × 10s and bolting them in place partially underwater would not have been possible if it had not been for Ron Smith's tremendous ability as a carpenter. He can drive nails better underwater than most carpenters can above water.

Pumps, of course, are a necessary ingredient of every salvage operation. Some people are convinced that diesel pumps are absolutely essential. Admittedly they are great and once they are started salt spray will not stop them. However, they are hard to find, heavy, and expensive. The standard old-fashioned centrifugal two-and-one-half-inch pump driven by an an air-cooled gasoline engine is easily carried and fairly reliable. But to operate a centrifugal pump you need a damn good mechanic as the carburetor will often give trouble. Also a gas engine will not operate in heavy spray as it immediately shorts out and stops if spray gets on the ignition.

It is hard to get a centrifugal pump to pick up suction; the suction line must be absolutely without any pinholes or cracks and there must be a foot-valve and strainer in the bottom of the suction line. When pumping, it is essential that the suction always be clear; this is sometimes difficult as the strainer easily becomes completely clogged. One way to keep the strainer clear is to stick the intake hose and strainer inside either a plastic trash can with plenty of holes cut in it or, better, inside a plastic laundry basket. In out-of-the-way areas if the pump suction should become clogged a large straw basket will act as the primary strainer which will make it easy to keep the pump strainer clear.

In salvage work you never can have too many pumps because if two pumps will just barely keep ahead of the water, three will do the job nicely and four will give you an anchor to windward if one pump should conk out. So always try to obtain more pumps than are necessary.

On the average forty-five-foot yacht with two pumps, even a badly damaged boat with a number of poorly plugged holes can be pumped dry.

If you are in an area where gasoline or diesel pumps are not available but labor is plentiful you would be astounded at how much water you can move by using plain manual pumps if those pumping can be periodically relieved.

Don Hack in Grenada in the West Indies made up a four-inch manual pump of PVC drain pipe (see Fig. 6). Hack had been unable to obtain a gasoline pump and had a "cocktail cruise" catamaran with a very leaky hull. He could not haul for a number of weeks; thus he had to pump every day. The PVC pump was so effective that when Hack measured how much water he had pumped and timed it against a gasoline pump when he finally did obtain a gasoline pump, he discovered that the PVC pump moved as much water as the gasoline-driven pump. Hack had needed three men, each pumping for fifteen minutes with thirty minutes off. If PVC is not available the same type pump could be made out of wood.

And of course the fastest and most efficient bilge pump is a scared person with a bucket knee-deep in water. A man should be able to dump ten buckets in a minute. Figuring a bucket is 2½ gallons, 10 bucketfuls is 25 gallons a minute × 60 is 1,500 gallons an hour. Because this rate cannot be sustained for more than 10 to 15 minutes, plenty of relief labor is needed. Five men working, with plenty of relief labor available, can bucket up 7,500 gallons an hour—an awful lot of water.

A flooded boat can be bailed out strictly by muscle power. This is illustrated well by the fact that in 1976 a boat bounced off the reef in the Tobago Cays and was holed. The Caldwells from Palm Island went out in their launch to help. They managed to pull the boat off the reef and to tow it into the anchorage between the two islands. The boat was rapidly sinking despite the efforts of two or three people bailing with buckets. As the Caldwells brought the boat alongside the beach, she was only showing about an inch of freeboard but crews from all the other anchored boats came over to help. Using nothing but buckets, within an hour the assembled multitude had the boat bailed out to the point where they were able to put temporary patches on her.

If the boat is sunk in water that is so deep that the possibility of pumping is eliminated you have a difficult but not impossible situation. If she has sunk in a tidal area where the tidal range is considerable, you should try to install patches at low water so the boat can be floated off on the incoming tide. If patches cannot be installed, flotation must be provided. In a tidal area at low water it should be relatively simple to lash flotation alongside in the form of dinghies or 55-gallon drums. Before doing this, you should carefully ascertain how much buoyancy you need.

A 55-gallon drum weighs roughly 50 pounds and provides roughly 400 pounds of flotation. A boat of any size will require a lot of drums. Another way to solve the problem is to use inflatable dinghies as they can be placed inside the boat and then inflated. The exact amount of flotation varies from dinghy to dinghy, but Avon reports the following figures:

Size	Cu. Ft.	Buoyancy
2-man raft	15	960 lbs.
6 man	23	1,472 lbs.
8 man	30	1,920 lbs.

Dinghies

8'	14	896 lbs.
9'	18	1,152 lbs.
10'	20.5	1,312 lbs.
12'	31	2,048 lbs.

A flooded wooden boat is much easier to salvage than the average fiberglass, steel, aluminum, or ferrocement boat because the wood in the boat will supply enough buoyancy to compensate for the weight of the engine and other non-floatable equipment. You only have to supply enough buoyancy to float the ballast keel. In other words, a 40-foot wooden boat (auxiliary) displacing 10 tons (20,000 pounds) with a ballast-displacement of 40 percent means that 8,000 pounds is in the ballast keel; therefore roughly 8,000 pounds of buoyancy must be provided. This may be done by providing 125 cubic feet of buoyancy in the form of dinghies lashed alongside as camels, or rubber dinghies stuffed inside the boat or by twenty 55-gallon drums.

However, a glass, steel, aluminum, or ferrocement boat will require about 312 cubic feet of buoyancy or fifty 55-gallon drums. It is very difficult to obtain or to secure this number of drums to the boat since each drum is 36 inches high and 24 inches in diameter and is almost impossible to fit through a hatch. This means they must usually be lashed alongside the boat which is not an easy operation.

Also a wooden boat is easier to salvage than steel, fiberglass, aluminum, or ferrocement because it is relatively easy to nail temporary patches to a wooden boat even underwater. Trying to secure patches to steel, aluminum, or fiberglass boats, either awash or underwater, is extremely difficult.

To salvage a boat that has sunk in very deep water is a different and much trickier project. Such a vessel cannot simply be filled with flotation unless you take into account the problem of expansion when she is

Fig. 6. Effective hand pump with large pumping capacity can be fabricated of wood with valves of rubber or leather. Alternative materials include PVC pipe or galvanized steel down-spout pipe. BRUCE BINGHAM

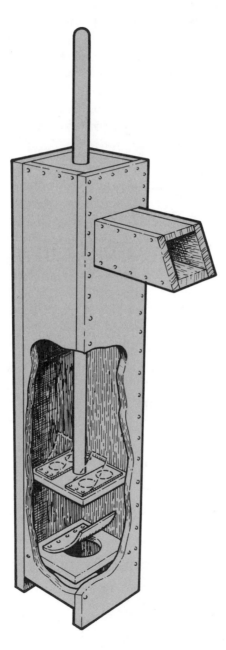

brought to the surface. A deep-water salvage job is one for experts and should not be attempted without considerable study.

Just because engines and generators have been underwater does not mean that they are ruined. Engines, generators, and starters will survive immersion if they are properly stripped down *immediately upon surfacing* and are completely rinsed out in fresh water.

When a yacht goes on the beach and appears likely to fill, the dip-stick holes of the engine and generators should be securely plugged, then covered with a plastic bag lashed in place. If the crankcase oil can be kept in the engine and not allowed to float around, the interior of the boat salvage work can be immeasurably expedited.

Finally, don't despair should you put your boat on the beach. If you use your brains, your brawn, and your perseverance, you can probably get her off. Keep the faith and your wits about you and you'll soon be sailing again.

22 ❈ Anticipating Emergencies

BY FAR the most common emergency at sea is the failure of the engine and/or generator to start. But if you have wind and if your rig is in good shape, unlike the more unfortunate powerboat man, you should be able to get home. Nevertheless, there are several things of an emergency nature that might happen to a sailboat and we will talk about a few of them.

A very common emergency onboard the average sailboat is a main halyard failure. There should be an easy solution to a halyard failure without having to send a man aloft. If you have a flag halyard block at the top of the mast, make it oversize—large enough on a very small boat to take a ⅜-inch line and on a large boat, a ½-inch line. You can secure the flag halyard to the end of a spare line, preferably tapered as in Figure 1, run it aloft through the halyard block and secure it to the head of the mainsail. You are underway again in a matter of minutes. Similarly, if

Fig. 1. Tapered rat-tail halyard end will go through block easier than full-size section.

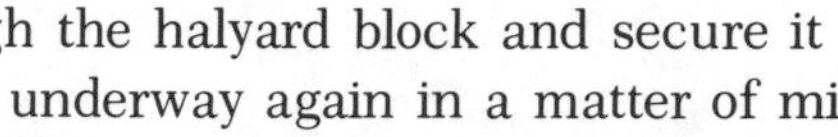

you do not carry two jib halyards you should have a spare block, again with a messenger through it, to enable a spare jib halyard to be rigged if necessary by using the same method.

On a double-headsail-rigged boat, the spinnaker pole topping-lift block should be located just below the staysail halyard block. It should be strong enough so that if the staysail halyard lets go, the end of the spare halyard can be run through the topping-lift block and the staysail re-hoisted.

Of course if the main boom topping lift lets go, you can rig a spare topping lift without sending a man aloft by running a spare halyard through the oversized flag halyard block.

Losing a stay is the next most common occurrence on a sailboat. On a properly designed cruising boat with an adequate-sized mast and plenty of rigging, you should be able to lose a single stay or shroud and still keep the mast in the boat. If a shroud does go, and sail is taken off the boat immediately and you manage to get on the other tack, a spare halyard can be set up tight as a substitute stay. This rig will usually keep the mast in the boat while a new stay or shroud is being rigged.

If the stay should break in the middle, or over a spreader tip (a relatively unknown occurrence on well-maintained boats) it is a case of getting an entire new wire in place. Have in your log a list of the lengths of every stay on the boat. Staylock, Norseman, or Nicopress end fittings or wire rope clamps should be on board and be the correct size.

You should carry on board one length of wire that is longer than the longest stay on board. If you do, making a new stay is easy even though a man will have to go aloft to install the replacement stay.

Sending someone aloft is always a tricky job at sea. He must be suitably tied into the boatswain's chair, and he should have plenty of clothing to absorb the crashing and banging around that he will inevitably receive. Two snap shackles should be attached to the boatswain's chair and they should be snapped to a stay, shroud, or halyard that is still under tension (Fig. 2). Two shackles should be provided so that, as the shackle approaches a fairlead or spreader, the second shackle can be snapped on before unsnapping the first shackle.

The most important thing to remember on any rigging failure is to make a temporary repair that is adequate for the immediate future, and until the first port of refuge is reached.

If a headstay goes, ease the mainsheet and run downwind. This will take the load off the mast while jib halyards, spinnaker halyards, and other spare halyards can be set up to take the strain for a fairly long period of time until something more permanent is rigged.

If a backstay goes, come into the wind, drop the jib, and switch to a very small headsail. The main sheeted in hard will tend to hold the mast in the boat. You can then rig up a spare main halyard and the topping lift as a temporary backstay.

Fig. 2. Boatswain's chair should have at least two snap shackles for safety.

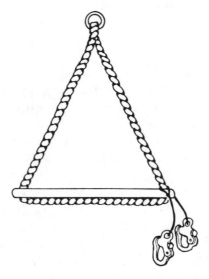

A spreader failure is one of the most difficult things to repair, particularly in a single-spreader rig. It requires a really fast helmsman to get the boat on the other tack before the whole caboodle goes over the side. This is one reason why a double-spreader rig is so often favored by a cruising sailor.

Usually the best temporary solution for the loss of a spreader is to rig a spinnaker pole up to the top of its track (Fig. 3). Then take the shroud that was led over the collapsed spreader, lead it through the end of the spinnaker pole back toward the chainplates, then set up a tackle to the chainplate. The lead of course will not be right, but put a shackle through the chainplate toggle, clamp a four-part tackle on it, lead it to a winch, and crank up tight. With modern winches and gear this will be more than adequate strength.

If the chainplates are mounted fore and aft you will have a foul lead, but remember this is an emergency. If they are mounted athwartship there will be little or no difficulty (Fig. 4). It goes without saying that the spinnaker pole should be guyed both fore and aft, as well as topped up to hold it securely in position.

This puts a severe strain on the spinnaker pole track and if you are on a racing boat with a reaching strut it is worthwhile to think about un-

Fig. 3. Tackle led to winch takes up strain on broken shroud.

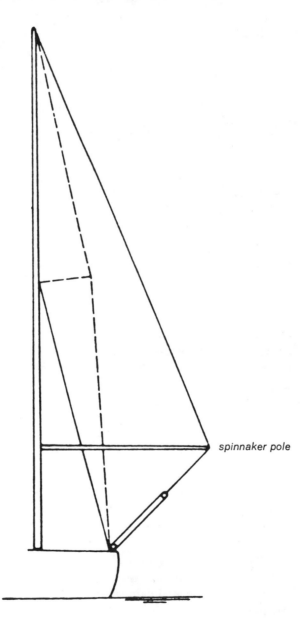

spinnaker pole

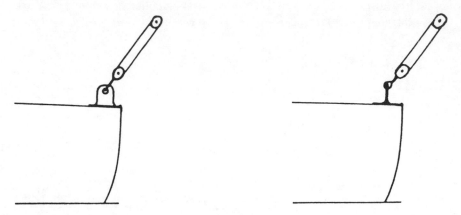

bolting the strut fitting on the mast and relocating it on the mast high
enough to give a better lead for the stay over either the reaching strut or
pole.

A spinnaker pole on its track supporting a stay puts the track bolts directly in shear and this is very bad. But if the spinnaker pole is set in the
reaching strut socket on the side of the mast, everything will be in com-
pression and it works far better.

Despite all these precautions sometimes a mast does go overboard
and exactly what to do when this happens varies with the individual cir-
cumstance, weather conditions, the size of boat, and the size (and ability)
of the crew. Whether the mast is wood or aluminum will also influence
the action taken.

Many times a wooden spar goes over the side and it ends up in two or
three pieces. If it goes over the side in a single piece, weather conditions
are often such that it must be disconnected and cut loose immediately so
that the butt end does not knock a hole in the boat.

However, many seamen feel that if it is at all possible, all the rigging
except for one stay or shroud should be disconnected and the mess
should be allowed to trail out to windward as a sea anchor until everyone
gets his wits about him. Then an intelligent decision can be made about
whether the rigging and mast should be salvaged or abandoned.

Many times a cruising boat that had a split rig, stayed so that either
the main or mizzen could go overboard without dragging the other mast
with it, has picked up the fallen spar with the aid of tackles.

An aluminum spar, however, except in the small sizes, should be cut loose as fast as possible. If the water is not too deep it is worthwhile trying to buoy it for it may be retrievable at a later date. If there is rod rigging it must be disassembled, and this job is facilitated if the rig has properly installed split pins. Split pins should be spread, not bent back on themselves, as in Figure 5. If they are bent back on themselves, it will be all but impossible to remove them. When split pins are removed the clevis pins must be knocked out and the best way to do this is to use a hammer and a drift pin: a good reason to have two or three big drift pins (punches) on board.

Fig. 5.

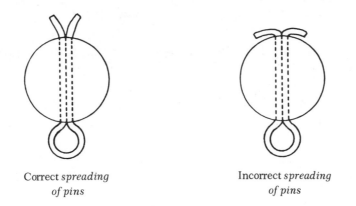

Correct *spreading
of pins*

Incorrect *spreading
of pins*

If the aluminum mast has not broken all the way across, there is a major problem in cutting the aluminum for it will work back and forth and will tend to bind on the hacksaw blade. Bolt cutters will sometimes work—each case will be slightly different.

On a large boat, a small oxyacetylene portable unit is sometimes carried. It weighs no more than thirty to forty pounds for both bottles and is useful in cutting through an aluminum spar.

But the primary thing to do first is to look at your spars and rigging on the boat and discuss the various methods of meeting with the emergency of a spar overside *before it happens.*

Serious leaking is the next most common failure. The first thing that must be done is to ascertain that the bilge pumps aboard are capable of staying ahead of the leak. It must be remembered that the most effective bilge pump in the world is a really scared man knee-deep in water with a bucket!

The subject of pumps is an article in itself, but certainly no boat should be cruising without at least one big diaphragm pump; the size of the diaphragm pump depends on the size of the boat. What is sufficient for a twenty-footer is obviously insufficient for a forty-footer.

Once it is ascertained that you can stay ahead of the leak, find out where it is coming from. Every skipper should know exactly how many through hulls there are and where they are located. Check them first, then look at the stern gland. Failure of any of these should be relatively easy to fix once the area is located.

On old wooden boats, frequently the leak can be traced to a bad seam. A leak in the hull can happen to the best of boats. In one of the Bermuda races shortly after the war, *Baruna* was leaking so badly she almost dropped out of the race. The leak was found behind the ice-box, and the late Captain Olle Bergendahl and the other professionals on board, with the aid of a wrecking bar and hatchet, demolished the very expensive ice-box and refrigerator, threw the pieces overboard, and plugged the leak with lead sheeting and bedding compound. She continued to sail and finally won the race.

A fiberglass boat, once it begins to come apart at sea, is more difficult to repair. If hull reinforcements and bulkheads shake loose, it is impossible to glass them back into place until calm weather arrives or a sheltered harbor is reached.

One thing to remember about a fiberglass boat is that if plenty of material is available—given calm weather—and if the boat stops flexing, a tremendous amount of work can be done in a short time. If larger quantities of activator can be added to the resin that is normally called for, glass can set up much faster than normal. Admittedly, this does not help the strength, but remember, we are thinking about emergency repairs. When port is finally reached, the major repairs can be done.

One problem that has cropped up on fiberglass boats is the top half (the deck) coming off the bottom half (the hull). There are various solutions, none very good, and one is rather drastic. In one case, the crew wrapped the anchor line around the hull four times. They chopped up some of the wooden interior to make windlass bars, and they wound up the bights of line with Spanish windlasses and this held the boat together (Fig. 6). In another case a skipper had an even more drastic solution. He chopped holes in the hull, put the line through the holes in the hull up through the portlights, and again made Spanish windlasses that held the top half to the bottom half.

Steering failure is all too common and there should be on all boats with wheel steering an emergency tiller-steering system which should be tested. If you have not tested the emergency steering, take the boat out under power, rev up the engine to maximum rpm, install the emergency tiller, and see if you can slam the tiller hard right and hard left. If you can't, it's time to redesign your emergency steering system.

If you have a good emergency system, loss of wheel steering is a minor problem. Emergency tiller steering can be installed and the boat sailed perfectly adequately until the regular steering system can be repaired with the tools and spares you ought to have on board.

If the boat is tiller steering, there should be a spare tiller on board. And I mean not only a spare tiller, but also a spare rudder head fitting, for there are numerous instances of the casting failure.

The most serious thing about any emergency at sea is that it probably will be one you have never contemplated. A good seaman should review ahead of time all the emergencies that could happen to the boat he is sailing on. He looks at the emergencies and then considers what will be

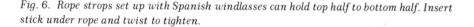

Fig. 6. Rope strops set up with Spanish windlasses can hold top half to bottom half. Insert stick under rope and twist to tighten.

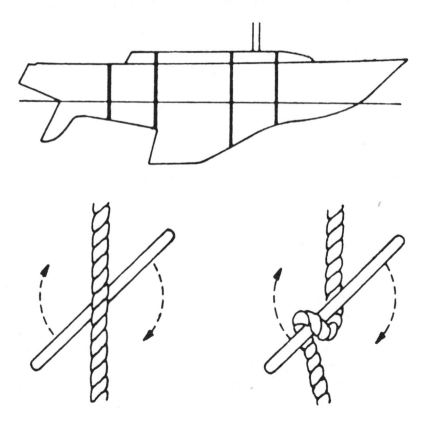

the best solution. In practice, the solution may not actually work but it is surely the best point of departure.

Then when an emergency finally does happen, the good seaman can instantly start organizing for he or she has anticipated the problem and figured out the solutions many times before while sitting on deck during a night watch, while becalmed, or just quietly contemplating the sunset.

23 ❀ Electricity without an Engine

ENJOYING wind, water, and sun is basically what sailing is all about. What most sailors forget is that wind, water, or sun can also produce enough electricity to supply electrical needs of the average cruising sailboat up to forty feet, provided she does not have electric refrigeration.

Wind has been providing power for hundreds of years. The Dutch windmills date back to the 12th century or possibly earlier. Wind has powered electric generators ashore since the 1920s when the Win charger was designed. This is a simple twelve-volt generator driven by a two-bladed eight-foot wooden prop producing maximum of fifteen amps with about twenty knots of wind. This generator is simple and completely reliable. Witness the fact that the electricity in our house in Grenada has been produced by this Win charger for the past ten years with a minimum number of failures.

When I first arrived in the Caribbean twenty years ago, Kit Kapp had one of these big Win chargers mounted on a mizzenmast of the forty-eight-foot ketch *Fairwinds*. Although it did produce more than ample electricity, the noise vibration and weight (about sixty pounds) made it rather impractical. It made the *Fairwinds* not only uninhabitable while it was running, but it also made the whole anchorage uninhabitable.

What was obviously needed for the cruising sailor was a small wind charger which would be light, vibration-free, reliable, and capable of putting out smaller amounts of electricity.

In the early 1970s small windpower chargers came out but they were just trickle chargers, producing a maximum 1/4 amp per hour at twelve volts, a total of six amps per day—not useful for anything but keeping a trickle charge on the batteries.

I approached dozens of people trying to get them to put together

Sail, June 1977.

some sort of small wind charger for *Iolaire*. Although everyone had
various ideas, no one succeeded in putting one together. However, in
December, 1974, I discovered that Hugh Merewether, a former British
test pilot and owner of the Nicholson 38 *Blue Idol,* had an experimental
wind charger mounted on his mizzenmast. He claimed it put out adequate supplies of electricity; it kicked in at 9 knots of wind and produced
a ½ amp at 10 knots, 1½ amps at 15 knots. I did some quick calculating
and figured that would produce enough electricity to provide for *Iolaire*'s
everyday needs while sailing if we were careful with our electricity, and I
persuaded him to lend me his generator for *Iolaire*'s seventieth-birthday
cruise.

Merewether's wind charger proved practical. It weighed eighteen
pounds; the windmill diameter was twenty-six inches, and the pivoting
radius was eighteen inches, small enough to be practical and vibration-
free. The unit was mounted on top of the mizzenmast where it pivoted in
all directions clear of everything.

From April 1975, until November 1976, when we replaced the original experimental unit with the Ampair production model, the wind generator produced all *Iolaire*'s electrical needs for the boat except when we
were moored alongside docks in areas with little wind. Under these conditions we connected up a twelve-volt battery charger to shore power.
Anchored out in the harbors in the Caribbean, the wind generator produces about twelve to eighteen ampere hours per day at twelve volts.
While sailing in the Caribbean, as long as the wind is forward of abeam, it
produces twenty-four to thirty-six ampere hours per day. Thus, while sitting at the mooring for a week, the batteries may be slowly losing their
charge. But all one needs is several days' sailing, and the batteries have
rebuilt their charge.

As long as the wind is forward of the beam, the wind generator works
excellently. However, once the wind goes aft of the beam and the apparent wind falls off, the amount of electricity generated also drops off.
Going dead downwind, the wind generator does not produce electricity
unless the wind is blowing extremely hard. Sailing back across the Atlantic downwind before the trades, we had to be extremely careful with our
electricity.

At this point I realized while watching the log spinning away that the
water is a thousand times more dense than air. Moreover, in the 1976 Observer Singlehanded Transatlantic Race a couple of boats had towed generators. Thus, when we replaced the original Ampair wind generator with
a new model, we took the old generator apart. We removed the propeller,
cut the jaw fitting off the end of an old turnbuckle, drilled a half-hole in it,

and threaded it onto the generator shaft. We then found a piece of $^9/_{16}$-inch threaded steel rod, heated one end, flattened it and drilled a ¼-inch hole in it, for a shackle. On the other end we put a nut, jammed on the first propeller we found (an old Evinrude outboard motor propeller), put a nut on the end, and secured 40 feet of $^5/_{16}$-inch braided Dacron line to the shackle on the rod. We lashed the generator to the stem pulpit, secured the line to the turnbuckle fitting, and while sailing, threw the line, rod, and propeller overboard.

We were most pleased to discover that at 3 knots the device started to generate; at 5 knots of boat speed it produced ¾ amp; and, as we sailed off toward Grenada at about 7½ knots, it was generating 1½ amps per hour, but no more. At 7½ knots the propeller began to break the surface of the water frequently.

When we arrived in Grenada, we replaced the Evinrude prop, which had the wrong pitch, with a four-bladed Seagull prop and discovered that the Seagull propeller started generating at around two knots and was up to 2½ amps at four knots and 3 amps at six knots. The next step was to experiment with various propellers to see how much they would produce at what speeds, a project that Hugh Merewether is again involved in, having designed a special low-drag prop that produces 3 amps at 6 knots on a drag of 28 lbs, meaured with a spring scale.

Now Hugh has come up with the best of both worlds: a towed generator to use at sea while cruising long distance; when at anchor it is removed, and replaced by a fan that will continue to produce electricity while in port.

I personally prefer a permanently mounted Ampair unit on a mizzen-mast and a towed unit for whilst under way, rather than switching back and forth. When going to windward, the wind generator produces ample electricity without having to tow the water-powered generator. However, once sheets are eased and wind's abeam or aft of the beam, propeller drag is relatively less important. Then the water generator can be towed and the necessary electricity produced even off the wind.

With the towed unit producing 3–72 amps per day it will be possible to have 12-volt refrigeration at sea without running the engine continuously. The newest 12-volt refrigeration systems, using 12-volt motors with permanent magnets rather than the old reduced magnetism motors, reduces the electrical needs of the unit to 18 amps under a full load, 12 amps under partial load. A good unit should only have to run a maximum of two hours a day. Thus it is within the realm of possibility to power an electrical refrigeration system off a towed generator!

The idea of a generator-alternator running off a freewheeling propeller shaft is a very old one. Marcy Crowe on *Langsyne* turned a low-rpm generator off his propeller shaft while happily crisscrossing the Pacific numerous times, running his auto-pilot and refrigeration system with the electricity produced. It must be remembered he did this back in the late 1940s when autopilots and refrigeration systems used large quantities of electricity, yet he had ample electricity. It is difficult to understand why so few have copied his system.

In September, 1976, I stumbled across a South African boat, *Agbwe*, owned by Doug MacIntyre, who has had a similar installation for the last four-and-one-half years. He runs an alternator belted from his prop shaft and swears it works perfectly.

His shaft with a three-bladed, 18 x 10 propeller does 450 rpms at 5 knots with the gear box in neutral. The alternator starts charging at four knots; at five knots it delivers on upwards of fifteen amps at twelve volts to the point where it gives thirty amps at seven knots. This is more amperage than he can deal with, and to keep from boiling the plates in the batteries he cuts back the alternator to where it only charges fifteen amps. He achieves the necessary rpm for the alternator by placing a ten-inch diameter, V-belt pulley on the prop shaft driving a two-and-one-half-inch pulley on the alternator.

With this rig one could easily run 12-volt refrigeration from the electricity generated from the prop shaft. This installation would appear to be practical as when alongside a dock one can run the 12-volt refrigeration through an inverter cutting down 220 or 110 ac to 12 volts. Then, when sailing, it runs off the prop shaft, and there is no necessity to run the engine to run the refrigerator—a great asset.

At this point, considering the problem of prop drag (who likes towing a three-bladed prop?) and the amount of electricity available from an 18 × 10 prop, one wonders about another possibility.

One answer is an adjustable-pitch prop, especially if the shaft has a disconnect clutch that lets the propeller freewheel. The pitch could be adjusted on the prop to maximize generator rpm, permitting electricity to be generated when desired, yet the prop can be fully feathered when electricity is not needed, thus minimizing propeller drag. Saab has such an adjustable-pitch, fully-feathering prop with a disconnect clutch.

Guessing how much torque a freewheeling propeller will develop is rather complicated and involves a lot of "guesstimating," but shaft rpm is a little easier to figure. As a rough rule of thumb, the shaft will freewheel at about one half of the rpm that the shaft would turn to propel the boat in calm water at the same speed. For instance, if under power the boat does six knots at 2,500 rpm with a 2:1 reduction, shaft rpm is 1,250.

At six knots under sail the freewheeling prop will turn approximately 625 rpm, approximately because the accuracy of engine alignment, the stuffing gland and gear bearings, as well as the generator/alternator installation all cause friction and slow down rotation speeds.

The sun can also produce enough electricity for the average cruising boat if one is extremely careful with the electrical use. Solar cells developed for use in outer space are now available for providing electricity on sailing craft. Basically, four square feet of solar cell can produce about 1.5 amps per hour in bright sunlight. The great advantage of solar cells is that one installs them, runs the wires from them, and forgets about them. Provided the sun shines, they produce electricity. The chief disadvantages are their cost and fragility; they are quite expensive and they are prone to damage. For instance, you cannot walk on them. They must be protected by a Lucite or Plexiglas panel which cuts down their efficiency by twenty percent.

In this respect, multi-hull craft have an advantage over mono-hulls. The multi-hull has areas of the boat which seldom feel the feet of the crew, areas such as the extreme ends of the outer hulls of the trimaran or the extreme ends of the hulls of a cat. These places do provide an area where solar cells can be installed and can be the answer to cat or tri's electrical needs.

In the tropics they work best with the bright sunlight although it must be remembered the tropic day is basically only twelve hours long with enough sunlight to produce electricity on a solar cell probably closer to ten hours. Conversely, in the northern climates, especially in Scandinavia, England, and Ireland where daylight can be from sixteen to twenty-four hours during the sailing season, they certainly would produce a considerable amount of electricity. However, in foggy weather they will produce little or no electricity. While sailing transatlantic on *Iolaire,* we never saw the sun (and some of the crew claim we did not even see the bowsprit) for the first nine days out of Halifax. Had we been relying on solar cells for electricity, we would have been out of luck.

Solar cells are also rather expensive. A panel of solar cells, 24 inches square, weighing 3 pounds, and producing 18 ampere hours in 12 hours of sunlight cost approximately $800 in 1977. However, in time as the state of the art improves and the number of units increase, the cost should come down.

Thus, there are a number of methods of generating electricity other than using a noisy diesel or gasoline generator. For a yawl or ketch with no engine the obvious solution is the wind-powered generator mounted on the mizzenmast head. On sloops and cutters, it may be installed on a stub mast secured high enough above the afterdeck so the crew will not get whacked in the head by whirling blades. A towed generator over the stern or possibly a combination of wind- and water-powered generators would be the best.

For those boats that already have propellers and shafts installed, the obvious solution is to consider belting an alternator off the shaft after first checking that the gear box will not be damaged by a freewheeling shaft.

For a new boat under construction the obvious and most efficient solution is to go to an adjustable-pitch prop fitted with a disconnect clutch so that prop may be freewheeled to generate electricity when desired and feathered when electricity is not needed.

Wind, water, and sun are free; the equipment to utilize their power to generate electricity is definitely not free but not inordinately expensive, especially when considered in comparison to the cost of engines or generators. The time has come to start thinking, investigating, and experimenting.

24 ❊ Reducing Electrical Needs

REDUCING electrical energy consumption, especially aboard an offshore cruising boat, goes hand in hand with devising an alternative way of restoring battery charge whether by sun-, wind-, or water-generated means. These methods can produce enough electricity for the cruising boat under forty feet, provided one makes a wise choice of electrical installations and is conservative in their use.

There are a number of electrical devices that are worth considering for the amount of electrical drain they can reduce. The first and most obvious means of reducing electrical load is to install one of the three-way masthead running lights now available on the market. These three-way lights incorporate red and green sidelights and a white stern light in a single unit. At present they are legal in international waters for sailboats of twelve meters LOA or less.

Since a single bulb instead of two or three is providing the illumination, these lights can have a bright bulb of, say, twenty-five watts, drawing two amps per hour, about fifty percent less drain than the total used by three bulbs normally used in three separate running-light installations.

The saving is even more if the three-way installation can use a

Sail, August 1977.

smaller bulb, for instance of .9 amps, and still have a range of two miles. Add to this the standard compass light which draws only .1 amp and the total drain during a 10-hour night of sailing is only 10 amps. In turn, this amount can be reduced if the running light and the compass light switches are easily accessible to the helmsman. Often on a clear, starlit night there is need for a compass light only occasionally to check the course as one can steer an accurate and frequently less fatiguing course by the stars rather than by the compass. Similarly in areas where there is little or no ship traffic the running lights can be switched off except when another boat or a ship are visible. Switching off navigation lights, of course, should never be done in crowded waters, in coastal waters, or when the helm is unattended and no careful watch kept.

There are other advantages of the masthead-mounted three-way running lights. At the masthead they are high above corrosive saltwater spray and thus more reliable than normal running lights mounted on the side of the hull, on the cabin top, in the pulpit, or on light boards in the rigging. The disadvantage of the masthead-mounted light is the difficulty in replacing a burned-out bulb or in tracing a short in the connecting wiring. However, even these are not serious disadvantages when one considers the comparable difficulty of replacing a bulb or a corroded socket in the type of running-light installations that have been standard on small boats.

Of course, any cruising boat should have a back-up set of running lights that can be temporarily but securely mounted in case the three-way masthead system fails, but the double set is needed regardless of the type of primary system installed.

In installing running lights remember that when under power one needs lower port and starboard lights (the three-way masthead light is not legal), a stern light, and a steaming light, four bulbs that produce considerable power drain. However, since these lights are needed only when you are running under power and thus when the engine is generating electrical power, the electrical load is not a significant factor.

The three-way masthead light has an advantage that may outweigh the savings in electrical consumption. As they are high in the air—as much as twenty-five to thirty feet even on a small boat—they are far enough above sea level so that they may be better seen from the bridge of a large ship. Also, at the masthead they are free from obstruction by the sails, the hull, the bow wave, or high swells. Therefore, in offshore waters the masthead unit has a decided safety feature, especially when the brightest possible light is used for illumination.

Nor are three-way running lights the only way to reduce electrical drain. Below decks the drain can be cut down by switching from incandescent bulbs to fluorescent lights. Compact, efficient fluorescent lighting fixtures are readily available for use on boats although they do cost more. Fluorescent lights normally draw .5 or .9 amps at 12 volts, considerably less than effective incandescent lights. Moreover, they give roughly four times the amount of light of an incandescent lamp of the same amperage drain. Thus an incandescent bulb of one amp is a ten-watt bulb with minimum light; usually, for anything but dim cabin illumination a two-amp bulb is required. On the other hand a fluorescent light drawing .9 amps gives the same amount of light as four amps of incandescent bulbs. For lighting in such areas as the galley, the chart table, and in berths for reading, fluorescent lights provide comfortable illumination without taxing the electrical capacity.

In minimizing electrical needs don't overlook using a kerosene lamp below. A good gimbaled kerosene lamp properly maintained can provide ample light below decks for almost all uses except detailed work at the chart table or extended reading for people whose age has caught up with them and whose arms are too short. For satisfactory light for the galley, the head, or for just gamming in the main cabin, the light from a kerosene lamp is economical and pleasant.

One of the best advantages of kerosene lighting is that at sunset a lamp can be lit and left turned down low for just the right amount of dim cabin illumination. Then, when more light is needed for making coffee or for the change of watch, the light can be turned up to give enough light to see yet not enough to destroy night vision as bright electrical light might. In northern latitudes the kerosene lamp can also give off enough heat to keep the night chill away and in the tropics the heat from a lamp turned low does not become uncomfortable if there is ventilation over the chimney.

Even with considerable use of fluorescent cabin lights plus three-way running lights the daily electrical consumption remains so reasonable that recharging using solar cells or a wind or water generator is feasible and certainly avoids the need to run the engine or power generator regularly. If you opt for refrigeration, the situation changes, however. Generally, the electrical demands of refrigeration are so strong that auxiliary power generation is needed; but even this demand can mean running the engine for only a short time at convenient intervals if the refrigeration system and box insulation are made as effective as possible.

It should be noted that a revolution is occurring in electric motors—a revolution that some electricians claim will do for marine refrigeration what the transistor has done for marine electronics.

Normally, a twelve-volt DC motor's field coils are magnetized by power from the battery. Thus whether under a load or not the electric motor drew the same amperage. However, this is not true with the permanent magnet motor. This draws less current when first started and as the load is reduced, so the power requirement is reduced.

With a fairly good installation the twelve-volt system would have to be run only for an hour in the morning and the evening. However, if one really concentrated and designed a superbly insulated system I am sure the running time could be cut down to half an hour in the morning and evening. This would make a reliable, correctly designed and installed refrigerator worthwhile if you can afford the expense.

Apart from lights and, for some, refrigeration, there are other electrical demands that should be considered. One of these is the use of an auto-pilot. Vane self-steering powered by the wind uses no electricity, but it does have the disadvantage of being cumbersome, vulnerable to damage, expensive, and difficult to adapt to some types of stern and rig configurations such as reverse transoms and split rigs with overhanging mizzenbooms. For these reasons some offshore sailors think of an electrical powered auto-pilot as an alternative.

The electric auto-pilot has a reputation as a consumer of large amounts of electrical power. Yet this need not be so. For small boats, say up to thirty-five feet, small auto-pilots that connect to the tiller or to steering wheels are available and at a price that is considerably below the price of an effective vane-steering system. These cockpit-mounted units can be mounted and removed readily and they do not pose the threat of damage at sea *or* during docking that the exposed vane-steering system does. Furthermore, many users of electric auto-pilots see their most advantageous feature in the fact that some of these units can be electronically operated off either the compass or a wind indicator to suit varying conditions.

The power drain with these small units is advertised at one amp per hour or less. The drain is dependent especially on how well the boat is balanced and on how carefully the sails are trimmed. The power drain is greatest when the motor in the steering unit is operating and the less time and less effort needed to correct the course with the helm the less the power drain. Thus a boat with a light helm and a hull that is directionally stable will use less power than one that is heavy on the helm and unstable.

One method of reducing the load on the helm and hence on the battery drain is to install an adjustable trim tab on the after edge of the rudder. Incorporating a tab controllable from the deck on an inboard rudder is difficult but not impossible, while a tab on an outboard rudder is a much simpler matter. A few stock cruising boats offer the trim tab on the rudder as standard equipment. The use of this tab connected to an auto-pilot minimizes the load on the auto-pilot and therefore the electrical drain needed to operate it.

Several years ago John Mathias had such an arrangement on his Tahiti ketch *Coryphiena*. He used an auto-pilot fitted into a small plastic box about the size of a shoebox mounted on the head of his outboard rudder and linked to a trim tab on the aft edge of that rudder. With this system the power drain was so minimal that he charged a 240-amp truck battery in the Canary Islands and sailed all the way across the Atlantic and then up the Lesser Antilles to Martinique before he finally decided the battery needed recharging. The drain with such a system was so little that the amount of amperage needed could easily be replaced by electricity produced by the sun, water, or wind.

25 ❖ Tools and Spares

THE DAY SAILOR who always takes off from his own mooring in the morning and comes back to his own mooring at night might squeeze by with a screwdriver and a pair of pliers as his total tool kit. The world-girdling sailor must have a set of spares for practically everything on board the boat plus the tools either to make what he does not carry as spares or to install replacements. Basically he should be able to rebuild his boat from the keel up with the tools and spares on board. Between these two extremes lie the vast majority of cruising and racing sailors.

The yachtsman who goes on weekend cruises, perhaps leaving his boat in a distant harbor to be picked up on a subsequent weekend, and makes a two- or three-week summer cruise is well advised to keep an adequate set of tools and spares on the boat.

The basic element in making up a list of tools and spare equipment for short cruising is to have enough to make at least temporary repairs. For instance, spare gear can consist in part of worn equipment that has been replaced before it became totally useless. Rope, wire, fittings, and fastenings can thus make up a collection that can prove most valuable for emergency repair.

Sail, August 1977.

A word of warning is necessary, however. Make a distinction between spare gear and tools that can be useful and that which just accumulates. Many boats, as the years go by, become loaded with short lengths of wire, rusty tools, corroded fastenings, and broken fittings. These odds and ends might conceivably be useful, but more likely they will make finding a piece of useful gear or a needed tool more difficult. Moreover, they make rust prevention more difficult and take up space out of all proportion to their value.

During each layup sort out the toolbox and spare-gear lockers, disposing of the excess, preserving the useful, and perhaps adding items that experience has indicated could be worth having.

Remember, too, that tools have a limitation. A tool alone cannot make a repair; the person using it has to have the skill to make proper use of it. If no one aboard has ever tucked an eyesplice in wire cable, there is little sense in having a splicing vise aboard.

This list I compiled for such a cruising boat looks long and the expense of purchasing the tools and spares may seem great, but over a period of years all the spares are apt to be used. With inflation and hence the increasing price of all marine supplies, money tied up in spares is probably money well invested. Furthermore, when your plans are set and you have looked forward all the year to a vacation cruise it is a shame to have your cruise delayed or shortened because a needed spare part is not readily available. You waste a week of precious vacation time swinging to the anchor while the essential part is found.

A prime example of this is a starter. Sooner or later the starter is bound to go, and replacement starters for most marine engines are difficult if not impossible to buy off the shelf of the neighborhood garage while rewinding facilities are few and far between. A starter can be switched in a matter of minutes or, even at the worst, in a matter of hours. Then you are on your way again. When the solenoid fails, it can be shorted out. If necessary, a good mechanic can adapt an automotive generator or alternator, and pumps usually can be substituted—*practically anything can be made to work for a marine engine except the starter.*

It is essential that the manuals—not just the owner's manuals but also the repair manuals—for every piece of equipment be on board the boat. A good mechanic can fix an engine he has never seen before with little difficulty, given the manuals and the spare parts.

Similarly, it is only with a really complete manual that you will be able to order spare parts. Speaking of ordering spare parts, it is much better to telegraph the manufacturer listing the spare parts needed and then follow up with a phone call a day later. Trying to read a list of parts numbers over the telephone is a guaranteed way to make sure the numbers are garbled and the wrong parts sent.

The older your equipment is, the more essential it is to have ample spare parts. Owners of small old gasoline engines are likely to have trouble finding ignition parts, starter motors, and generators. Similarly, old diesel engines spring leaks in their injector lines; these can be replaced easily if the injector lines are on board, but they are not readily available except from the manufacturer.

When one has a complete set of tools aboard, one is more inclined to do more of his own work. This cuts down substantially on one's yard bill. When I bought my set of taps and dies, the set paid for itself in the first week they were aboard.

It is no use having a pile of tools and spare parts on board if one does not know where they are. Many people recommend tool storage roughly as follows: small toolbox, approximately 12 × 6 × 7 inches, made of stainless steel with wooden lid and stowed in a handy place such as under companionway steps. A removable wooden top provides a working surface on deck and yet permits clapping the top on the box, keeping the tools dry in event of a rain squall.

In this box should be stowed the everyday tools—a couple of sizes of screwdrivers, crescent wrenches, hammer, cold chisels, wire-cutters, punch, a few small files, pliers, hacksaw, knife, plus a collection of common fastenings. Thus the toolbox has the tools that are apt to be needed for small jobs.

Elsewhere in the boat should be a separate toolbox, size depending on the size of the boat, of mechanic's tools for the engine, another box of woodworking tools, and a third box with electrical equipment.

Toolboxes should be either of plastic or wood. Wood has the advantage of letting the toolbox be built to a specific size to fit in the space in the boat and the right size to hold the tools that are most useful. Metal toolboxes are rather useless, as often the tools will rattle around letting all the paint flake off inside the toolbox; rust begins, and everything including tools becomes a mess.

Tools must be kept absolutely dry and periodically be cleaned and oiled to protect them from the dampness. The hardest thing to keep in any shape is the wood saw. Many recommend it be kept oiled and wrapped in a brown paper bag.

The sail kit sold in specialty shops is a little rolled-up kit with various pockets for various bits and pieces of equipment. Many sailors prefer a good canvas bucket with pockets sewn around the side and a strap so that various tools can be placed outside the pocket and are thus readily available and visible. An easy way to keep sail needles from rusting is to stow them in a baby-food jar half full of ground coffee.

Sail repair kit should be a canvas bucket with a drawstring closure. Bucket holds spare twine, fittings, shock cord, etc., while tools fit into pockets sewn around outside.
COURTESY OF *Sail* MAGAZINE

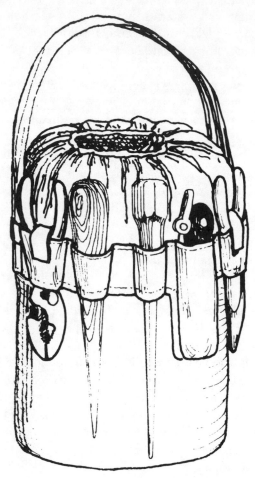

Wire-cutters are considered vital equipment on any proper cruising boat that is making any sort of long trip. However, seldom are the wire-cutters tested to see if they are strong enough to cut through the largest diameter wire used on board the boat. Everyone should definitely check this piece of equipment to make sure it does the job it is designed to do, remembering that if it takes two men to cut through the largest diameter standing rigging when you are sitting on a level deck, the cutter is not large enough.

The cutter should be large enough so that one person can operate the cutter on the largest wire even when he is tired and encumbered by foul-weather gear, sea boots, and safety harness while the boat is rolling around in a heavy sea.

It is seldom possible to have too many tools on board a boat, but of course everything is a compromise. Tools will have to be chosen after reviewing the type of boat, her owner's bankroll, the crew's abilities at repair, the space available for tools, and the type of cruising contemplated.

TOOLS

General Tools

A small clamp-on or suction-vise
Claw hammer
Small wood saw
Hacksaw, extra blades
Mallet
Chisels
Six-foot tape-measure
Small square with adjustable bevel
Whetstone
Brace
Screwdriver bits
Hand drill
Drill set $^1/_{16}"$–$^3/_8"$
Bits $^1/_4"$–$1"$
Screwdrivers
Countersinks
Wood rasps: flat, round and oval
Electric drill: The standard $^1/_4"$ drill is generally too small and the more powerful $^3/_8"$ is preferable. A 12-volt drill that can be powered from the ship's electrical system is excellent and not expensive. (Order one from Foulkes in England.)
Small crowbar
Large magnet

Rigging and Sail Repair Tools

Special tools for dismantling winches
For rigging up to $^5/_{16}"$, crimping tool for Nico-press and necessary sleeves
Hollow fids for splicing braided rope
Splicing vise
Hydrochloric acid for cleaning stainless wire
Marline
Dacron sail twine, plain and waxed
Serving wire
Hand-powered sewing machine
Marlinespike
Serving mallet
Rigging knife

Cold chisel with piece of bronze for cutting wire (cutting against bronze protects
    edge of chisel)
Wire-cutters capable of cutting largest wire on board
Palm
Needles in various sizes
Grommet tool

Plumbing and Electrical Tools

Tubing cutter
Flaring tool
Wire-cutters and strippers
Crimping tool
Pipe wrenches
Test meter and light
Soldering iron (12-volt)

Mechanical Tools

Mechanic's tool set including assorted sizes of socket, open end, Allen wrenches
Files—rat-tail and flat
Taps and dies to ½"
Set of "easy outs"
Adjustable open-end wrench large enough for stern gland and rudderpost stuff-
    ing box
Punch
Slip-joint pliers
Vise-grip pliers
Bottle gas torch
Wire brush
Hand pump for engine oil

Engine Tools

Special tools for particular engine
Tappet, ignition, fuel line, carburetor wrenches
Feeler gauge
Small hand pump for engine oil

SPARE PARTS

Hull Repair

For wood hulls
    Sheet plywood cut to stow under bunks
    Sheet lead, fastenings
    Bedding, caulking compounds
For metal hulls
    Quick-drying cement, epoxy, underwater epoxy
    Primer paint
For fiberglass hulls

Fiberglass mat, cloth
Polyester resin, activator
Patching compound
Epoxy resin

Plugs, Fastenings, Tape

Tapered wooden plugs to fit through-hull fittings
Assorted bolts, nuts, and washers
Assorted wood, sheet metal, and self-tapping screws
Assorted galvanized nails
Duct, adhesive and vinyl tape

Spare Rigging

Turnbuckles
Toggles
Cotter pins
Clevis pins
Serving wire
Shackles
Blocks
Wire, one length at least as long as the longest stay
Halyard
Rope
Winch springs, pawls
Winch, roller-reefing handles
Nico-press sleeves
Norseman-type end fittings

Sail Repair Materials

Rip-stop tape
Sailcloth in various weights
Leather for chafe protection
Sail twine, serving wire
Jib hanks
Sail slides plus shackles, plastic chafe protection
Grommets
Sail stops
Battens

Mechanical Spares

For gasoline engine
    Complete gasket set
    Carburetor rebuilding kit
    Points
    Distributor cap and rotor
    Coil
    Condenser

    Ignition leads
    Spare plugs
    Waterpump and belts
    Alternator, waterpump belts
    Filters
    Gasket cement
    Penetrating oil
    Engine oil
    Transmission/hydraulic fluid
    Grease
    Waterproofing spray
For Diesel engine
    Injectors
    Injector lines
    Filters
    Belts
    Waterpump impellors
    Gasket cement
    Transmission hydraulic fluid
    Engine oil

Plumbing

Repair parts kit for heads, pumps
Hose
Stainless-steel hose clamps
Nipples
Adaptors
Reducers
Pipe fittings
Teflon tape

Electrical

Wire
Fuses
Bulbs
Gasket material
Sealant
Crimp-on fittings
Battery lugs, cable
Hydrometer
Distilled water
Brushes for starter motor, generator
Diodes for alternator
Starter motor
Generator or alternator
Voltage regulator
Electrical tape

 26 ❋ Collision at Sea

MANY YEARS AGO when West Indian cargo schooners were all strictly sail, a certain well-known yachtsman received a basic lesson in avoiding collisions at sea. It was a clear moonlit night. He was standing north on a starboard tack when he spied a large native schooner reaching to the southeast on a port tack. A few quick checks of the compass showed that they were on a collision course, but since he had the right of way, his running lights were burning brightly, and the moon was out, he held his course. The schooner held hers, too, and as the distance closed he lit up his sails with a spotlight, but received no recognition or change of course from the schooner.

Finally he bore off and ran down the starboard side of the schooner. As he rounded up under her stern, he asked angrily, "Don't you farmers know anything about the rules of the road?" To which the helmsman replied, "Yes, mon, but you and I are sailing by different rules. 'Round here, we sail by workboat rules—the biggest boat got the right of way!" . . . which, of course, in restricted waters has been spelled out in a tentative way in the new International Rules of the Road. If you wish to survive, the "workboat rules" should be observed at sea . . . because they seem to be the rules observed by steamers the world over.

Sailing between Martinique and Dominica in mid-afternoon, *Zambeze*, a fifty-five-foot schooner, was almost run down by a freighter of a prominent line. The ship never altered course or gave any sign that the boat had been seen. Many freighters and tankers have passed me close aboard in broad daylight with no sign of having seen me at all, and I have often wondered what would have happened if I had been in their path and unable to maneuver out of their way.

At night, in an area that fishing boats frequent, it must be expected that the fisherman will be cruising along on auto-pilot or with helm lashed and everyone asleep below, but one Caribbean charter skipper was almost run down at night by one of Her Majesty's destroyers!

In my own experience I have had enough near misses to begin to think that for some reason or other merchant ships just have a general dislike for yachts and would like to eliminate them from the sea. During the Cuban crisis I was delivering a forty-foot ketch from New York City to St. Thomas. The third night out of Morehead City we were reaching along on starboard tack, with a moderate sea, a clear night, and an almost-full moon, when I spotted port and starboard lights with range light and masthead light in line between them.

Since I knew our running lights were not working (a result of heavy weather, light boards slatting in slack lee rigging and being hit by jib sheets) I lit up the sails with a twelve-volt spotlight. But the lineup of the ship's lights remained the same. After a few more minutes of this, I altered course to port and a big tanker passed to starboard, about 200 yards off, with no sign of life aboard anywhere. Less than an hour later the same situation arose again, and again I lit up the sails, and again I had to alter course to port, again the tanker passed close aboard with no sign of life. Still later a third ship appeared—again the same routine. This time we passed down the starboard side of the tanker no more than fifty yards off and played the spotlight down the side of the ship and right onto the bridge—no sign of life whatever.

Evidently these ships had been rerouted up special lanes by the Navy in order to keep track of them during the crisis. The ships were probably running on auto-pilot, with the officers watching the radar set only and not making any attempt to maintain a visual lookout despite the fact that it was a clear night. Since we were a wooden boat with wooden masts and had no radar reflector, we didn't produce a good echo and probably wouldn't have been spotted even if we had been run down.

These are not isolated incidents. In my own boat, *Iolaire,* I was almost run down by a French banana ship despite the fact that I was continually illuminating the sail with a powerful flashlight. In another instance, we were being overtaken from astern and had to alter course to avoid being run down despite bright masthead and stern lights, and excellent visibility. In this case we were sailing an aluminum boat with aluminum spars—she should have stood out well on radar.

In another case, we ran into very rough weather while delivering a thirty-five-foot sloop from Curacao to St. Thomas. It was single-reefed main for the first three days, double-reefed main for the next three days, with the working jib giving us a bad lee helm and a problem in tacking. We should have been using a smaller headsail, but didn't have one on board.

On the last night of the trip I was alone on deck about 0200, the other two crew members asleep below. It was blowing hard and we were beating to windward on the port tack. Every once in a while I had to luff and feather her through the worst puffs. In spite of the wind, however, the visibility was excellent. On a routine search of the horizon I spotted a bright white light fine on the starboard quarter. I watched it for a few minutes, and the bearing remained constant. Through the glasses I could see two lights, one above the other—range-lights of a steamer heading right for us.

I lit up the sails with a bright spotlight. After a few minutes both port and starboard running lights became visible. I was afraid to tack because of the weather and our unbalanced rig, so eased the main a trifle and bore off, intending to run across the bow of the ship, and let her pass to windward. The port light soon disappeared, the range-lights opened, and I relaxed. Then suddenly the range-lights closed again and the port light reappeared—she had altered course to starboard and was heading right for us again!

The range was now closing fast, I was afraid I couldn't get downwind of her if she continued to turn to starboard, so I sheeted in the main, came hard on the wind, and prayed. She was now much too close to risk tacking and getting caught in stays.

The ship—she turned out to be a large tanker—came storming by at fifteen to eighteen knots, passed no more than fifty yards to leeward, and her bow and quarter waves filled the cockpit. She never gave any indication of seeing us, even when I aimed the spotlight right into the big glass windows on her bridge.

Exactly how all these near misses occurred became less of a mystery when I did some checking with merchant marine officers. It seems that there is a tremendous amount of paperwork on a well-run ship—and the officers tend to do this work on watch. Crews are getting smaller while ships are getting larger and, especially in the good lines, the ships are being maintained to a higher standard than ever before. As a result whenever the ships are out of the traffic lanes and the weather is good, the helmsman and lookout are busy doing ship's work, so that the mate of the watch has the whole watch to himself.

But he spends most of his time in the pilothouse rather than out on the wing of the bridge. He looks at the radar every twenty minutes, and he should go out on the bridge wings for a visual check, but that is all too often ignored. Since he is deep in paperwork, it is frequently more than twenty minutes between inspections of the radar set. With chart corrections, cargo manifests, and just plain navigation—and almost to a man the foreign merchant marine officers use the long, tedious Marcq St.-Hilaire method of navigation—the officers spend more time in the pilothouse than on the bridge. Today there are many twenty-knot tankers and freighters. If the yacht and the ship are on reciprocal courses, in twenty minutes the distance apart will close eight or nine miles. If the watch officer misses you on his quick look from the bridge you may be run down before he comes on the bridge wing again, twenty to thirty minutes later.

Not only are the cards stacked against pleasure boats by these watch-keeping practices, but on many ships the engineering gang also adds to the problem. Once they have left crowded waters many ships keep only a minimal watch actually in the engine room. The rest of the watch is standing by on call in their staterooms, with the result that if the ship needs to back down it may be five minutes before enough men can be assembled to stop and reverse the engines. This system is of course not universal, but the fact that it does exist on some ships makes one stop and think. Watch-keeping standards at sea today are rather lax.

However it must be remembered that when a pleasure boat is run down it is not always the fault of the steamer. Often there is contributory negligence on the part of the pleasure boat's crew. They have failed to keep a good lookout, failed to hoist a radar reflector, or have even themselves turned on the auto-pilot and gone below.

There is one famous case of a boat getting run down from astern on a squally night. Supposedly the owner–skipper was on deck, steering and keeping a good lookout, but this boat had a very comfortable doghouse and a good auto-pilot, and many suspect that at the time of the collision the owner–skipper was asleep or reading in the doghouse. Though the boat sank, the crew were lucky and survived.

The same skipper with his new boat later ran smack into some exposed rocks that rise out of deep water. He was doing seven knots under power, it was broad daylight, and the rocks are clearly visible—but the boat was running on auto-pilot and her skipper and crew were below. Luckily it was a heavily constructed steel boat—and though the bow bent horribly out of shape, the watertight integrity was not damaged and they were able to back off the rock. Had it been a wooden boat she would have sunk at once.

The one difficulty with auto-pilots and vane-steering gears is that though both are excellent relief helmsmen they do not take the place of a lookout. Yachtsmen have the same obligation to keep a good lookout as do watch officers on the bridges of steamers.

With these facts in mind it is easily seen that the pleasure boat is the vessel that must keep a good lookout and take evasive action to avoid collision. A sailboat's running lights are usually visible about two miles. If the freighter and the sailboat are on reciprocal courses, the closing speed will be twenty to twenty-five knots. Thus the freighter's watch officer, if he is relying on visual rather than radar contact, has from four minutes and forty seconds to six minutes from the time he first spots the sailboat's running lights until he has passed her or run her down.

If a twenty-knot freighter is overtaking a five-knot sailboat the watch officer has still only eight minutes from the time he could spot the stern light until he has passed her or run her down. This is assuming that he is a very alert watch officer, that he spots the lights at their maximum range of visibility, and that the boat's lights are efficiently mounted and working. That's a lot of assuming.

A large freighter cannot possibly stop in this short time, although she can alter course. Any delay on the part of the watch officer in determining the pleasure boat's course and speed may leave him with little or no time for evasive maneuvering. And these figures are based on optimum conditions—clear night and calm sea. If there is fog, a low haze on the water, a rain squall, or a large sea running, visibility may be so reduced that it is physically impossible to avoid collision if visual contact is relied upon.

Many boats hug the steamer lanes because they get a sense of security from passing ships and feel that if they should have trouble they'll be able to get help. I feel the opposite. But if anyone must hug the steamer lanes, let him at least hug the lane that is going in the same direction he is—the closing speed will be less, and the chances of being spotted and avoiding collision are increased.

It will help to avoid collision if you make yourself visible at the maximum distance possible. A metal boat with an aluminum mast gives a good echo on the radar screen but a wooden boat with a wooden mast is all but invisible to many ships' radars. If you are cruising in a heavily traveled area, especially when visibility may be bad, I think it is essential to have a radar reflector permanently mounted aloft. One hoisted on a flag halyard to the spreader is good, but it is easy to put off hoisting it until the visibility gets really bad. In heavily traveled routes, the reflector should be up always at night, and whenever visibility is the least bit bad in daylight.

Where to mount the reflector is always a problem. If it's at the spreader, the headsails tend to foul it; it it's on the masthead it fouls the wind pennant or burgee. On ketches or yawls it should be mounted permanently on the mizzen masthead, and on most sloops or cutters attached with wire rope clamps to the permanent backstay.

Wooden or fiberglass powerboats should be protected, too. A portable radar reflector can be hoisted on the mast, or permanent radar reflector panels can be incorporated in the superstructure, as high up as possible.

Two or three square feet of light sheet aluminum mounted on each side of, say, the flying bridge, will return an excellent radar echo.

The visibility of running lights could be vastly improved. The law sets minimum ranges of visibility, but I would advise installing bulbs of the greatest intensity practical. Care must be exerted here—if the bulb is too strong it will heat up and blow out.

The location of running lights is often poor, sometimes useless. Old-fashioned light boards in the rigging are worse than useless because the one on the lee side is usually obscured by the headsails, and since the lee rigging is slack the light slats around until either the wire chafes through and shorts out, the wire breaks, or a jib sheet fouls the board and flips the whole thing overboard.

Some boats have lights mounted in or on the bulwark, in order to make the light visible under the low-cut genoa. This is an improvement, but in heavy weather so much water pours across the foredeck that it is all but impossible to keep the lights watertight, and they frequently short out. Pulpit lights are less likely to short out but they too receive their fair share of spray. There is the added disadvantage that all these lights are too low for good visibility.

Recently, a number of stock boat manufacturers have begun mounting their bow lights below the rail cap, in the hull. This is absolutely useless as only a porpoise or someone sitting in a rowboat can possibly see these lights.

Under the newest international laws, any boat of fifteen meters or less (and it is in the works to amend this to twenty meters) is allowed to carry under sail a single, three-way masthead light—port, starboard, and stern. This really puts the running light where it belongs, thirty or more feet in the air where it is easily visible from a steamer. The reliability of running lights of this kind is greatly increased when they are so positioned, out of the way of salt spray.

The three-way light also allows one to put in one very bright bulb, and the battery drain is much reduced from what it takes for three smaller lights.

Admittedly, this is *not legal under power* as then the bowlight must be above the running lights. In this situation, one must switch back to the old-fashioned port, starboard, and stern running lights. Here of course you are running four bulbs but it does not matter as the engine is generating more than enough electricity to compensate for the battery drain.

Bow and sternlights should be mounted as high as possible—in the pulpit for the bowlights and on the top of the stern pulpit, or maybe on the top of the mizzenmast, for the sternlight.

Sternlights are almost always mounted too low, at best on the stern pulpit, frequently on the deck, and sometimes on the transom. On ketches and yawls the sternlight can be mounted on the mizzen masthead, on sloops and cutters it can be clamped twenty feet up the permanent backstay, which will improve the range of the light considerably. Some means must be found, of course, to keep this light facing aft.

At the present time there is a great deal of fuss and furor about the display of illegal, unshielded lights while racing—masthead light, spreader lights, etc. I think that is all rather ridiculous considering that the merchant ships of the world charge about the sea lit up like a town ready for carnival. Unshielded white lights are almost always visible before running lights are. When bow on or stern on it is very difficult to see which direction the vessel is going until careful bearings have been taken. If you want to leave your masthead light on all night to see the wind sock (I am old-fashioned, and prefer it to an electric wind indicator) or to make yourself more visible to steamers, I see no reason why the racing rule makers should prohibit it and thereby lessen your chances of survival.

Your best chance of avoiding collision, however, lies in keeping a good lookout. On a crystal-clear night, steamers with all their lights are sometimes visible at a range of twelve miles, although the range will decrease rapidly as conditions deteriorate. With the speed of modern ships it is important to check the bearing immediately upon sighting and to ascertain as soon as possible if you are on a collision course.

When trying to determine the range, course, and speed of a ship, be careful. What you think is a large ship at a great distance may be a small one very near. A submarine on the surface used to appear like a large ship far off and caused many collisions. Nowadays the danger is largely eliminated, from U.S. submarines at least, because they display a rotating white light when cruising on the surface.

Avoidance of collision is the best possible reason for owning a good pair of 7 × 50 night glasses—not cheap ones, but the best you can get. Under certain conditions the cheap ones tend to fog up, and once they have they are useless and might as well be thrown overboard. (I have never been able to fathom why the owner of an $80,000 yacht will equip his boat with a $20 pair of binoculars. A rough rule of thumb among jaundiced professional skippers in the delivery business is: the more expensive the yacht, the cheaper the binoculars!)

Instantly upon determining that you are on a collision course take evasive action. Make your change of course at least 20° or 30°—large enough to show up at once on a radar screen. Light the boat up to make it visible at the greatest distance possible. Sails should be lit by floodlight, spreader lights, or flashlight, whatever is available. One very good steamer scare sometimes overlooked is the man-overboard light. When trying to light up the boat, grab both the man-overboard lights and turn them upright—a strobe-light is visible for miles.

Some yacht-owners have taken this one step further and installed a strobe-light upon the mizzen masthead to be switched on in emergencies. If a ship cannot see this, the watch is either blind, drunk, or sound asleep—or maybe, all three at once. If necessary, and the other vessel is perilously close, use a parachute flare to alert her. The confusion is better than being run down.

Avoiding collisions at sea is a matter of careful mental preparation on your part and material preparation of your boat in the way of radar reflectors and lights. A well-equipped boat with an alert skipper is seldom run down.

27 ❊ Abandon Ship

STORIES OF SMALL BOATS having to be abandoned by their crews have been commonplace over the years. More recently, the dramatic accounts of the ordeals suffered by the Baileys and the Robertsons have made sailors, both offshore and coastal, conscious of what they should be prepared to face in event of the ultimate catastrophe at sea: the sinking of their craft.

The first consideration of the skipper planning to take his craft offshore should be, of course, does he have the means by which he can keep his craft afloat despite a serious leak, dismasting, collision, or fire? The boat must be equipped with the proper tools, pumps, spare gear, and repair materials. Moreover, the crew must have the know-how to effect emergency measures in an effort to save their boat.

Once he has assured himself that he does have the means to do everything possible to avoid abandoning his boat, he then must have equal assurance that he and his crew can survive should those measures fail.

These measures fall into three categories, each of equal importance. The crew must be able to stay afloat, to withstand the effects of heat and cold and lack of water and food, and to attract attention to their plight to

Sail, July 1974.

facilitate rescue. Moreover, as the Bailey and Robertson tales clearly reveal, the crew must have the will to survive.

Few if any yachts go offshore nowadays without some kind of emergency life raft. Offshore racing yachts are required to carry a life raft that has been certified as being in good condition and most cruising boats have adopted a similar practice.

Personally, I prefer to go to sea on a boat with two smaller life rafts rather than a single large one. On a boat with a crew of six to eight this means a pair of four-man rafts instead of a single eight-man raft. Thus if a raft fails to inflate, there may be overcrowding but not immediate calamity.

Whatever size life raft is carried, though, its condition should be completely checked at least annually. The cheapest form of examination is by the skipper and consists of simply unrolling the life raft, checking that the equipment stored therein is in good shape, weighing the CO_2 cylinder and noting whether the life-raft fabric appears to be in good shape. The life raft is then rolled up and repacked. A more expensive procedure is to unroll the life raft, inflate it for forty-eight hours, repairing any leaks, then deflate and repack. The latter procedure is to the best of my knowledge a standard American procedure. In the United States the people who service life rafts for yachts are also the same people who service life rafts for aircraft. Their procedure follows the FAA regulations which require the life raft be inflated for a full forty-eight hours.

This is fine and dandy in the United States, Europe, or Australia. But getting a life raft checked in an out-of-the-way area is all but impossible. Thus frequently the offshore sailor must do it himself. If you are in an area where your CO_2 cylinder can be refilled just yank the cord and see what happens. In an area where a CO_2 cylinder cannot be refilled, the best procedure is to unroll the life raft and inflate it fully with vacuum cleaner or hand pump. Leave it inflated for twenty-four to forty-eight hours, check equipment, repair weak spots in the fabric as necessary, weigh the cylinder, deflate, and repack.

Three things to remember when deflating and repacking are to deflate the raft with the aid of a vacuum cleaner to suck all the air out, secondly to be sure the life raft is absolutely dry, and to dust it liberally with talcum powder as it is repacked.

Life-raft stowage is a problem that varies with every yacht. If it is stowed in a cloth valise I think the raft must be stowed where it will stay dry and out of the sun but yet be readily accessible in an emergency. If stowed in a cannister, it may be stowed on deck but it must be firmly secured. The flat cannisters are much easier to stow than the round ones.

It is essential that life rafts be equipped with a canopy. In cold weather without a canopy the crew may expend most of their energy keeping warm and even die of exposure. In the tropics the lack of a canopy may cause massive dehydration and sunburn.

The color of the canopy is also important. For many years the European manufacturers of life rafts manufactured a life raft that was dull gray in color, practically impossible to spot floating in the water. The life raft should be of a highly visible color—yellow or bright orange.

The canopy also should be made of radar-reflective material. It should be noticed that the Robertsons, who spent 37 days in a life raft, and the Baileys, who spent 117 days in a life raft, saw numerous ships pass close by. The ships didn't see them and failed to stop. Although watch-keeping standards on merchant vessels today are abominably poor, watch officers occasionally do look at the radar screen. If they see a target on the radar screen, yet see no ship on the horizon, they may get inquisitive and therein lies a good chance of a floating life raft's being spotted.

A life raft also should have pocket flares, a Very pistol and rockets, and a stainless-steel mirror all stowed in a durable, waterproof container and secured to the life raft. In addition a small strobe-light should be in the life raft. It can be one of the small, individually operated strobe-lights of the man-overboard type which can be flashed to attract attention at night. A good powerful waterproof flashlight is also essential, the more powerful the better.

A freon horn is an effective daylight attention getter, more effective than shouting at the top of your lungs—but hope that a ship's crewman is on deck as even a horn is not easily heard inside a closed air-conditioned pilot house.

A life raft, in order to make it small enough to be easy to pack, is made out of very thin material basically designed to keep afloat for a few days until rescue arrives. However, since yachts are frequently off the beaten track you may have to float around for weeks or longer.

Thus despite all the stress today on life rafts, a rigid dinghy has a lot to be said for it as a lifesaving craft. The dinghy should certainly be taken along with the life raft. The Robertsons would not have survived if they had relied on a life raft alone nor would have the Baileys as they did have to make major repairs on the life raft at sea. In both cases survival can be attributed to a back-up dinghy.

The dinghy should have enough built-in flotation so that two persons can sit inside the dinghy and bail it if the dinghy swamps. Additional flotation material may have to be attached under the dinghy thwarts and a couple of buckets should always be secured to the dinghy for bailing.

The amount of food and supplies carried within the average life raft is the absolutely bare minimum. For offshore delivery trips, my standard procedure has been to take a spare sail bag and put in it a case of canned beer plus durable, but compact, foodstuffs, fruit juice, extra flares and rockets, and a couple of life jackets to give the bag flotation. Tie the top tightly and leave it in the cockpit locker where it can easily be reached. Also leave in the locker five gallons of water, with a small air space at the top so it will float, as well as one, but preferably two or three, salt-water stills. As Siegle of Survival Systems has proved, if a person has the will to live, and he is in reasonably good health to start with, the shipwrecked sailor can survive on a pint—even half a pint—of water per day.

The cans of water in the life raft hold a meager supply and may corrode through. Furthermore, tropical cockroaches will eat through aluminum foil to raid the life-raft food supply, thus the necessity of pre-packaging supplementary supplies in a sail bag.

Another piece of emergency equipment a skipper should consider is a compact radio designed for transmitting a distress signal and capable of being carried on a life raft. Some are so small that they are no larger than a carton of cigarettes; most made for the aircraft industry are referred to as ELTs (Emergency Locator Transmitter). The cheapest cost about $150 and the most expensive range up to $400 and $500.

Some are merely automatic transmitters of a distress signal; others have the capacity to permit voice transmission on a distress frequency.

But ELTs are by no means the be-all and end-all of survival systems. They usually broadcast on a civilian distress frequency of 121.5MHz and on a military frequency of 243MHz. They are useful only if someone is listening to these frequencies. The contention that all aircraft listens to the emergency frequency is absolutely false. I have personally checked with a number of crews on transatlantic, inter-caribbean and New York–Lesser Antilles flights and they point out that whilst their radios are tuned into ground control, all their radios are busy and they do not have a frequency spare for listening to the emergency frequency.

Thus on the transatlantic run, from the time the plane takes off on the East Coast of the States until the time it has cleared Labrador the ELT emergency frequency is not being monitored. It is only monitored from about Labrador to approximately 400 miles out of Ireland, where again they come under ground control and, once more, all frequencies are taken up. Europe is so small that the planes are always under ground control and the emergency frequency is definitely not monitored. Similarly, from New York to the islands, it is not until 400 or 500 miles out of New York that radios are free to listen to the emergency frequency; and then, 400 or

500 miles out of San Juan aircraft are again tuned into ground control and therefore the frequency is not monitored.

Again, on the transatlantic run, from the Canaries to the Lesser Antilles is an area which has no regular overflights of commercial aircraft—thus the ELT is practically useless. However, the ELT is useful if a yacht becomes overdue and search aircraft are sent out. In this case all aircraft in the vicinity are requested to make sure they are listening on the distress frequency.

Although the ELT have helped in rescues, they have also caused a number of false alarms to the point where people have cried wolf so much that ELT distress signals are frequently discounted until three or four different sources have reported hearing what sounds like a genuine distress call. It should be noted that in certain areas like Alaska, at least two reports must come in from an ELT distress signal before a search is initiated.

A larger battery-operated unit is available that sends out an automatic keyed message on 500 KHz. Because of the size of the set and the short antenna it has a relatively short range of thirty to fifty miles depending on the set. This unit will trigger the automatic alarm on any ship in the vicinity.

Both the Robertsons and Baileys probably would have been picked up in a relatively short time had they had radios of this type. The radio could have been turned on when ships passed near by, the automatic alarm would have been tripped on their radio receivers and a search instituted.

Thus in a life raft having a radar reflecting canopy and with a radio that will trigger the automatic alarm on a passing ship, the chances of a crew of a sunk boat *not* being rescued should be minimal.

It is of course essential that you survive long enough to be picked up. Attitude has a tremendous amount to do about this. All comprehensive survival studies have proven that if victims of a sinking survive the first twenty-four hours their chances of being picked up increase. If they survive forty-eight hours, the chances increase even more. Thus if you have the ability, equipment and attitude to survive the first seventy-two hours with no real trouble, your chances of surviving are quite good.

In order to offer maximum chances of surviving this period the problem of proper clothing is foremost. In the northern climates you should of course be wearing every piece of gear you can manage to get on including foul-weather gear, sea boots, and life jacket.

Five layers of damp or even soaked clothing are a lot warmer than one thin layer of wet clothing. Even in the tropics it is essential to wear warm clothing and plenty of it upon abandoning ship. At night at sea the temperature will be down to between 65° and 70° which does not sound cold until you realize you may be forced to sit motionless in a puddle of water after a long day in extreme heat. The heat loss will be considerable and the energy consumed fighting the heat loss is more considerable. Also in the tropics each crew member must have the clothing to keep the sun off the skin plus a broad-brimmed hat.

In the tropics a medical kit on board the life raft should have plenty of sunburn cream; although burnt lips, hands, and face may not actually kill you, they can become so uncomfortable and discouraging that you will begin to lose the will to survive.

The final and most important thing that should be remembered is that the best equipped life raft is still much more difficult to spot than a derelict yacht. Do not abandon ship until you are absolutely sure that the vessel will not remain afloat. *Curlew* was abandoned off Bermuda supposedly in a sinking condition. A large ship came alongside and the crew jumped into a cargo net slung overside and scrambled up the sides of the freighter. They endangered their lives by the risk of getting crushed between the schooner and the ship. Despite the fact that she was abandoned and supposedly sinking, *Curlew* was found afloat three days later. The crew would have been better off staying where they were. Similarly *Integrity,* a replica of a coasting schooner, was en route south and ran into a bad gale. Her crew decided that the vessel was in a sinking condition. Again a passing freighter came alongside, again the crew tried to scramble up cargo nets without getting crushed.

However, they were unable to get aboard the freighter via cargo nets and, at risk to the ship's crew, a lifeboat was launched and the crew of *Integrity* taken off. Finally, the life boat had to be abandoned as weather was too bad to get it back aboard. Like *Curlew,* the boat was found floating unattended about a week later and towed into the Bahamas.

It takes a lot of water to sink a boat, even with no one pumping. Do not abandon ship until you are sure there is no hope of saving the vessel. The speed that water may be bailed out of a boat is in direct proportion to the depth of the water inside her. When the water gets ankle deep a crew can bail fast; when it gets knee deep it can bail with superb speed. Most important though is the obvious fact that a boat, even if her decks are virtually awash, is easier to spot than a raft.

Although you probably will never have to abandon ship, every yacht should be equipped to do so, and should have the necessary gear packed and ready to go.

28 ❧ Tender + Fenders = Back-up Life Raft

MOST SAILORS are familiar with the survival stories of the Baileys, who were adrift for 117 days after the sinking of their yacht, and the Robertsons, for 39 days. In both cases it is highly doubtful whether they would have survived if they had not had their normal yacht dinghy as a back-up for their rubber life raft.

In each case the life raft was considered the major means of survival; yet the Baileys had great difficulty in keeping their life raft inflated, while the Robertsons' life raft became unable to retain air. As a result of their experience, many sailors now insist that the dinghy should be adapted to serve as an auxiliary life raft.

Normally, a rigid dinghy is not thought of as an adequate lifeboat. The average rigid dinghy, once it is capsized or swamped, is all but impossible to bail out without beaching or lifting on deck and certainly incapable of being bailed in ocean conditions. Standard wooden dinghies seldom have any built-in flotation other than that afforded by the wood structure. Fiberglass dinghies usually do have flotation built in but the flotation is seldom sufficient to do anything more than float the dinghy with gunwales awash.

To serve as an auxiliary lifeboat, it is essential that a swamped dinghy float high enough so that one or, better, two persons can climb in and bail it out. Moreover, even when a considerable amount of water is sloshing back and forth, the dinghy should retain some stability.

To achieve this amount of positive flotation, some sailors secure racing dinghy airbags or inflated inner tubes inside their tenders. This is an easy solution, but the bags or tubes can puncture. Others add block styrofoam which is expensive and bulky.

A much simpler method of giving the dinghy flotation is to secure standard air-filled vinyl fenders under the dinghy thwarts rather than stowing them in a seat locker or lazarette. If there is not enough room to fit them under the seats they may be secured with heavy shockcord fore and aft below the gunwales.

The Telltale Compass

A large fender has considerable buoyancy. For instance, an inflated fender 10 inches in diameter and 30 inches in length has approximately 82 pounds of positive buoyancy (87 pounds of buoyancy minus the five-pound weight of fenders). Four fenders of this size would give any dinghy enough additional positive flotation (328 pounds) to make the dinghy into a back-up life raft.

Another time when additional dinghy flotation is useful is when it is necessary to row out an anchor in rough weather, either as a second

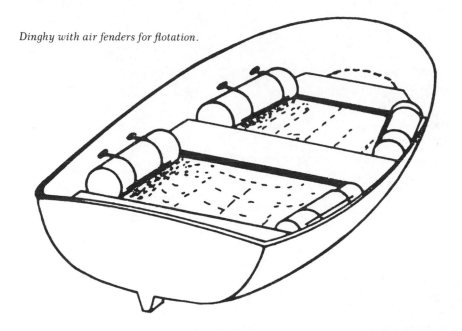

Dinghy with air fenders for flotation.

anchor in heavy weather or to kedge off. The dinghy may have to be launched in a hurry, just the circumstances that make it all too easy to swamp a dinghy.

Moreover, there is the risk of overturning the dinghy while handling ground tackle under such conditions and then having to get the swamped craft back and emptied alongside, a potentially exhausting exercise.

Using fenders to provide additional flotation also reduces the possibility of catastrophe if the dinghy swamps when carrying crew members in its role as tender.

None of the above is meant to suggest that even with fenders as flotation a rigid dinghy replaces the need for a good canopied life raft on offshore passages. Nor should the additional flotation encourage the substitution of an ultra-light cockle shell for a stable, seaworthy dinghy. And certainly it does not justify overloading or careless handling.

Like many aspects of good seamanship, the fenders are merely being put to good use when they are not serving their primary purpose.

VI

Street Speaks Out

[The Telltale Compass *calls itself a newsletter of information, evaluation and opinion for the yachtsman. It carries no advertising, so its watchdog editors, Victor and Betty Jorgenson of Lake Oswego, Oregon, need pull no punches for fear of economic reprisals when discussing boats, equipment, and other aspects of the yachting industry. Don Street is a regular contributor to TTC and in its pages has expressed many outspoken, not to say controversial opinions about nautical matters. The following reports provide a cross section of his authoritative views—some pro, some con—on various facets of his favorite subject. The italicized notes preceding some of the articles were penned by the editors of TTC. —Ed.]*

29 ❧ Cruising Designs Seen at Boat Shows

COMPROMISE, an old philosopher once said, is the mainspring of living which may, or may not, be so, but when it comes to boats, it is as essential as the caulking in a wooden hull. No boat ever built has been able to do everything well, nor is it likely that such a paragon ever will be launched simply because the extremes of the sea and her uses are limitless.

A boat built for speed will not have the qualities of weatherliness in a gale. Lightly built craft that may be a pleasure to sail in the upper reaches of the Chesapeake will not have the sturdiness to survive an ultimate wave. The perfectly constructed boat will cost so much that no one can afford her, while the boats economically stamped out, cookie-cutter fashion, these days in manufacturing plants instead of builders' yards, most often wouldn't be wished on the experienced yachtsman's worst enemy if he planned an open water passage.

The Telltale Compass, November 1974.

It is manifestly ridiculous to buy a boat that is rigged and equipped to weather a gale off Cape Horn, as the Westsail 32 is supposed to be able to do, if one is never going to sail anywhere except between western Long Island Sound and Edgartown. On the other hand, it is equally ridiculous to go offshore on some boats, such as the Columbia 45, that obviously should not venture outside of Long Island Sound, although they are advertised as offshore cruising boats.

All this was brought back to me in the course of wandering around the so-called in-water boatshows in Newport, Stamford, and at Annapolis in the last month or so where I saw things that were simply unbelievable.

Almost universally fat cruising boats were rigged with wide spreaders and with the chainplates out by the rail cap, making it impossible to effectively sheet the headsails for going to windward. Swage fittings were found as terminal ends on boats that, the salesmen claimed, were designed and able tropical cruisers despite the fact that any surveyor in the tropics gives swage fittings an average life of no more than three years. Anchor windlasses were almost universally inadequate, or notable for their absence.

Hatches were too few in number and only opened one way, guaranteeing poor ventilation. There are a few double-opening hatches, almost all of which necessitate going on deck to pull the pins and reverse the hatch. This operation nearly always takes place in the pouring rain, which can be rather bothersome, to say the least. However, someone always builds a better mousetrap. Gigiot (800 Aquidneck Avenue, Middletown, Rhode Island 02840, is the U.S.A. address) builds a double-opening hatch with a cleverly designed hinge so that the hatch may be opened fore or aft and reversed *from below decks*. Why this sort of hatch is not universally installed on all stock boats I don't know—the slight increase in price would certainly be repaid in customer satisfaction.

Dorade ventilators were notable for their small size and the few provided. Few, if any, life-line stanchions were put in so that they would stand the strain of a heavy man falling against them. Most showed signs of movement even under a light tug which guarantees leaking. What will they be like in a year?

Electrical installations, although better than a few years ago, obviously were not designed by competent electricians. Engines were beautifully hidden under ladders, boxes, bulkheads, and cockpits. They took up next to no room, but to work on them, one would have to tear half the boat apart. Simply changing a starter motor on some installations probably will cost $500 instead of $50.

The federal government claims it will be strict in enforcing its new ban against pumping oily bilge water over-side, yet few engines had integral pumps for pumping the engine oil directly from the engine when changing oil. Drip pans were poorly designed, and few, if any, included a small sump from which the last dregs could be bailed with a small portable pump, much less a separate small permanent pump for the engine sump.

The heavy cruising boats were guaranteed not to sail well since all were towing sea anchors behind them in the shape of big, solid, three-bladed props. The designers and builders seem to have forgotten that the Scandinavians have been using adjustable-pitch props for approximately seventy years. The excuse that they are too expensive does not hold water, either. If a European engine is purchased complete—engine, gear box, shaft, prop, and stern tube—the adjustable pitch prop unit, which does not require a gear box, is for all intents and purposes the same price as the solid prop with the gear box. Not only can the adjustable-pitch prop provide minimal drag when feathered under sail, but also it can operate with peak efficiency at various engine revolutions and under various sea conditions. A solid prop is only truly efficient at one rpm and in one sea state, efficiency dropping off markedly when the ideal conditions are not met.

Admittedly, in northern climates north of Long Island or Puget Sounds, one can cruise comfortably without the aid of an ice-box, but if one is buying a fifty-thousand-dollar boat that is advertised with an ice-box, one should expect that a proper ice-box be installed. Trying to find a properly designed ice-box was nearly fruitless. Almost universally there was no insulation in the top; side insulation was usually an inadequate two inches rather than the minimum four inches, and generally consisted of poorly fitting styrofoam bats rather than poured styrofoam—in short, an almost complete waste of time, money, and energy.

Refrigeration systems were even worse. The best holding plates in the world will not hold the cold unless they are installed in a properly insulated box, and all too many of the refrigeration units were constructed as above. Some were criminally bad, and were little more than the uninsulated fridges used in cheap house-trailers. The average refrigeration unit would require three to four hours a day of engine time to make it work, a great waste for either a sail- or motorboat.

Cockpits were noticeable for improper seat locker scuppers (despite what some builders say to the contrary, you can't make water run uphill) and large cockpits with small drains still were the norm rather than the exception. Probably none of the boats will be out in conditions where they are likely to be pooped running off before a gale, but many a boat taking a knockdown with spinnaker up or in a sudden squall has filled the cockpit and ended up half swamped when the boat finally righted herself.

A cruising boat is supposed to go to sea and stay at sea. She will heel under sail day after day. Meals must be cooked and eaten with convenience and comfort if the cruise is to be a pleasure. So where are the gimbaled tables, the fiddle rails, the gimbaled stove, the stove with an oven, and the oven vent to remove the smoke from the oven when roasting? What are you supposed to do, wire a deep pot to the stove, eat stew out of the bowl three meals a day at sea?

Heads and showers were, in general, magnificent, but we often asked an embarrassing question: "How much water does she carry?" The reply was all too often: "Thirty or forty gallons." With that little water capacity, what good is a shower?

Bunks were invariably too many; stowage space for sails, anchor rodes, spare gear, and clothes was grossly inadequate. Bunk boards and lee canvases evidently have not been invented. Most of the salesmen told me that they could be added by the owner, but on these new fiberglass boats with thin decks, and thinner head liners, how does one know where one can secure pad eyes for lee canvases?

The honest cruising boat, as the British say, should be able to "take the ground": intentionally to dry out on a hard alongside a pier; or unintentionally . . . it happens at some time to all of us. Yet few modern cruising boats can "take the ground." Almost universally, the lead or iron ballast is encapsulated inside the glass hull. Once the boat runs aground, the gel coat is broken, water enters into the glass and passes along the fibers, and an expensive repair job is needed instead of grinding and painting.

As Erick Hiscock says, "A true cruising boat should be able to work to windward off a lee shore under reduced canvas even in the teeth of a full gale." Other yachtsmen also point out that a true sailboat should be able to tack with confidence in restricted water in five knots of wind. Few of the new cruising boats are able to do either.

Not only are they dragging the big three-bladed props, but also most have the high freeboard which may provide wonderful and airy below-deck space, but also creates excessive windage that can turn any boat into a dog in either light or heavy air.

Rigs generally are too short to spread adequate canvas, and spreaders and staying bases, as already noted, are too wide to allow decent sheeting of headsails. The ketch rig, which has acquired an almost faddish cachet as a cruising rig, is inefficient except on a reach, and the biggest part of the stamped-out cruising boats are light in draft so that excessive leeway is encountered.

On top of all that, so many goodies are loaded aboard in the shape of freezers, air conditioning, loran, radar, washing machines, hi-fi systems, and what not, that there is little room for proper ballast so it is small wonder that few of them can either claw their way off a lee shore or even come about smartly in the light air of a protected harbor.

But one thing does stand out for the foot-weary pier thumper at the shows and that is the "decor," of which much is made, of course. It would seem there isn't a major manufacturer who hasn't hired a team of interior decorators to "color-coordinate" everything below decks and to add the gimmicks and gadgets that seemingly are designed to make the boats look more like Hilton Hotel rooms than boats at sea. Even such laughable . . . if they weren't so lethal . . . items as tall pottery-based lamps were common and not a one with any apparent means of securing them. It doesn't take any deep thought to imagine what happens to those things in a deep roll, but they leave no doubt that the interior decorator who ordered them never has gone cruising and they raise some question as to either the ethics or the knowledge of the manufacturers who display them.

Altogether, the decor emphasis and the lack of qualities that do make an able and comfortable cruising boat indicate that few, if any, of today's manufacturers have any direct knowledge of cruising or what is needed. Isn't it time that they leaned less heavily on the decorators, and asked the people who do cruise? As it stands, the compromises are going the wrong way.

ℬ⓪ ❧ Shore-bound Naval Architects

MANY EXPERIENCED YACHTSMEN that I have talked to here and there along the waterfronts feel that one of the major problems in yachting today is the fact that all too many naval architects and designers spend too much time at the drafting board or crawling over the test tank and far too little time at sea. It is a comment that equally holds true for the vast majority of builders and manufacturers.

When the designer does go to sea, it is almost invariably on an ocean race when he is accompanied by a good, experienced crew. He spends

The Telltale Compass, July 1975.

most, if not all, of his time on deck supervising the sail trim, rigging adjustments, and attending to the fine points of making the boat go fast. Little, if any, time is spent below decks, and immediately upon the finish of a race, the owner and designer decamp to the nearest good hotel for hot showers and comfortable, dry, steady beds.

Money is unimportant to the designer. He designs a boat to win. Generally, he is paid a percentage of the craft's costs, and as a result he is not greatly interested in cutting them. His go-fast gear includes expensive rod rigging, grooved luff headstays, a vast array of sails, electronic gear that costs a fortune, all put aboard a boat that is so lightly built that her life expectancy most probably will be five to ten years at the most. The boat's cruising potential is nil so she cannot be converted to a fast cruising boat once her prime racing life is over.

Witness the 1974 Bermuda Race. It was not a particularly hard race. Major gear failures were few and far between. But some crews reported the boats were so poorly ventilated that it was impossible to sleep comfortably below decks in the heat. Others reported so much water from deck leaks that not only were the bunks soaked but electronic equipment was flooded out and failed.

In one extreme case on board a standard, popular and successful racing design, an Ericson 37, the crew reported so much water came through the hatches at times that the cabin sole was awash. Water trapped between the deck and the headliner completely ruined five thousand dollars' worth of electronic gear. That made for an expensive and uncomfortable race.

But even those few racing designers who did make the race were so intent on ship speed and tactics that few took much notice of such conditions, a situation that brought a prime suggestion from one of the grizzled veterans aboard. He suggested that the designer be leg-shackled below for the race instead of being allowed to act as God on deck.

"Let him cook, serve and wash up for the crew with three meals a day for a week," he grunted, "and I am sure that galleys, ventilation systems, ice-boxes, refrigerator, and stowage systems very shortly would be radically different."

And he could have added: Let the designer sail the boat back to her homeport shorthanded. Let him try to change headsails single-handed on the foredeck in a squall at two in the morning. Let him try to steer his short-keeled monster four hours at a stretch with no relief helmsman. That would give him some insight on the troubles delivery crews have with those dream ocean-racing machines, and the problems that owners, who like to cruise as well as race, encounter when four people attempt a passage in a boat that is raced by ten experts, four to six of whom will be not only expert sailors but also one size smaller than gorillas.

Cruising boat designers suffer from the same difficulty. They, too, spend too much time clamped to the drawing stool and not enough time sailing to find out how their designs work out in the hard, cruel test tank of constant cruising, whether it be alongshore or offshore. And even a succession of weekend sails won't help much because if a man does not sail three to four thousand miles a year on a variety of boats, he does not encounter the conditions that produce the ideas necessary to design a really good boat.

Obviously, though, this basic problem puts the designer firmly between the horns because it is readily apparent that the less time he spends behind his drawing board, the less gelt flows into his pockets. Still, I strongly suspect that would be a short-term disadvantage since the architect who designed from a foundation of down-to-the-water experience no doubt would quickly build a name for himself that would offset the losses he took acquiring that knowledge.

Even so, there are other ways of tilting with that big problem which, although not as good, would provide better results than the current practice by most stock boat manufacturers of letting designs be determined by so-called "market surveys" which most often are made among people who have never owned a boat, let alone made a cruise.

The solution is painfully simple. Why don't the designers consult with those who really know: the people who cruise regularly, who visit various areas of the world, who see different boats and who indulge the cruising man's favorite pastime of discussing the incidents and problems of life aboard, of passages made and passages to be made, with the cruising sailors they encounter. Those people know what works, they know what they want and most probably what other sailors will want in a cruising boat, whether the latter have the experience to know it or not.

It is a simple and obvious technique, and it does work. Witness the fact that the best cruising boats afloat today ordinarily are custom built by good yards, designed by good architects, but—and it's most important—they are built for experienced yachtsmen who already have the cruising experience to know precisely what they need and want. It's a triumvirate of designer, builder, and knowledgeable owner that seldom misses, and particularly so when the owner is as strong-minded as cruising men are inclined to be.

If the manufacturers who are building cruising boats by the hundreds would employ that simple technique instead of relying on the fashion experts, the color coordinators, and the market analysts who compile statistics by asking a thousand outboardmen what they want in a fifty-footer they most likely will never own, then perhaps we will begin to see some good, honest cruising boats that will be a pleasure to take to sea and to live aboard, in place of the horrors that now crowd our waters.

There is another method of achieving the same end. The designer, as previously mentioned, spends too much time ashore behind his desk. The builder is worried about production, thus is not able to spend enough time at sea. He is usually not concerned enough to really attack the problem of what is going to happen at sea, or about accessibility and the ability to easily service and repair gear. The owner is too busy to fight the battle or lacks knowledge. This is where the design consultant can pay for his charges ten times over.

On new designs, the owner, designer, and builder are well advised to go and find someone who knows a moderate amount about yacht design and has been around for many years, preferably an experienced delivery skipper with plenty of offshore experience. They should have him sit down with them and they should listen to his suggestions and criticisms. Were this done in the majority of stock designs today, the improvement in the boats would be substantial.

31 ❀ What's Wrong with Boating Magazines

[The author has been twitting us about the following article which he sent us a good many months ago, and which we have been sitting on. Not because we don't like it or don't believe it—we agree completely—but because we have spent long enough in the business to know that many of today's boating editors also will agree with him . . . but only privately . . . and that most of them suffer frustrations of a greater or lesser degree in fighting the system, or what is known as "City Hall." The core of the problem is an industry exercising its considerable economic clout, but editors and publishers can't be complimented for the stiffness of their backs, or the clearness of their purpose.

Nevertheless, Street is due the right to complain, although we did discourage comparisons, odious or otherwise, with The Telltale Compass *since they would be unseemly. He explained that his singling out of* Yachting, *which long has dominated the boating press, is not because those incidents are singular, but simply because he doesn't maintain a file of* Motor Boating & Sailing, Rudder, Boating, *or the rest and the incidents he picked were the ones that had stuck in his memory.—Ed.*]

A GOOD PART OF the experienced yachtsmen I meet here and there on the water feel that many of the problems boatmen encounter with their gear and boats can be laid directly on the laps of the publishers and editors of American yachting magazines, of which there is a plethora.

Few boatmen don't read one or another, or two or three of them—at least one old duffer I know, who is retired, tries to read them all—but I seldom encounter one who admits to finding much profit in the effort. In fact, most of the veterans tell me they do little more than "leaf through them, just in case" and the "in case" usually seems to mean that they sometimes find a tip-off on some new bit of gear or gadget that has come on the market while they weren't looking, and that they think might be worth investigating.

It hasn't always been thus. There was a time when writers like the late Herbert L. Stone, W. H. "Bill" Taylor and Alf Loomis of *Yachting,* and Thomas Fleming Day and L. Francis Herreshoff of *Rudder* were followed with close attention by any boatman worth his salt, and what they had to say was worth considering. At times, they laid into the yachting industry, or the scene, or into yachtsmen themselves in no uncertain terms. Unfortunately, those days seem to have gone, and whether or not they ever will return is anyone's guess.

It may be naive on my part, but it always seemed to me that a publication . . . any publication . . . was in business to inform its readers; to advise them on what was happening in their field of interest, good, bad, and indifferent; to report to them on the discoveries in techniques, gear and what not that they otherwise might take years to learn, and on occasion to entertain them. Nowadays, even the entertainment is thin and most often consists of some chronicle of stupid mistakes that befell a hapless neophyte . . . can anyone find that entertaining, no matter how humorously presented, or how well?

But it seems obvious that the kingplank for any publication has to be the reader. Without him, there is nothing except an expensive collection of paper and printing. Without him, all the carefully contrived messages from advertisers go to waste.

A majority of present editors, and advertisers, seem to have forgotten or, at least, they ignore that basic tenet, and I suppose it is not hard to understand since the readers supply but a small part of a publication's gross revenues. Most times his payments don't cover the costs even of finding him as a subscriber, and the business office is inclined to regard him simply as a necessary evil. His complaints may be source of amusement, but if he gets angry enough and leaves, the single loss seldom is significant.

On the other hand, the advertiser is the one who makes up the difference, and supplies the wherewithal that not only pays the salaries and expenses, but also provides the profits. Because there are far fewer of him, and because he pays in bigger chunks, his loss is something to upset the business office and the editorial office, if at fault, hears about it for weeks on end. So it is not surprising that the most common saying in publication precincts is that hoary adage: "Don't bite the hand that feeds you."

As a consequence, the advertiser ends up with immense power to get what he wants, and since his chief interest is to sell his goods, it is small wonder that editorial material shows up more as a mirror of the advertiser's claims than as an impartial evaluation designed to help and inform the reader. And that despite the fact that the strong editors of yesterday long ago proved that honest criticism was as useful to the manufacturer in bettering products as it was to the reader.

As an instance, take the so-called boat tests that appear in many of today's boating magazines. Ostensibly, these are critiques designed to inform the reader on the salient characteristics of the craft which, to be really useful, would have to include both good and bad points. It is seldom you hear anything bad except now and again that such and such a thing was missing, but that "George Applewiffer, the sales manager, told us this would be corrected in the next boat off the line." (Maybe it was, which should point out to those writers and builders the value of criticism.)

But with few exceptions, those reports are nothing more than advertising, disguised as editorial material, and it is rare they show up any of the true attributes of the boat, let alone any of her problems . . . and there are few boats ever built that are without them.

The series, though, that has amused me for a long time is *Yachting*'s—the mother-hen of the tribe—which very carefully never "tests" a boat, but, as their department head reads: "*Yachting* Eyes a Boat." It is a bemusing phrase, and while I suppose it is meant to imply that *Yachting* isn't claiming to make a test, but simply is taking a look, it is rich in other implications. It brings to mind a gnarled veteran of the typewriter keys sighting down a hull, but I have never seen them mention the lumps and hollows that can be found in more than one of today's production boats even by the rankest tyro. At other times, though, I have wondered if the editor who cooked up the phrase wasn't a punster, as editors are inclined to be. Does he, himself, read it, "*Yachting* Ayes a Boat?" In that case, it is a more honest heading than most.

Not that the tests are outright dishonest. Most of the time they warn the careful reader, by implication at least, in reporting that they picked up the boat at the factory float so that you know it was factory tuned, and cruised down Biscayne Bay, which was so flat they had to run back on their own wakes to determine her "rough water performance" . . . as if that would do it. Or they take a weekend sail to Catalina and back with light air all the way, so light that much of the passage was made under power. Then they make kind comments about the layout, or the decor, or the electronic gear. Such passages won't tell you a thing about what the boat will look like after a 2,000-mile beat into head seas; or what it is like to try to serve chow aboard her with the rail down; or whether the boat will steer in heavy weather under emergency gear; or whether she will heave-to quietly; or such simple things as how long the refrigeration system runs, or whether it is possible to adjust a generator belt underway in a troubled sea.

Most of those pieces end up in an enthusiastic glow that no doubt brings a shine to the eye of the manufacturer who sees the light reflected in his pocketbook, but they are of very little use to the man who is looking for answers to even the basic questions about a boat.

On the other hand, it also is clear that to do a proper and useful job would be tremendously expensive for the magazines, but there are ways of collecting real information about such stock boats without so much as the costs of a weekend trip to Florida or California. I often have wondered why the magazines don't send their writers to talk with men like my old friends Bob Lamson or Chuck Reid, both of whom make a profession of delivering yachts and have thousands of miles at sea under their belts in an incredible variety of boats. Lamson, a retired Coast Guard chief, has spent his life at sea in small craft, and at last count had put in 30,000 miles delivering Hatteras and other power boats from the States throughout the Caribbean, and Reid is not far behind him, if at all. Either one could tell those writers what they had learned about this or that boat, and it would be something of solid use to the magazine's readers.

There is no question that the advertiser's wrath would bloody editorial heads for a time after any such report, but I think it still is the responsibility of any publication pretending to inform its readers to educate its own advertisers on the positive value of criticism . . . and I use that word in its broad sense to include the good as well as the bad. After all, criticism is an honest and valuable function in art and literature and even the movies, and although a bad report might make them unhappy, authors and publishers have learned the value to everyone, including themselves, of honest criticism. Why shouldn't the same thing apply to boats, or winches, or gadgets, or even knives and forks, or anything else that is manufactured and sold for everyone's use? With the exploding complexity of living these days, it is high time we had it.

Almost every one of the magazines makes a pretense of criticism in the design reviews, of which, perhaps, the less said the better. Most of them are written by the designer himself, or the firm building or selling the boat. No one would expect them to point out problems, but even where there are additional comments from another designer, there seldom is anything but pleasantries or the arcane gobbledygook of prismatic coefficients, sail area-wetted surface ratios, etc., that means little to the average boatman. Seldom does a commentator take apart the design, or point out the stupidity of having two showers and a total water capacity of eighty gallons; nor does he mention the shortage of ventilation, or the lack of double opening hatches; or point out that, while the boat has berths for eight, there is no stowage space for sails or even the personal gear for eight, and I have yet to see anyone comment on the fact that if you load one of the currently popular light displacement craft with all the crew they have berths for as well as the necessary food, fuel, water, and gear, you no longer have a light displacement boat. Obvious, but unmentioned.

All told, I have seen few attempts at real criticism in American boating magazines. I know it is difficult to find a naval architect who will critically analyze another designer's work out loud. It is much the same as getting one doctor to testify against another in a malpractice suit, so much so that it seems the club of yacht designers, although more informal, is more tighly knit than the American Medical Association. Nonetheless, it again is the clear responsibility of the magazines to develop such critical talent, just as book and art critics have been developing elsewhere on the scene.

There is still another standard magazine "department," as they are called under various cute headings, that calls for criticism on the part of the writers and editors if it is to be of any real value. That is the new products section, so-called, which covers generally not only new products but also old ones that some advertiser apparently thinks need a publicity shot to get sales rolling again. Seldom is any attempt made to evaluate the usefulness, quality, or efficacy of the gadget and at times, I have noted ones that simply reprinted the manufacturer's publicity handout, mis-punctuation, misspelling, and all. Bad as they are as a rule, they do serve a purpose in flagging the new items and, as noted earlier, are the things most oldtimers check in the boating magazines, just for clues.

But I think the most frustrating boating article I have read was on a really first-rate subject that *Yachting* dug up some time back. It concerned life rafts and safety equipment, and apparently was brought about when Jeff Hammond, one of the magazine's associate editors, made the horrifying discovery that one of the emergency life rafts on the market not only wouldn't inflate properly, but was ill-equipped for the job it was supposed to do, as well as being quite shoddily put together.

Hammond arranged a test of that gear and some of its kindred at Larchmont Yacht Club, and his piece called a spade a spade. He found little right and much wrong—almost everything was below par and some of it totally unacceptable—even though every boatman has to bet his life on the quality and reliability of emergency gear. *But,* there wasn't a single manufacturer's name in any part of the piece, nor any identifications, so it was only the rare few who could recognize a picture or two and put one and the other together. Even so, no one, I expect, was completely sure, and it had to be something more than frustrating to new boatmen who had no clues at all.

I have little doubt that article was the subject of some heated editorial conferences, and I suspect the advertising department was there in force . . . certainly in spirit . . . but that piece, other than providing a broad warning, did little but blacken the entire emergency gear market for *Yachting*'s readers. Without saying which item was bad and why, and who made it, *Yachting* succeeded in getting across—to me, at least—only that all emergency gear was suspect, which isn't either true or fair.

Subsequently, Jeff Hammond became editor of *Motor Boating and Sailing* and, as editor, attacked the problem of life rafts, except this time he tested them and called them by name. This almost resulted in a lawsuit, but in the long run it improved the quality of the Winslow life rafts. Since then, he has written good articles on various aspects of the yachting business, articles that were real sizzlers. They have made a lot of people mad but also made people think. At last, we have an editor of a leading magazine with enough guts to say what should be said.

Nevertheless, timidity, born of avarice, seems a common quality for the majority of the American boating press. It is long past time for them to take a hard look at their critical responsibilities if the game is to go anywhere. It is long past time for them to stop sweet-talking the advertiser just for his revenues, and to start educating him on the values good criticism can provide in his own interests. It is time to stop sweeping it all under the rug. The rug is much too lumpy.

32 ❧ Paper Coast Guard I

[Most old hands have their favorite yarns about encounters with the Coast Guard, but few will want to match those that Don Street narrates here in the first of two articles on the subject.—Ed.]

THROUGHOUT my sailing career, I unfortunately have been on the receiving end of some magnificent manifestations of Coast Guard incompetence, several of them bordering on the unbelievable. So much so that these days I strongly question the old belief we were brought up with that the Coast Guard is, if nothing else, the mariner's alter ego.

In truth, I long ago decided, as have many boatmen, that basically there are two Coast Guards: the "Paper Coast Guard" and the "Working Coast Guard." The order seems proper since the Paper Coast Guard appears to be in control. They are the legions of desk-bound characters who give the orders, mine the tons of paper the Coast Guard produces, and who spend their time writing rules about some matters they seem to have little knowledge about . . . in the practical sense, at least.

Years ago, the Paper Coast Guard was the lesser part and boatmen had little contact with it, but in the past few decades that has changed decidely, as we all know only too well. But I still remember my first real encounter with them a bare twenty years ago when, in a moment of supreme idiocy that I lived to regret, I installed an engine in *Iolaire*. At that point, I had been sailing and chartering her for something over two years around the eastern Caribbean, sailing on and off moorings, alongside and off piers, and in and out of the smallest ports happily and with no problems except for missing an occasional connection for lack of wind. So I convinced myself *Iolaire* needed an engine, and then my troubles began.

First off, the Coast Guard area commander told me that in order to skipper and charter for hire a boat carrying six or fewer passengers, I would need a Motorboat Operator's License, and to get that I would need to get a job on a motorboat and work for a year under "competent supervision" before I could even apply.

The Telltale Compass, September 1977.

"You are not qualified to sail her now that you have put an engine in her," he told me with a perfectly straight face.

Well, I had neither the time nor the resources to spend in getting the Coast Guard's sanction so I am afraid I sailed illegally for many years, but six years ago, after warring with that cold-hearted hunk of metal in the bilge for nearly fourteen years, I ripped it out and tossed it overboard. Today, I am legal again because the Coast Guard doesn't require qualifications for a skipper who only sails.

Sometime after that initial contact, I had another encounter with the paper legions down in St. Thomas Harbor in the Virgin Islands when one of the minions threatened to write a citation because I had no life preserver cushion in the dinghy. I squeaked out of that one by pointing out such cushions were being stolen faster than I could buy them and, besides, I could see no reason for supporting Basil Symonette's "Sea Saga Enterprises" just because of a regulation.

Nonetheless, the paper boys weren't finished and shortly after boarded *Iolaire* for an "inspection." They hadn't been aboard ten minutes when one sat down in the cockpit to write a citation for "Lack of fog horn." I promptly dug up my battered old conch shell, and practically blew that guardsman's ear out. Whereupon, he scratched off that citation and substituted "Lack of fog bell."

And I didn't have one since no fog has ever been reported in St. Thomas, nor in any of the Lesser Antilles, for that matter. Yet, "It's the law," so I had to pungle up twenty-five dollars, which was a true fortune in those days.

Despite such encounters with the Coast Guard's unbending paper, though, I still felt the Working Coast Guard, those stalwarts who manned the search-and-rescue boats and who carried out the Coast Guard's ostensibly prime mission of aiding mariners in distress, were seamen and boatmen with few equals. But that opinion has been subjected to some rude shocks over the years.

The first was around 1960 while I was helping the owners deliver to Florida the old schooner *Abenaki,* which was one of John Alden's fifty-foot Malabar schooners and which then was already thirty years old. Beating down the Florida coast, we managed to shred both her mainsails which were cotton and had been cut before the beginning of World War II. At this inopportune moment, her old six-cylinder Universal also cashed in its chips and refused to sputter. Then, since schooners do not work very well to windward against the Gulf Stream with storm trysail, foresail, and headsails, we anchored directly off Cape Canaveral like many an old coaster waiting for a wind shift.

Late in the afternoon, a Coast Guard launch came alongside and offered us a tow into Cape Canaveral which we accepted with considerable thankfulness since it was October, the wind was south at fifteen knots and freshening, and the sun was sinking fast in the west. They asked for *Abenaki's* draft and although it was slightly over seven feet, we told them ten feet to be on the safe side.

As soon as the towing hawser was rigged, the Coast Guard took off at full bore, a good ten knots or better, and *Abenaki* tailed along in as close an approximation to a Nantucket sleigh ride as I hope to see. Just as darkness closed in, the Coast Guard took a sheer to starboard and entered the channel at the inner end of the shoal extending south from Cape Canaveral which the chart noted as a shifting channel with no more than ten feet at best. We were horrified, and even more so when the old *Abenaki* charged down one of the big swells that were running and tapped the bottom in the trough. In the next few minutes we must have bottomed out at least thirty times, and some of them were hard enough that I was certain the old boat was going to open up and sink.

The owner went forward with ax in hand, but by now we were in the middle of the shoal with breakers to port and starboard, and not far off, so he didn't dare drop the tow and all we could do was scramble into our life-jackets, ready the dinghy for fast launching, clutch the old rabbit's foot very tightly, and pray. Amazingly enough, the old *Abenaki* held together, and we did get into Cape Canaveral, but my respect for the Working Coast Guard's seamanship went down about as fast as the stock market.

It took another dive a few years later while I was delivering a little thirty-foot Abeking & Rasmussen yawl named *Stout* from St. Thomas to New York via Bermuda. We had our troubles on that voyage and bypassed Bermuda, but we were getting along fine under a jury rig for the starboard mizzen chainplates, which had pulled out, and for the rudder stock which had broken off at deck level during a particularly vicious squall. Because we had gone by Bermuda, we were afraid the Coast Guard would start an unnecessary search for us, and we spent a couple of days trying to stop passing freighters to send word to the Coast Guard since we had no radio. We finally succeeded after using up all our flares, and we asked one freighter to tell the Coast Guard we were proceeding directly to Norfolk under jury rig, with a non-operating engine, but that we were in no danger. I also asked that they notify my sister about our delay and gave them her phone number and address.

The wind was northeast, our course northwest, giving us a good beam reach under which we comfortably logged a hundred miles a day for the next three days into Norfolk. As we approached the Chesapeake, a Coast Guard Albatross circled overhead and dropped a float on a long streamer that we picked up. Inside was a note directing us to signal if we were alright with the mirror enclosed in the cannister. We would have been happy to do so except that it was raining, under which conditions the signal mirror was somewhat less useful than a broken oar. So we simply broached the rum bottle and the Albatross took off finally, although he left us completely frustrated because he didn't seem to understand our arm signals.

Later that day, the wind backed to north and we hardened up to close hauled on the starboard tack, bucking the tide running out of the Chesapeake. It was a Friday and the ocean was splattered with U.S. Navy vessels inbound for the weekend so, both to stay clear of the channel and the tide, we headed in along the Virginia shore. We spotted one of the large Coast Guard cutters lying near the lightship but didn't speak her and continued in to the Norfolk Yacht and Country Club where we tied up at dusk.

I promptly called the Coast Guard to report our arrival and was a little nonplussed by the concerned astonishment of the Officer of the Day who fairly screamed: "Gee, we haven't been able to find you for the last three days! Where are you? How did you get in?"

I told him we had come in on the rhumb line and asked him where he had been looking. He told me they had figured our speed of advance at 150 miles a day even though our message, which he confirmed had been received, carefully specified that we were a thirty-foot yawl under jury rig. He seemed amazed when I told him that it would be only under the best of conditions that anyone would expect a thirty-footer to average 6.25 knots for long, and certainly not one under jury rig, as we were. In any case, they had been looking for us fifty miles ahead of our position the first day, and a hundred the second. Even so, if the search plane had simply flown down the rhumb line they would have found us in short order, but the Coast Guard in its wisdom knew exactly where we should be.

The O.O.D. also couldn't understand how we had gotten by the cutter which had been alerted by the Albatross. I told him we had seen her, and gave him her number which we had logged, but I certainly had no explanation unless the watch had a particularly hot rummy game going.

Yet the worst part of that particular incident was that the Coast Guard had called my sister and told her they had been unable to find us and consequently we were presumed lost. They also passed the word to the Norfolk papers which explained the rather odd look the dockmaster had given us on arrival . . . a bit as though he were seeing Marley's ghost.

Fortunately, my sister is one of those unflappable types, and I suspect she rather shocked the Coast Guard when she advised them not to worry, and added: "Bad pennies always come home to roost. He'll turn up sooner or later."

She was right, of course.

That wasn't the only time the Coast Guard has buried me at sea, though, and sometimes I wonder if they aren't indulging a bit of wishful thinking. The second time was during the year of the Cuban crisis while I was taking the typical thirty-six-foot Casey ketch *Catalina* down to St. Thomas as a favor for a friend.

Patrick Ellam has a cardinal rule that no yacht should depart Morehead City headed for the Caribbean beyond mid-November because the chances of getting caught in a northwest gale are too great, and he is quite right. However, a series of circumstances led to our being in Morehead City at the very end of that month, waiting while one of those gales raged along the Atlantic seaboard. Finally, the weather reports announced the gale had moved out into the Atlantic and would not return, and we, as well as a dozen other weather-bound yachts, took off.

The first twenty-four hours were beautiful sailing but then that gale turned around and came right back on us. It was a dandy, with tremendous seas, and we later learned that about every boat that had left at the same time was in trouble . . . either sunk, with ships standing by, or sending frantic Maydays on the radio. We weren't comfortable, but we rode it out under a small staysail, and were blissfully ignorant of the trouble around us because we had no radio. However, every day at least one or two U.S. Navy spotter planes would drop out of the sky and circle us, checking us out which didn't seem too amazing in view of the trouble in Cuba.

But when we finally sailed into St. Thomas, we were flabbergasted by a cheering throng on the pier, and one old friend who kept shouting over his bullhorn: "Hey, Lazarus, where the hell have you been?"

We couldn't understand what it was all about until our friends trotted out a handful of newspaper clippings reporting that the "Yacht *Catalina* was missing with all hands." We hadn't raised a peep. In fact, without a radio, we couldn't, but the Coast Guard had decided we were missing because everyone else was having trouble and they hadn't heard from us. They obviously didn't bother to check with the Navy who knew exactly how we were getting along, and so consigned us to the deep.

There have been dozens of such incidents of Coast Guard idiocy in my career, including the particularly exasperating exchange with the skipper of a big Coast Guard cutter off the north coast of Puerto Rico when Percy Chubb's *Antilles* inadvertently crossed a seldom-used Coast Guard firing range. The cutter chased us down, and the skipper ordered us to clear the area on a course exactly into the eye of the wind. And he couldn't understand it when we told him there was no way a sailboat could sail the course he wanted, and seemed to think we were being recalcitrant in the face of authority. Nor was he convinced until we brought *Antilles* up to the course he designated when, naturally, she stopped dead with her sails thundering, to his astonishment.

That is far from the end of this story, though, and I will next recount a few more and some allied observations.

𝟛𝟛 ❧ Paper Coast Guard I I

IN A WAY, I suppose that every sailor has to be an optimist else he never would go to sea, so each year I keep hoping to see some evidence that the Coast Guard is changing for the better. But so far, it has been a mostly fruitless hope.

As recently as the 1974 America's Cup series at Newport, I watched one incident with the Working Coast Guard that had all the elements of a pure nightmare, but it clearly indicated that today's Coast Guardsmen know little, if anything, about sailing craft. Not that the Coast Guard has an easy or enviable task in shepherding the hundreds of boats that gather to watch that triennial bash. The quality of seamanship that many of the spectator boats exhibit is strictly unbelievable—and horrifying— and I think most of us end up forgiving the Coast Guard's officiousness during that madness. Nonetheless, in this case, a little more was revealed.

For one of the races in the series, I was invited to view the event from aboard the grand old ketch *Ticonderoga*. We had a glorious sail out to the starting line, but the race was canceled due to heavy fog and an increasingly strong wind. We turned back to Newport and charged along at nine or ten knots, passing a good part of the powerboat fleet slogging along in the building seas. Then, as we came abeam of Fort Adams at the entrance to Newport Harbor, we broke out of the fog into the sunshine, and the inner harbor looked for all the world like a sparkling stage set. *Mighty Ti*'s skipper couldn't resist it and promptly decided to make a few boards back and forth across the harbor to give the crowds a chance to see the grand old campaigner at her best. She is a magnificent boat to sail, and to

The Telltale Compass, October 1977.

watch, and both the crew and the crowds obviously were enjoying it immensely.

At one point we were on the west side of the harbor sailing eastward, reaching along at around nine or ten knots on the starboard tack, with one of the big high endurance Coast Guard cutters coming up the channel slowly so that we had at least a quarter of a mile to spare in crossing her bows. But at that point, the bullhorns came alive with the preemptory order: "Don't cross in front of the cutter!"

Ti would have been happy to give way, *but* the orders were coming from two Coast Guard forty-four-foot launches, one of which was coming in about thirty degrees off the starboard bow, and the other about thirty degrees off our port bow, and both at full bore. They had us as neatly boxed as a couple of cowboys riding down a bull. Old *Ti* could neither luff up nor bear off without crashing through one of them, and had we let everything go by the run, we would have ended up sitting directly beneath the big cutter's stem.

From the bow, we tried to wave them off while calling back to our rightfully nervous helmsman to hold his course. It was the only thing we could do, despite the angry shouts from the Guard boats which were yelling: "Back up. . . . Stop. . . . Back up!"

At the last possible second, the boat to starboard backed down hard, and we luffed sharply past her with only inches to spare, but as we roared by, the coxswain screamed across: "Why didn't you stop?"

Aboard the *Ti,* we were too shaken to think of an answer and besides how do you explain in a minute the ways of a boat like *Ticonderoga* while she is doing ten knots on a close reach in a good breeze? I don't imagine that to this day those cox'ns realized the nearly impossible and highly dangerous situation they had set up.

Yet such incidents aren't the only things that bother me about the Coast Guard. In theory, at least, another of their prime duties is to maintain a close and careful watch on the radio distress and calling bands, but during *Iolaire*'s seventieth-birthday passage to Europe for the Fastnet Race in 1975, we ran into three different situations where we had hell's own time raising them.

The first was on our initial passage from Bermuda up to Block Island, which was not one of our most brilliant . . . we set a record for slowness. We had two doctors aboard, both with operations scheduled ashore, and when we were still two-and-a-half days out, we started trying to raise the Coast Guard on 2182 KHz. We tried every four hours around the clock at the change of the watch, but never once got so much as a click in reply. Finally, as we sighted Block Island through the rain and mist, a helicopter appeared overhead and we gave him a shout, asking him if he could raise Block Island for us. Block Island immediately came on the air and told us they were reading us loud and clear but claimed they hadn't heard us at all in the previous two-and-a-half days. I was thankful that we hadn't needed to file a Mayday.

Then some days later after we left City Island headed for Boston in our preliminary running up and down the coast, we were smoking past Eatons Neck Point in a beautiful sou'wester that had us at hull speed. We spotted an eighteen-foot outboard just off the Coast Guard station, whose crew was frantically waving their arms. We swung in, and found that they were okay but couldn't get their engine started. Since they were in no immediate danger, we told them we would call Eatons Point for them.

For the next five minutes at least, and perhaps more, we tried to raise the Coast Guard on 2182 with absolutely no answer. Then, when we were about to give up and go back to the outboard, Fisher Island, which is some seventy-five miles farther out the Sound, came on the air and noted they were reading us loud and clear. They, too, tried to raise Eatons Point with no luck, but then apparently must have called them on the telephone because a few minutes later Eatons Point did come booming on as loud as might be expected since we still were in shouting range.

For the next few minutes, I had one of the most painfully slow and exasperating radio exchanges that I have ever had. That Coast Guard radioman wanted to know *first* the name of the boat reporting, the type, the size, the color, the rig, my registry, my name, my address, and precisely where I was, at which point I'm afraid I blew a fuse and yelled at him: "If you stick your bloody head out of the window, you can see us!"

It was only after that that he wanted to know about the boat in trouble, which certainly struck me as getting the cart rigged out before the horse. As it happened, while all that was going on, one of the Coast Guard forty-one-footers had boiled by us, heading in, and at that very moment was passing the outboard, which was some hundred yards off the buoy. I told the radio-man that fact in no uncertain words and when he continued to babble, I cut the set in exasperation.

I suppose those two incidents should have prepared me for our troubles trying to contact the weather ships while crossing the North Atlantic to Cork, Ireland, on *Iolaire*. We tried repeatedly to raise them to get weather and ice information and not once with any success, even though, at times, we were fairly close to them. On the other hand, we always were able to contact St. John's radio despite its being four or five hundred miles away.

We had a retired Coast Guard chief aboard for the passage who just shrugged his shoulders and said he guessed the weather ships had their radios turned way down either to avoid being blasted when the powerful sets of the big ships called them, or so that they could listen without interference to the music that was usually being played in the radio shack. God help the little guy with the little horn.

Also among the Coast Guard's many responsibilities is the maintenance of the buoyage system in American waters, and there, too, they seem to have their idiots. At least, judging by one incident we had when we stopped into New London on the same transatlantic cruise. We were taking our departure, and were working our way down the clearly buoyed channel when *Iolaire* came to a jouncing, grinding halt although we were well within the marked channel. We sounded fore and aft and found plenty of water, but amidships there was only five-and-a-half feet over a narrow ledge. We drew seven.

A Coast Guard launch pitched up and the cox'n was a bit belligerent with his claim we were out of the channel, but we pointed out that there was one buoy marking the reach, and there was the other and the line between them was at least fifteen yards in-shore from our position.

Later, we learned those buoys had been repositioned only a week or two before our arrival, and in that short period numerous boats had been aground on the same ledge.

In any case, he gave us a hand off, and we went on to City Island where we discovered the rudder heel fitting had been so badly bent it had to be completely replaced and that we had a permanent kink to port at the after end of the keel. If it hadn't been for the wonderful and speedy help that Wes Rodstrom and his crew at Consolidated Shipyard gave us, we never would have made the Fastnet in time.

From all this, it might be thought that I have given up completely on the Coast Guard. But how can you in view of their record of daring and brilliant rescues that goes back almost two centuries and often entailed the sacrifice of not a few dedicated Coast Guardsmen? It is a record that won't be duplicated by any other of our public service organizations.

So what is the problem? While I certainly am no expert on the question and can only watch from water level, so to speak, I suspect the real trouble is that the Paper Coast Guard with its computers, its forms, its reports, its niggling details, and its distance from the water, has taken over from the earlier-day Working Coast Guard under pressures and directives from an unknowing and certainly far-from-expert Congress.

Paperwork, in part at least, figured in the retirement decision of Master Chief Boatswain's Mate Thomas D. McAdams, the Coast Guard's "No. 1 Coxswain," who the press liked to call a "living legend," recently.

Chief McAdams had a long list of successful rescues in his twenty-seven years on the turbulent bars of the Oregon and Washington coasts and not only was responsible for the design of the Coast Guard's incredibly seaworthy forty-four-foot self-rescuing surf boats, which can be, and often are, rolled completely over in the surf, but who also ran a training program for small boat handling that was widely considered as the best.

Chief McAdams often complained at length, both colorfully and publicly, about the floods of paper he had to service while he commanded the Motor Lifeboat Station at Newport, Oregon, his last command, and ruefully noted the time involved interfered greatly with his rescue training work. Although only forty-five years old at the time of his retirement, the chief was the finest kind of seaman in the old tradition, and a type of boatman that seems to be disappearing from the scene.

There is little question that the Coast Guard's modern recruiting techniques also are a factor, although it could be an area in which they have little choice. In the old days, recruits were largely drawn from the ranks of youngsters who already were seamen—fishermen and watermen of all kinds. They ordinarily applied at the local lifeboat station and the old chiefs made sure the recruit had some inkling of what he was about on the water before he was accepted, and it was only then that he was sent to Cape May to learn to wear a uniform and carry a rifle.

Nowadays, they are drawn from all over the country under the Coast Guard's highly organized and sophisticated recruitment program, and many of them see deep water for the first time when they arrive for training which, at best, is a matter of a few months of largely class work and drill. Making true seamen out of such men under such circumstances would be an even larger task than the labors of Hercules.

Much the same applies to their officer recruitment, with candidates beguiled by the prospects of free education rather than a life at sea, and much of the training is behind a desk in a classroom or on the drill field. It is true the Coast Guard does have the magnificent old barque *Eagle,* and each class does get a six weeks' or two months' so-called summer "training cruise," which as often as not is more a pleasure cruise, but I would like to submit here that *Eagle* is grossly underused.

I have heard it claimed that the *Eagle* is not "cost effective," whatever that means, and that to use her as the backbone of Coast Guard training would be anachronistic in this age of power craft because few Coast Guard officers ever board another windship after leaving the *Eagle*. Most spend their time shuffling papers, or flying planes and helicopters, or serving on powered ships, so why would they need sail training?

The best and most cogent answer to that question I have heard came from the skipper of one of the Scandinavian Sail Training ships some years ago who pointed out that a sailor aboard a powered ship these days often spends his whole lifetime without encountering more than one or two real emergencies that put both himself and his ship in danger, but that aboard a square rigger, such emergencies had to be faced at least once a day, and sometimes several times.

He then pointed out the obvious, that no one can tell how a man will react in an emergency without exposing him to it, nor could a man learn to deal with emergencies in a calm, cool and efficient way without such exposure. Yet the ability to solve emergencies is the core for any good seaman, and it certainly stands one in good stead anywhere, afloat or ashore. It is an argument that I think is hard to refute and it still doesn't take into account the clear benefits that *Eagle*'s sailors gain by direct contact with the way of wind, and sea, and ships.

If, instead of making *Eagle* an incidental part of the training as she is today, she were used to full potential by, say, sending each and every freshman class to sea aboard her for a full year, and most of it underway, it would serve many purposes. First, it would provide a solid basis of seamanship and ship maintenance for the embryo Guardsman that only a square rigger can give; second, it quickly would indicate which of them had the qualities that make really good officers and which would be the washouts. Third, the prospect of a year at sea probably would narrow down the candidates to those who really were interested in a sea career rather than just a free education at the expense of the taxpayers. It also would give the midshipmen themselves a solid and real basis for deciding whether following the sea was something they wanted, rather than just a romantic illusion.

Such a program, in the long run, would be cheaper and yet more effective, I think, and no doubt would reduce the current problems of Coast Guard officers who get their four years' training, spend the minimum time in service and then leave.

It has always struck me as odd that the Coast Guard leans heavily on sea experience requirements in licensing professional seamen . . . even motorboat operators . . . and yet in filling their own ranks, the emphasis seems to be on books, classes, and grades, and the ordinary landlubber techniques in education.

There is an old adage that no one ever learned the ways of the sea from a book, and these few incidents, which are far from unusual from all I hear, demonstrate the truth of that adage.

It is time for the Coast Guard to burn much of its paper and go back to sea.

34 ❧ Buy British!

LAST YEAR during the course of *Iolaire*'s seventieth-birthday cruise across the Atlantic and back, I had the opportunity to once again check up on the question of buying yachting gear in England, and must admit that before we left England's shores, I was kicking myself roundly, in a manner of speaking.

By now, I imagine most yachtsmen know the usually high quality yachting gear the English manufacture is priced there at but a fraction of the cost of the same gear when it is imported to the United States. In its first issue ever, *The Telltale Compass* carried what probably was the first study of that situation in the U.S. boating press, but much water has gone down the river since November of 1969. Nonetheless, I found that little has changed, except for the prices themselves. Today, they are higher, but "Buying British" still has solid value. That is, if the boatman buys directly from English sources.

As was pointed out in the original article, English gear was available for direct purchase at prices that often were half or less of the prices for the same gear purchased from U.S. importers. While it may not be hard to understand the reason for some increase in cost on this side of the Atlantic since several more middlemen enter the picture, each with his hand out, plus the cost of shipping, insurance, duties, and so on, still double and triple retail prices in England are hard to fathom. At times it seems as though the importers start with the English retail price as a base, then compound all the various charges, and finally take a hefty percentage of the full total for their profit margins.

I once charged an importer with that sort of pricing gambit and he denied it, although not with much spirit, but he did tell me he had been amazed to find what a small markup the English work on. He said that a 30 percent markup from manufacturer to retailer was considered very good in England; that 20 percent wasn't unusual, and that in some areas it could be even less. He claimed no American retailer could live with such ratios and laid much of it to the high cost of advertising on this side of the Atlantic and to higher distribution costs.

That may be so, but it still doesn't change the fact the American

The Telltale Compass, March 1977.

boatman can deal directly with English firms, in some instances, or at least with English chandlers and come out well ahead.

As a counter to direct-buying advantages, it has been claimed that the U.S. representatives of English outfits—they have been multiplying at rates somewhat faster than the proverbial rabbits—will refuse to service English gear unless purchased through them. I have heard that claim often, but never have been able to pin it down positively and must say that, in my experience, the English—and their reps—seem a great deal more interested in their reputations than in worrying about how the gear was purchased. I have yet to find anyone who did buy directly who had difficulty getting service over here although I suppose it is quite possible. Even so, he could still go back to England with his problem, which would take longer, but generally is a happy experience, since many of the English firms still subscribe to some of the oldtime business ethics and have not allowed themselves to become valets to soulless computers.

By the way, that reminds me of one service I discovered while we were in England with the little Seagull outboard, which has no equivalent with U.S. motor manufacturers that I know about, and which also indicates the English take a somewhat dim view of the all too common American theory that everything should be built to be thrown away, sooner or later, and usually sooner. Anyway, they have a system that if you send your old, rusty, beat-up Seagull to them (British Seagull Co., Ltd., Fleets Bridge, Poole, Dorset, England) along with £25 ($50 at the rate today), they send back a completely rebuilt Seagull that looks brand new, and acts it. It is the best exchange program in the world for my money, and a plan that American motor-makers could copy for the benefit of everyone.

But to get back to the story and the reason I was kicking myself. Basically, I didn't follow my own advice. When we were getting *Iolaire* ready for the voyage, there were several things I needed. We had been sailing in the Caribbean for seventeen years with only one sojourn to the States, and had no radio direction-finder aboard since they are of little use in the area. For the transatlantic course we had laid out up the sometimes foggy East Coast, past Nova Scotia, Ireland, the southwest coast of England, though I felt that a direction-finder not only would be a help but nearly mandatory for a safe passage.

I long ago decided that the only type that made sense for me was the kind of hand-held direction-finder with a built-in compass so that you could get immediate and direct readings rather than battling the relative bearing problem which can introduce large errors in a bouncing small boat. Consequently, I wrote to Brookes & Gatehouse in England, certainly the Cadillac of the tribe, and was somewhat astonished when they offered to sell me one of their excellent Heron direction-finders at a fifty percent discount. It was an excellent offer, but time was running out and we had the immediate problems of the out-bound voyage, so when we arrived in the States on the initial leg, I called Brookes & Gatehouse U.S.A. (154 E. Boston Post Road, Mamaroneck, N.Y. 10543) and told them about the letter.

They were friendly and affable but pointed out they were a completely separate company and couldn't meet the English offer. However, they said they would give me the maximum 40 percent "trade discount" which I thought was a very good deal. So I gave one of my crew a blank check and told him to hop in his car and pick up the Heron. Imagine my shock when he returned and announced he had filled in the check for just shy of $600. It seems that the retail U.S. price for the Heron was some $980. Needless to say, it took me a few days to recover.

But the aftershock was even worse when we arrived in England and I found that I could have bought the instrument straight off the shelf at retail for $565 or $33 less than I had paid with the handsome discount. And if I had taken the English B & G's first offer and had them send it to me . . . well, there was some reason for kicking myself.

I also outsmarted myself when I bought a Japanese-made three-quarter size sextant from Nautech Maritime (111 E. Wacker Drive, Chicago IL 60601) which reported it was discontinuing the line and had a special price on one for $170. It seemed a good deal at the time, but later I found exactly the same instrument being sold in London for $125.

Yet, I recovered elsewhere, and particularly on flares. The standard American distress signal is the Very pistol flare, but in Europe there are several companies turning out hand-held flares that are a great deal more effective.

I learned about them in 1969 during a highly graphic demonstration at the sail-by when the Royal Cork Yacht Club celebrated its two-hundred-fiftieth birthday. A number of American boats went over for that affair, and one of the features was that everyone fired flares as they sailed by the original station. The Americans fired their Verys, of course, while the British touched off their rockets which went up three times farther than the Very flares and, naturally, stayed up three times longer. They would be visible over a much larger area than the Very.

At the time, I bought a fair quantity of them, but they were way over the hill on their expiry dates so when Revere Marine Supply was repacking our Danish-made life raft, I asked them to replace the rockets with fresh ones. They said they would be happy to do so, but told me the rockets were listed at $35 each in the U.S. Since I remembered I had paid something like three dollars each for them, I declined and bought some fresh Very shells, but when I got to England, I acquired a new set of rockets at the still-reasonable price of $6.71 each, which is a long way from thirty-five bucks. I have no idea the reason for the great difference and it is one of the worst ratios in the American-English prices I have found.

In any case, sometimes I think I would have been wise to pop on an airplane and take a trip to England to acquire the things I needed, and I suppose anyone fitting out from scratch might find that a savings despite the flight costs and some of the special problems it might present. In that line, the latest one is the additional tax English boatmen pay for gear under what is called the VAT. That stands for Value Added Tax, I am told, and while I can't say I understand it, it seems to be a massive sales tax in effect. Consequently, if you do buy in person in England, you have to pungle up either eight or twelve-and-a-half percent more to the government there, although if you take the gear out of the country you can get a refund by complying with Her Majesty's custom requirements. Having little stomach for such bureaucratic hassles, I didn't bother to find out just what Her Majesty required. In any case, gear ordered and shipped aboard from England pays no VAT.

So for the American boatman, it still seems best to be forehanded enough to buy via air mail, and the simplest procedure seems to be ordering direct from one of the English chandlers, because many of the English firms have set up U.S. distributors who follow the usual pricing practices. I stopped by Thomas Foulkes (Landsdown Road, Leytonstone, London E.1., England) and the London Yacht Centre (13 Artillery Lane, Bishop's Gate, London E.1., England) which are two of the leading outfits. Foulkes offered a fabulous variety of gear, and the Yacht Centre was a close second. Both have catalogs (Foulkes charges a dollar for theirs) and Foulkes especially are well accustomed and efficient in shipping gear overseas. It is a procedure that still is good and there is little reason to pay double for the stuff.

35 ❋ A Better 'ole

EVERY HOLE in the bottom of a boat is, or should be, a concern not only to the boatman whose life depends on the water-tight integrity of his boat, but also to the builder, if he has any vestige of either care for or pride in his craft.

Yet, the multitude of holes punched through many of today's production boats to accommodate head, galley and what not discharge or to allow intakes for engine cooling water, seem to be matters of least concern for many, both owners and manufacturers. It is far from uncommon to find such outlets with no means of closing them off at all, and even worse, to find plastic piping secured to through-hull tails by nothing more than a single pipe clamp.

That such unions can slip off, allowing the sea to rush in with all the force of a fire-hose, can be attested to by more than one boat owner who has arrived at his mooring to find his boat sitting quietly and sedately on the bottom. It seldom takes long, once such a fitting comes adrift.

Part of the trouble, of course, is that such fittings are tucked away in the hull, most often out of sight and often completely out of reach, although they shouldn't be. The other part is that the proper shut-off mechanism, the seacock, is expensive, ranging from $20 for the smallest seacock up to as much as $250 for a three-inch model, and with the most often used sizes ranging somewhere around $75 each. Consequently, uncaring manufacturers are inclined to give them short shrift, and the unknowing boatman doesn't ask.

All kinds of dodges have been used to bypass the problem, including one used by Morgan Yacht on the Out Island 41 we checked out early this year; it hooked the sump and bilge pumps and the cockpit scuppers together and piped the discharge through a two-inch through-hull just above the water-line. Since it was above, rather than below, Morgan contended no shut-off was needed even though it would be obvious to anyone the outlet would be underwater on the port tack, and most likely would be so if the boat were overloaded with gear, which is common.

But perhaps the most common ploy among the stock boats is to use a gate valve which is relatively cheap because so many are manufactured for use ashore. They also can run the entire gamut for quality, and the cheaper ones are entirely unreliable not only in care of manufacture but also in material, using second-grade bronze or brass and often fitting iron handles that disintegrate in short order. Gate valves are so prone to failure that they are universally condemned by competent marine surveyors. If there is any electrolysis present, the gate valve usually is one of the first places attacked, particularly the threaded stem. Then, too, most often the valves are normally left open year in and year out, and corrosion and barnacles find a favorite spot on the valve seat. Then when it is screwed closed, the valve fetches up and seems solidly closed, but in fact may be only partially so.

The better answer is the traditional 90° on–off bronze seacock such as those manufactured by Wilcox-Crittenden (699 Middle Street, Middletown, CT 06457) or Groco (Gross Mechanical Laboratories, Inc., 1530 Russell Street, Baltimore, MD 21230), among others. For years, most experienced yachtsmen, including myself, have regarded such seacocks as foolproof. But they aren't . . . always.

Not long ago, the galley sink drain aboard *Iolaire* clogged so I closed the two-inch seacock and pulled the drain pipe to clear it. As I disconnected the hose from the seacock, I was astonished, and a bit horrified, to find that despite being closed, the seacock was passing quite a substantial column of water. I managed to clear the blockage easily and quickly reassembled the thing, but at the next haulout that seacock was the first thing on the list for tearing down. I ground the tapered plug in with valve compound, but it set so much deeper in the seat I had to machine off an eighth of an inch from the bottom of the tapered plug. Even now, it still isn't perfectly seated and is still on the list for attention.

Discussing that incident with other cruising men, I found few who realized it was quite possible for a proper seacock to have a major leak, and most of them actually had given it no thought at all. But to me, it is clear that it is another of those hidden dangers, and that to be sure, all seacocks should be tested while the boat is in the water by closing them and then disconnecting the lines to be certain there is no leakage. Actually, most surveyors, myself included, have checked seacocks simply by making sure they were readily accessible and that they could be flipped on or off—they are prone to jamming—but it isn't enough.

There is an alternative that was developed some twenty years ago for commercial operations looking for a positive and reliable valve for either liquid or gas, but it is still little known in the marine field despite its apparent potential. That is the ball cock which operates somewhat in the fashion of the tapered cock, but employs a ball stop seating against one of the tough new plastics, Teflon, for a very tight, wear- and jam-free seal. They are available in a variety of materials: good bronze, stainless steel, aluminum, or in dozens of sophisticated alloys so they are particularly adaptable for aluminum or steel boats where the dissimilar metal problem is constant.

And, strangely enough, they are substantially less costly than the traditional seacock, ranging from a half to two-thirds the price roughly, depending on quality, which, too, can run the gamut. But, as an instance, a two-inch ball cock in bronze of comparable or even better quality than a traditional seacock, which runs around $100, will cost in the neighborhood of $70.

The first time I encountered the ball cock was some ten years ago while searching for a positive shut-off for my propane stove and was introduced to it by Howard Freeman, president of the Jamesbury Corporation (640 Lincoln Street, Worcester, MA 01605), a long-time sailor himself. Jamesbury is one of the largest valve manufacturers in the country, and Freeman was the original designer of ball cock valves for submarines which have an obvious need for reliable valves. The new nuclear subs now use nothing else.

I installed one of his valves on *Iolaire*'s stove over ten years ago, and I check it periodically by shutting the ball valve, disconnecting the stove line, and turning on the main gas valve. After an initial test with the usual soapy solution, I then give it the acid test of lighting a match at the valve. I have never been able to get even a glimmer of escaping gas, and that is after ten years of day in and day out use, year-round.

Even though the Navy and the space program have adopted the ball cock almost exclusively, they are rarely found on pleasure craft and I have yet to see the Jamesbury Company listed in the usual marine directories. A few yachtsmen have tried them, though, and Freeman told us that Ted Hood, who designed Freeman's *Snowbird III* some ten years ago, now uses them on his boats. Freeman, of course, insisted they be installed not only on that boat, but also on his newer forty-five-foot ketch, *Snowbird,* he had built five years ago. He says he has yet to have a failure or even a problem with any of them. Some years ago, too, Chris Craft's steel Roamer boats were equipped with them, and undoubtedly there are a few other individual sailormen who have discovered them, including one friend of Freeman's who for twelve years has followed the seamanlike practice of closing all through-hull valves every time he leaves his boat and has had no problems.

However, I have yet to find a manufacturer that makes a good ball cock valve with a hull flange for direct attachment to the hull, although it is a simple matter to screw them to the threaded tailpiece of a through-hull. Still, that makes for relative weakness at a vital point as compared to traditional seacocks although Freeman may be right in his contention that the old seacocks were built over-strong just to take the sledgehammer blows you had to use when they froze in position, open or closed. In any case, the ball cock assemblies are much lighter, much more compact, much easier to locate, and you don't need room for a spanner since they require only a slight increase in torque to operate even after years in one position.

The chances of someone manufacturing a complete ball cock seacock unit are slim, Freeman told us, simply because of the smallness and disparity of the market although he said that the tapered cock valve makers have all but disappeared from the general valve business because of the superiority of ball cocks.

Nonetheless, since the seacock is one of those unmentionables insofar as most manufacturers are concerned and yet is such a key element in basic hull integrity, I would think it would be worthwhile for at least the bigger producers to get together, decide on a few standard sizes, and arrange for one of the good manufacturers to turn out a ball cock valve with a hull flange. It strikes me it could be a bottom line solution to the bottomhole problem.

In a subsequent issue of *Telltale Compass,* a reader wrote in and pointed out that the Apollo Ball Valve Division of Consolidated Brass and Copper Company (P.O. Box 125, Page Land, South Carolina, 29728) has been making a proper ball cock with a flange for use in the marine field for many years. It was designed at the request of Hatteras Yachts who have been using them for a considerable time. Why other builders have not done so is beyond me. Perko (P.O. Box 6400D, Miami, Fla., 33164) has recently come out, as noted in *Sail* magazine, with a bronze throughhull based ball cock, on the Teflon seal principal.

Finally on the electrolysis and the ball-cock problem, ITT Marine, U.K. division, has come out with a plastic ball cock valve.

Progress is really being made in making a better 'ole.

𝟛𝟞 ❖ On Time

[The author completed a sentimental journey in mid-December of 1975, in his venerable yawl Iolaire. *The passage took* Iolaire *back to her birthplace in Rowhedge, on the Colne in England, just seventy years after she was built. The 12,000-mile voyage was spread over seven months with* Iolaire *departing Grenada in the Windward Islands and returning to Àntigua in the Leewards after having sailed up the Atlantic to Halifax, across to Ireland and England, and then home via the Canaries with time out in European waters to take part in the Fastnet and a half dozen other racing features. Such a voyage provided unparalleled opportunities for the practical testing of marine gear, and one of the tasks Street undertook for us was to check out a variety of time gear. Herewith, his report.—Ed.]*
The Telltale Compass, *March 1976.*

IT IS A BIT IRONICAL that sailors who make long passages at sea find one of the attractions is that they can abandon the tyranny of time—the eight-hour day ashore . . . the nine-to-five syndrome. But the truth is that, perhaps as nowhere ashore, time is the complete tyrant at sea, and an inaccurate timepiece can lead only to disaster because the wrong time applied to a celestial fix can position the boatman miles from where he actually is.

Sailors since the beginning have battled that problem, and it was such an acute one back in the early 1700s that England's Board of Longitude offered the staggering fortune of £20,000 (something near a $100,000 then) to anyone who could devise a timepiece that would enable a navigator to get a fix within half a degree of longitude. John Harrison, the son of a Yorkshire carpenter, did much better than that in 1735 when he put together a sixty-five-pound monster of a clock that was tested aboard HMS *Centurion* on a passage to Lisbon and back and came up with an error of only three minutes of longitude. But it took almost forty years, and three more astonishingly accurate chronometers, before he collected at the age of eighty.

Obviously, chronometers in those days were astronomically expensive, and they still are. But no matter how costly, and no matter how accurate they may be aboard large vessels, the chronometer art has not kept pace with the declining size and the resultant quickening of motion in small craft that now venture to sea.

Time after time, I have sailed on yachts with good chronometers that had been perfectly rated in the chronometer shop ashore. They worked beautifully as long as the weather was moderate, but as soon as a bit of heavy weather was encountered, the chronometer's rate would become erratic and unpredictable.

Typical was an experience I had in 1969 during a transatlantic passage aboard *Antilles* when we had an Accutron chronometer (Bulova Watch Company, Bulova Park, Flushing, N.Y. 11756) aboard. At that point, the Accutron tuning fork escapement was claimed to be the most accurate movement around, within limits of a few seconds a year.

At first, all was well, but when we reached the cold weather off the Grand Banks, the chronometer began losing, and within a week it was thirty seconds slow. Then later when the weather warmed, it began to gain so that when we arrived in Ireland it was only a few seconds off. But the unpredictable variation was enough to destroy our faith in the Accutron.

Consequently, in our last transatlantic round-trip in *Iolaire,* I was more than fascinated to have a pair of time instruments to test to see how they fared at sea. One was a highly sophisticated quartz crystal sextant chronometer made and loaned me by the Oxy Nautica Division of Oxy Metal Finishing Suisse in Geneva, Switzerland, and the other was a small radio, the Simex Time Standard, produced by the late Captain Svend Simonsen's Coast Navigation School (418 East Canon Perdido, Santa Barbara, CA 93101) which *The Telltale Compass* desk tested several years ago (Vol. II, No. 9) and found excellent, but had never tried at sea.

The Oxy Nautica instrument, which they dub "Astroquartz," is a novel instrument, the idea for which its inventor, Jean-Claude Protta, developed during a single-handed Atlantic passage when he suffered the usual frustrations of juggling both a sextant and stopwatch while taking his sights. It is designed to replace the ordinary sextant handle and besides the quartz crystal chronometer movement, made in West Germany, has an ingenious electronic accumulator circuit that enables the navigator to stop the sweep second hand as he gets his mark by the push of a button. Then after the navigator has noted his time, he trips another button and the second hand skitters around the dial at something like three times speed until it catches up to the correct second when it resumes its sedate second-by-second pace. If the navigator forgets to re-start it, the second hand automatically goes into its galloping act after about a minute and a half.

This feature worked out beautifully, and hasn't failed yet. It obviously could be a solution for the single-hander, and also would avoid the need for an assistant navigator holding the watch on a crewed boat.

The Astroquartz was delivered aboard about the first of July, and we thought our time problems were over and we wouldn't have to worry about time checks. Of course, we did check and were horrified to discover that the quartz crystal chronometer was gaining roughly a second a day, a rate far from the claimed accuracy of five seconds a month, which seems to be a common claim for all the breed. The rate remained the same through November, and then, what was even more disturbing, it started losing time erratically. At that point, we tucked the gadget away, but later ashore did a little investigating that turned up a couple of possible reasons for its erratic behavior.

Firstly the chronometer movement was powered by one heavy alkaline C-battery that was held in place by a single leaf-spring pushing the battery against a fixed positive pole. This spring obviously had been flattened by the battery shifting with *Iolaire*'s movement at sea to the point where finally, when the Astroquartz was held vertically as it would be when attached to the sextant, the contact was broken and the clock stopped. A simple bending back of the spring and a wood wedge fixed it, but it is clear that the battery holder should be redesigned to hold the battery solidly with spring contacts at both poles to obviate the problem.

But our second discovery on opening up the Astroquartz was more unsettling. Taped to the side of the movement was a label that warned in three languages—German, English, and French—"Protect Against Shocks." There was no mention at all of that in the Astroquartz instruction manual which, at best, gave minimal information. Elsewhere, though, we learned that this particular chronometer movement was especially sensitive to shock, and that if bounced too hard, the thin wires holding the controlling quartz crystal could be strained to the point where the frequency was changed, resulting in a major alteration of the rate. The movement did include a trimmer that could adjust the rate, but only by about a half second a day. If that adjustment was not enough, the clock had to be returned to the factory for readjustment of the frequency with special measuring equipment.

Somewhere along the line, our Astroquartz apparently had been strained, and we found that a solid tap would cause the second hand to skip ahead a couple of seconds. Such sensitivity to little taps completely disenchanted us because it would be hard to conceive any navigator being able to get topsides for a sight in dusty weather without jarring his sextant, no matter how careful he might be. To do it aboard a small boat, he would have to be the ultimate ballet dancer.

Hence, it also is clear the Astroquartz needs a more rugged movement to live up to its promise, so I was particularly happy the instrument was on loan and that I hadn't laid out the $895 fortune it costs.

As a matter of fact, there is some question as to the future availability of the Astroquartz since we learned on returning home that the Oxy Nautica Division of Oxy Metals had been closed down following the acquisition of the parent company by the conglomerate Occidental Petroleum. All of that happened while we were at sea, and at this point we have been unable to determine whether the nautical instrument division of the Swiss company will be continued, and are unaware of the ultimate fate of the Astroquartz.

With little faith in the reliability of the Astroquartz, we turned back to the radio and the little Simex Time Standard—it isn't cheap either at $199.50—which lived up to the desk test we already have mentioned . . . for part of the voyage anyway. The model we checked was one of the newer ones with frequencies in the 5, 10 and 15 mHz frequencies for

WWV and 3.3, 7.3 and 14.6 mHz for the Canadian CHU broadcasts. The three WWV frequencies had proven the most useful in the first set tested which also had the 2.5 and 20 mHz WWV signals and only the 7.3 CHU band.

Before we left the Lesser Antilles, we were very pleasantly surprised to find the Simex regularly pulled in WWV day or night, which has been impossible on our other radios ever since the government moved WWV from Maryland out to Boulder, Colorado, back in the sixties. That move left the lower Caribbean, at least, in a radio shadow.

Up the Atlantic, the Simex worked perfectly and we could get a time check at will, but on the crossing when we reached 30° West Longitude, south of Greenland, the signals began to fade. By the time we were at 20° West, south of Iceland, we lost both WWV and CHU all together.

We did begin picking up the European time ticks, though, from the Spanish and Italian stations, but they are broadcast in their native language and by Morse code and no one aboard was competent enough in either to read them with any reliability.

So we went back to our old standby, a beat up and decrepit Sears Roebuck multi-band portable, and either the BBC, the Voice of America, or the Armed Forces Overseas stations, all of which provide time ticks at intervals, and which we could receive more or less faithfully all the way across the Atlantic.

On the return voyage, though, we again started picking up WWV on the Simex when we reached 30° West, and it proved reliable for the rest of the way.

Our only other objections to the Simex were that the aluminum case tended to corrode quite quickly and that some of the fittings and fastenings appeared to be of plated steel and rusted ripely. Unlike many of the better marine radios now, the Simex does not seem to be waterproofed nor even splash-proofed, although the unit we tested didn't fail for being a little wet on occasion. Still, in time, it could be a problem.

In the past few years I have delivered boats south with an interesting little gadget on board—a Time Cube, 2″ square, run on a very small battery with a whip antenna. This instrument costs $30 and is quite reliable. The last one was used and abused on about seven trips from the States to the Lesser Antilles and is still working. Admittedly it will not pull in time signals down in the St. Vincent–Grenada area during the day, but it will pull them in at 0200 and 0400. It's a small, cheap, and effective time machine.

So time still is a problem at sea, even though somewhat less so than in Harrison's day. We decided that the simplest solution is a couple of the more inexpensive multi-band radios, if one can't afford the classic Zenith Trans-Oceanic which most sailors regard as the best of the multi-band receivers, and a couple of good, ordinary watches. Those plus a copy of the Trans-Oceanic booklet that lists all the time frequencies and the hours of best reception, or a copy of the HO 117 A and B, "Radio Navigational Aids," which does the same, will get the ship there in time and perhaps even on time.

37 ❧ Stone Horse I

IMMEDIATELY AFTER the Newport Boat Show this year, my wife, Trich, and I took an Edey & Duff-built, Crocker-designed, Stone Horse twenty-three-foot cutter off on our second honeymoon. The Stone Horse was ideal for the job because going to sea in the Stone Horse is a little like sailing in a double bed. It is best to have an affectionate mate.

The Stone Horse stands out from her modern sisters for various reasons. First of all she is a good-looking boat. Secondly, she sails well without having to be bound up with big genoas, winches, and fancy spinnakers. Thirdly, her builders have not tried to cram a quart into a pint bottle. She is just a well-filled pint bottle having good accommodations for one couple, or at the most a couple with two very small children. She is definitely not a two-couple boat, unless you are extraordinarily good friends and sailing in a warm climate where one couple could sleep on deck.

The Stone Horse was designed by the late Sam Crocker, of whom it has been said, "Crocker never designed a crock." And it is true that most of his boats were beautiful as well as fast and handy.

The little Stone Horse is 23′4″ long overall, approximately eighteen feet on the water with only 340 square feet of sail area pushing 4,500 pounds of displacement (2,000 pounds ballast). She still sails extremely well despite having a large wheel aperture, and dragging a solid prop. At one point, with only her standard working sails in light air and despite towing a dinghy and that two-bladed sea anchor, we still held our own against a Ranger 27 sailing with her largest genoa. When it blew up, the Stone Horse was as mannerly, as we found beating from Vineyard Haven all the way up to Sippican Harbor, north of Mattapoisett, hard on the

The Telltale Compass, December 1976.

wind. Under double-reefed main, reefed staysail and no jib, she punched straight through the Buzzards Bay slop in an authoritative fashion. When we came out of Woods Hole, we caught up with a forty-two-foot schooner setting her club jib and reefed main, no foresail. As the schooner sheeted everything in, we slipped into a safe leeward position which we managed to maintain for forty-five minutes before the schooner finally tacked off in disgust.

Earlier, sailing dead downwind from Cuttyhunk to Woods Hole with double reefed main and reefed staysail, she was as docile as a lamb.

At times, she did develop weather helm, which could have been trimmed out by various alterations of sheet leads, a proper boom vang, and a loose footed staysail. Her hull shape allows her to track so nicely that I am sure, given a little more experience with the boat, we could have made her self-steering on all points of sail without the aid of self-steering gear.

We used the engine only twice, both times very briefly; both times it was not essential. It is a little single-cylinder Westerbeke seven-horse-power, which gives more than enough power.

The anchoring gear is excellent. Not one of the lightweight toys, but rather a twenty-five-pound Wilcox Crittenden copy of the Herreshoff anchor which held so well that one morning I could not break it out until

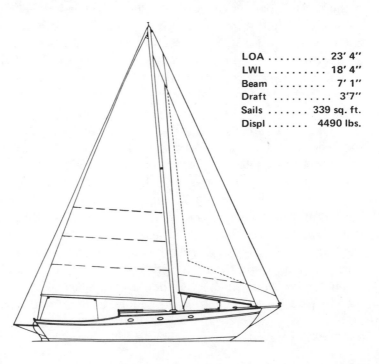

LOA	23' 4"
LWL	18' 4"
Beam	7' 1"
Draft	3'7"
Sails	339 sq. ft.
Displ	4490 lbs.

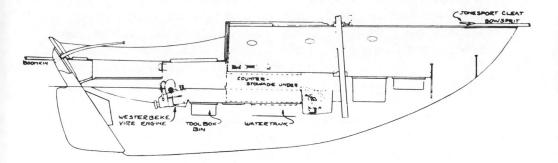

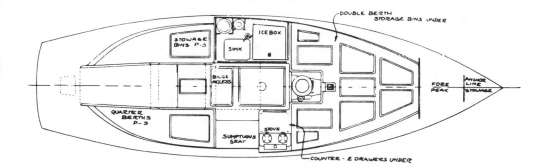

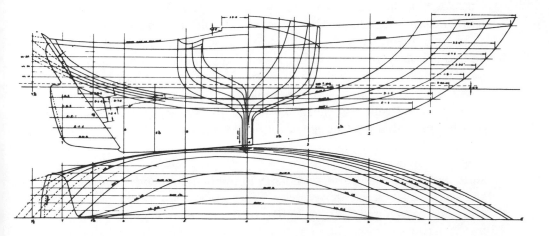

I had sailed around the anchor five or six times. Once broken out, it can be two-blocked to the end of the bowsprit from the cockpit and be allowed to hang there until one is clear of the anchorage.

The sail handling and rigging was back to basics . . . no winches, no wire halyards, strictly lines to cleats, roller furling jib luff set up by a turnbuckle, staysail rigged with a downhaul, staysail boom, and main boom fitted with topping lifts . . . simplicity itself, a far cry from all the winches and wires on many modern-day cruising boats, which are usually basically IOR takeoffs.

She has a decent-sized mainsail of about half the total sail area and it has an aspect ratio of roughly two to one which really has push in it. Not one of those tall narrow ribbons that is only efficient to windward.

Below decks, she is admirably laid out for two. Food stowage in the lockers was sufficient for two people for two weeks. Seldom, if ever, does one expect to go cruising in a small boat for more than two weeks without a good shopping stop en route. A two-burner stove with an adequate icebox allowed preparing more than adequate meals. A small charcoal stove kept the cabin warm on even the coldest, wettest, rainiest days.

Although she is of fiberglass construction, there is nothing tupperware or frozen snotty about her. Good solid construction of fiberglass and Airex foam give rigidity, strength, lightness, and insulation, reducing tremendously the tendency of glass boats to sweat. In the interior, wood is used liberally, almost concealing the fiberglass, and on deck teak is used extensively for trim and for hatches, cleats, and so on. It is a wonderful wood, easy to maintain, and the teak, unlike the teak in many snot boxes, appears to be very good quality instead of bits and pieces left over from a furniture factory. The fit of the joiner work, and the little details that most often are forgotten on today's boats, indicate that the Stone Horse is built by people who are interested first in turning out a good boat, and only after that in how musically the till rings in the office.

In truth, the Stone Horse's builders are a remarkably enthusiastic and straightforward gang which comes through clearly not only in the boat, but also in the singular little twenty-page pamphlet they put out to describe her and their reasons for doing what they do. It is a far cry from the usual advertising pap, and it shows that about every detail in the little boat has been thought through sanely, agreed or not.

The Stone Horse most often is categorized as a "stock boat," but it is a loose designation that doesn't fit her precisely at all. Where the usual stock boat is stamped out in numbers without benefit of order and then is stocked by dealers, the Stone Horse construction is started only after the order has been signed and an initial thirty-five percent payment made, just as has been the tradition in boatbuilding for centuries. This means that alterations in the accommodations can be made to suit the buyer's whims or tastes within the limits, of course, of the molded hull, and the Stone Horse people, in their price schedule, even list their hourly labor rates ($13.50) for making changes or special work.

The Stone Horse is a great little cruising boat, tough enough to weather rough seas sedately with a fair degree of comfort instead of tossing her crew about like beans in a teacup. She is fast enough in light airs to keep the enthusiastic sailor happy and she is small enough to be single-handed.

She is expensive, especially if the price is judged on a per-bunk basis—$20,000 for two bunks. No two ways about it, $10,000 per bunk is expensive. But $20,000 for 4,500 pounds displacement equals $4.40 per pound, which is not too bad for quality construction. If one is willing to forego the engine, the boat can be had for approximately $16,000 which brings the price down under $3.60 per pound. That is very reasonable, considering the Stone Horse is a first-class non-production boat, and remembering that her standard equipment list is about as complete and all-inclusive as any we have seen. It includes all her sails, of course, running lights, fire extinguishers, life vests, compass, anchor, a Porta-Potti toilet, galley stove—to name a few—and even such usually ignored essentials as a gurry bucket and samples of all finishing materials used.

After our honeymoon cruise, we decided the Stone Horse was an unusually excellent boat, and for a cruising couple possibly the best on the market, but that does not mean that we approved of everything absolutely. Some things were a matter of taste that we would want to change; other things we felt were so essential that they should be changed, or, at least, offered as options, to improve her, although none of them would really change the boat. But we will go into that in the next chapter.

38 ❈ Stone Horse II

As WE NOTED previously, there are some things about the little twenty-three-foot cutter Stone Horse, built by Edey & Duff in Mattapoisett, Massachusetts, that we would change, even though we found her a most satisfactory little cruising boat and ideal for a second honeymoon. No doubt others would change different things, but allow us our say.

Firstly, we haven't done it, but one of these days we want to go back to Sam Crocker's original design to see how he rigged the boat. Peter Duff told us that he discovered Sam had drawn up ten different rigs for her—some tall, some short—but strangely enough, all variations of her Bermudian rig and not a single gaff rig in the lot. I'd like to compare those to see how he juggled the centers of effort and lateral plane because under her modern rig we discovered with a double-reefed main and the staysail, she had so much lee helm as to be difficult. Tucking a reef in the staysail at that point made her much easier to handle, but she still had a light lee helm which is just what one doesn't need in a big, steep sea where you want her to come around quickly and positively.

To my way of thinking, if the staysail stay were fitted lower on the mast and made parallel to the jib stay, that would reduce the staysail area enough so that probably she would balance properly on a reefed main and staysail, or double-reefed main and reefed staysail. The forward mast bend thus produced could be countered by running intermediate shrouds down to chainplates about twenty inches abaft the mast line, which would act as shrouds as well as backstays.

The mainsail, as already noted, is a good driving, low aspect ratio sail and the sheet is a simple, practical arrangement running from the end of the boom to the stern traveler, back to the boom, along it and down to a cleat in the middle of the cockpit. It is excellent in light airs and to windward in moderate airs, but once the boom is eased beyond the quarter in any sort of a breeze, it tends to kite and the sail to twist, which ends up in overtrimming and a buildup in weather helm. If snatch blocks were rigged abeam the cleat on the rails, the sheet lead through the appropriate block would have a more direct downward pull and would do much to keep the boom from kiting while reaching. Also, when going to windward in heavy weather, flattening the main can be a bit of a workout. This could be lessened if another block were added about eight inches abaft the mid-boom block so that the bight of the main sheet between the two blocks could be brought down and rove through the snatch block. That would provide enough power that even a small girl could flatten the main.

In place of the two-part halyard on the main, I would prefer a single with a sliding gooseneck since it is much easier to pull down on the boom, or stand on it, than to haul up on the halyard.

The main was rigged for slab reefing, which works well but we felt the cleat could have been farther inboard so it could be reached even with the sail broad-off. Also, if she were my boat, I would take a page from the racing sailors and fit her, in place of reef points, with a wire from the clew to the tack earings. It makes for much simpler and faster reefing.

The Stone Horse's roller furling jib was set on a wire halyard tensioned by a turnbuckle which worked fine except that we felt the halyard was slightly undersized in diameter and thus had more stretch than was proper. A larger wire would be better, and if it were secured with a high-field lever rather than the turnbuckle, it would simplify either dropping or changing the jib. It might be lily-gilding, but I would like to have the option of a larger jib for real light weather, and it certainly is better to be able to stow the jib below if the boat is left long on moorings.

The club staysail is supposedly self-tending but is, in my estimation—and that of many seamen—a complete abomination. It cannot be backed when tacking in tight quarters unless someone goes forward to manhandle it, or unless extra lines are rigged. When reaching, as soon as the sheet is eased the club pops up, the leech falls off, all drive is lost and weather helm builds up. Running off, if one is a bit by the lee, the staysail collapses, the club charges across the deck, tries to uproot the traveler, and attempts to break the ankles of anyone imprudent enough to be on the foredeck. Since the Stone Horse's staysail is only seventy-six square feet in area, it seems to me that if the sailor is too feeble to trim it, perhaps it is time to take up a bathchair. Proof of the pudding: I have talked four boats into *temporarily* removing the clubs from staysails. Not one has put the club back on.

The wooden cleats mounted on the after face of the cabin trunk are classically beautiful, but would be more practical mounted on the cabin top. If so mounted, the sheets or halyards could be hauled aft and snapped around the cleat without loss. As it is, the lines have to make a right-angle turn across the cabin top and down to the cleat, making it hard to get that last fraction that gives a proper set to the sail. I even would consider a couple of the small-sized winches to provide fine adjustments when it blows up.

The tiller rig on the Stone Horse is admirably practical. The wooden tiller simply slips snugly between the cheeks of the rudder head and that's it, no catches or anything. Wriggle it forward and out it comes. The tiller is quite short, which is all that is needed since the boat is light on the helm, and it gives plenty of room in the cockpit. However, when sailing alone, the helmsman cannot reach the lines belayed on the forward bulkhead, so we felt that there should be two tillers with the longer tiller to be shipped for single-handing.

The little Westerbeke seven-horsepower diesel is flex-mounted and has an excellent reputation for reliability, but when it is running, it sounds quite literally like a machine gun. Possibly some of that comes from the apparent lack of a flexible coupling tying the engine to the shaft.

But the most serious fault was the lack of a drip pan under the engine, which is practically universal these days, although why is beyond my comprehension. I hope Edey & Duff will rectify that and while they are at it, look into an engine equipped with an adjustable-pitch, fully feathering prop, which would substantially reduce the prop drag under sail.

As I said earlier, below decks the accommodations are well laid out and comfortable, but there is one change that both Trich and I are definite about despite the feelings of Peter Duff, who is justifiably very proud of what he calls his "throne." That is a form-fitting fiberglass seat lodged over the Porta-Potti that indeed is very comfortable for reading or lolling below. But to use the potty, the throne has to be lifted clear and it becomes a most awkward thing to get out of the way. We hope Peter can be persuaded to redesign it with some sort of fold-up seat to avoid the gymnastics.

Very justifiably, neither Crocker nor Edey & Duff have insisted on more than sitting head-room below decks. More not only is a near impossibility, but really not needed in a boat the size of the Stone Horse. But it is nice to have some spot where one can stand up to put on one's pants. While anchored in Vineyard Haven in a howling northeaster with sheets of blowing rain and the companionway hatch firmly closed, we both decided that if the Stone Horse's main boom were raised about eighteen inches to allow a collapsible dodger over the companionway hatch, it would have made life more pleasant. With such a dodger, there would be a spot to stand to take care of the pants, to stoke the stove, or do the dishes. Furthermore, while sailing in bad weather, one could lash the helm and stand under the dodger in the companionway, keeping a lookout—dry, warm, and comfortable as the Stone Horse took care of herself, which she does admirably.

While there is adequate stowage for two for two weeks, as we have said, we still feel if the cabin could be lengthened twelve to fourteen inches without destroying the overall beauty of the design, it would greatly improve below-decks accommodation. The cockpit still would be an ample six-foot six-inches, but the extra cabin space would allow a foul-weather hanging locker on one side, and another for shore clothes opposite, making a truly complete cruiser.

With the Stone Horse's present small ventilators and hatches, ventilation was more than adequate in the cold northern climate. But whether the small foredeck hatch would be adequate down south, I am not quite sure although a wind scoop certainly would help. What is needed is proper hinging so that the hatch could be opened fore or aft, and hatch bars to hold it instead of being propped on beer cans as at present.

The Stone Horse has an awning to rig over the cockpit, making it habitable in rainy weather, but the less said about it the better. It is typical of awnings made for northern climates with long spreaders, guys, lifts, etc., that mean a major operation to set up. As I noted in *Ocean Sailing Yacht,* no northern sail or awning maker seems to know how to make decent awnings. If a good awning is wanted, try a sail–awning maker in business in the tropics. His sails may be poor, but his awnings will be great.

As Peter Duff points out, the sailor spends most of the time in the cockpit, so it should be big and comfortable. The Stone Horse's is, with enough room for four to six people. However, it also creates problems. We found the lee side of the cockpit carried a bucket of water at all times when going to windward in heavy weather—but then in a twenty-three-foot boat, who sits to leeward in heavy weather?

The foot-well also rides below water when the boat is heeled down, but the ample two-inch drain leading through the stern can be plugged with a large cork, making the cockpit watertight but not self-bailing. This is an acceptable compromise on a boat of her size. We did discover, though, while beating to windward reefed down, that the engine room hatch is less than watertight. Rail down, we had a small lake to leeward in the cockpit, and each time we tacked the water poured down through the less-than-watertight engine room hatch. It needs a good gasket and four strong hold downs, but possibly we were pushing the little girl a bit hard since Peter said it hadn't happened before.

All in all, looking back on a week's sailing in conditions that varied from light air to a good strong nor'easter, we found the Stone Horse very close to an ideal pocket cruiser. While the changes we would make in her might be something near to gilding the lily, the closer you come to a truly satisfactory boat, the more any sailor would be driven to apply the finishing touch. It is a disease much akin to that suffered by women in kitchens.

𝟛𝟡 ❊ Freedom 40 I

[Don Street has earned a name for himself as a rather acerbic critic of present-day boats and nautical gear—most often with very good reason—and has proven a hard man to please. Consequently, we were more than a little astonished recently to receive his report on the new

The Telltale Compass, January 1978.

*cruising cat-ketch Freedom 40 that was conceived by Gary Hoyt, drafted
by Halsey Herreshoff, and is being built by Tillotson-Pearson in Warren,
Rhode Island. Here, in the first of two parts, is that happy report—and a
few things, of course, that he would change.—Ed.]*

A FEW YEARS AGO, Gary Hoyt was sailing through the British Virgin Islands aboard a friend's sparkling new IOR-type cruiser–racer when they
encountered one of the shaggy native Tortola cargo sloops that usually
appear to be but a step from the boneyard with their baggy, patched sails
and battered hulls. They were on the same course and although the new
boat already had indicated she was quite fleet of foot, it took hours for
them to overhaul the seemingly lumbering Tortola and they had great
difficulty in getting by her.

They did, finally, but she was close on their heels when they turned
off to anchor for the night which the new boat had to do well offshore
because of her six-foot-plus draft, while the Tortola, drawing something
like three-foot-six, saucily slipped under their counter and put her bow
almost on the beach.

At that point the new cruiser–racer discovered they had some sort of
massive short in the electrical system that had drained the batteries and
very effectively had cut off every one of their sophisticated comfort systems. There was no water, no stove, no refrigerator, no lights, the head
wouldn't work, and there was no possible way of starting the engine.

They were rescued from the immediate predicament of a cold, light-
less, waterless supper by the broadly grinning skipper of the Tortola who
lent them an old primus stove, a kerosene lamp and a jug full of water.
But while he was passing that gear down to Gary in his dinghy, he observed: "Mon, all them conveniences gotcha all bound up. On the sea,
you gotta be free."

That quiet pronouncement hit Gary with all the delicacy of a poleax,
but it led to the Freedom 40.

Gary is no tyro, being well known in Puerto Rican waters for his
sailing and racing skills. He has put in his time battling Mother Ocean,
having sailed *Mahjong* from Hong Kong to Miami some twenty years ago
and having cruised his big 53-foot modern center cockpit ketch
Mandarin up and down the Lesser Antilles. *Mandarin* had all the
goodies, including batteries of winches, big headsails, an engine tied to a
huge three-blade wheel, pressure water, high-fi, electric rotisserie, and
what not, but every time one thing or another broke down, which was
often enough, it set him thinking, and then the skipper of that old sloop,
quite unknowingly, brought it all to a head.

Back in port, Gary sat down and listed all the conveniences he had aboard, and then opposite them all the troubles they had caused him and carefully weighed everything from his sails to the soft music. Then he went to Halsey Herreshoff with his thoughts, and together they worked out the Freedom 40.

The Freedom 40 is not truly a new concept, but, rather, a blending of a great many old ideas, most of which already had proven themselves, but had been passed by for one reason or another. She is forty feet overall, thirty-five on the waterline, with a twelve-foot beam, and three-feet, four-inch draft, board up, six-feet, six-inch, full down. Her hull lines are more mindful of those that were common in the last quarter of the last century, and her rig, properly, is a cat-ketch (her mizzen is a few inches shorter than the main) which might appear odd to modern sailors, but which was something more than common in earlier days. Almost all the sharpies from New Haven to Florida and way points had similar rigs as did the Crotch Island pinkies, the No Man's Land and the Kingston lobster boats, to name a few. And there were reasons for their popularity since there are few rigs that call for less strings to pull.

The Freedom's masts are unstayed, which again is nothing new. Chinese junks have used them for centuries; the Block Island cat schooners sailed with them for a hundred years, and even in modern times, *Jester,* a junk-rigged Folkboat, crossed the Atlantic a half dozen times and Bill King's *Galway Blazer* went right around the world with stayless sticks.

For simplicity of rigging and maintenance, they are hard to beat, and their natural flexibility does just the right thing when the breezes swing from light to heavy—the mast bends aft and to leeward, freeing the leech, and greatly softening the punch of any puff. But unlike her forerunners, Freedom's sticks are aluminum, ten inches in diameter, and either one could lever the boat onto her side without damage, according to the designer's calculations.

Still another beauty of the unstayed mast is the fact that the whole rig is not laced together as with modern rigs so if one were to go by the board, the probability of the other remaining unaffected is high. And it would be simple knife work to cut a downed mast adrift since it would be held only by the sheets rather than an exercise with bolt cutters trying to get through a tangled web of wire. The safety factor there in such a hard chance is a great deal better.

Her booms are wishbones, again novel but not really a novelty. Originally, they probably were a development of the early sprit rig, but Fritz Fenger popularized them in the thirties with his wishbone ketches;

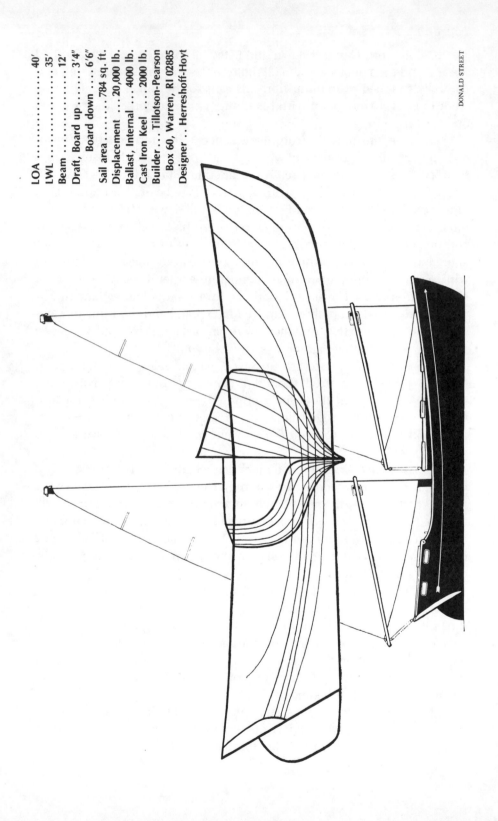

LOA . . . . 40'
LWL . . . . 35'
Beam . . . . 12'
Draft, Board up . . . . . . 3'4"
    Board down . . . . 6'6"
Sail area . . . . . . 784 sq. ft.
Displacement . . . 20,000 lb.
Ballast, Internal . . . 4000 lb.
Cast Iron Keel . . . . 2000 lb.
Builder . . . Tillotson-Pearson
    Box 60, Warren, RI 02885
Designer . . Herreshoff-Hoyt

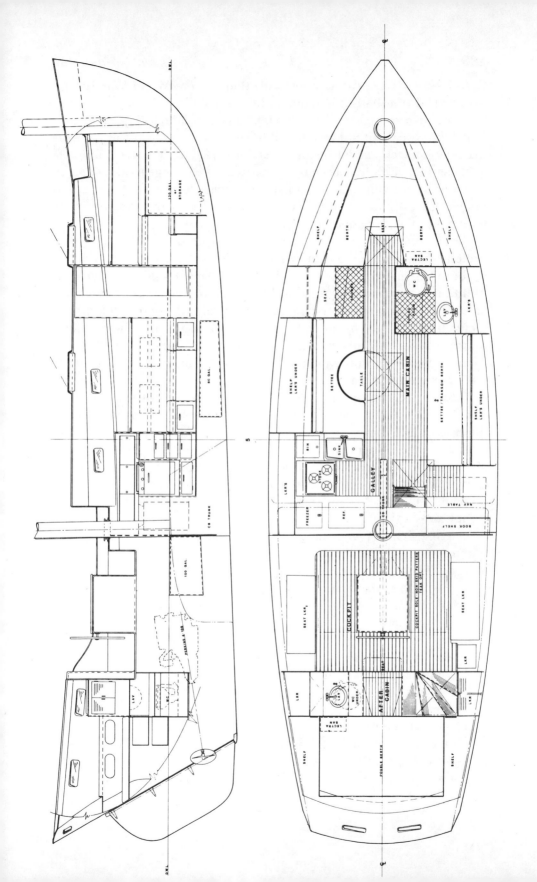

Vamarie raced very successfully with them before World War II, and Sydney D. Herreshoff used them on his Fisher's Island sloops.

The wishbone allows the sail to take a perfect airfoil shape but, more important, because the forward end of the boom is considerably higher than the sail tack, the wishbone leads downward to the clew and, in effect, the foot of the sail becomes a natural boom vang. As the sheet is eased, the sail swings out like a barn door with no twist and no need to change leads, set vangs, or perform any of the other scrambling exercises required by conventional rigs.

Freedom's sails are wrap-around double luff, another idea that sketches back into antiquity but which Manfred Curry analyzed, reduced to formulae, and concluded was the most efficient since it provided a blunt but smooth leading edge to the airfoil and got rid of turbulence around the mast. At times, racing rules have ruled the double luff illegal, including a proposal by an early *Shamrock* to use it, but there is little question on its efficiency. On the technically attuned open C-Class catamarans, double luffs long have been standard and the solid wing sails are an extension of the idea.

But all told, the Freedom 40 is really back to basics as Gary conceived her. No engine; electricity provided by twelve-volt batteries; lighting fluorescent and backed up by kerosene lamps; a straight, old-fashioned ice-box (it needs attention); alcohol stove; hand-pumping water system plus a gravity-fed, solar-powered hot-water arrangement for the shower. Gary would like to see her kept that way, and so would I although I have no doubt that some owners will have to have this or that to introduce complexity and problems.

At first sight of Freedom with her approximation of a sterncastle that reminds many of an antique Spanish galleon, more than one sailor has opined: "That tub won't get out of her own way!" But they are wrong —dead wrong, as was indicated in the last two Antigua Weeks. In 1976, Freedom creamed the cruising division with five straight firsts, and last year she did nearly as well with three firsts and two seconds. At the same time she beat, boat-for-boat, such larger craft as the fifty-two-foot, Hood-designed *Blue Light* and the Gulfstar 50 *Mai Tai,* manned by a hot SORC crew and fitted with everything in the book in the way of racing sails and gear.

Perhaps the second most common off-the-hip reaction the Freedom draws is that she won't go to weather because of the lack of headsails. Again the wiseacres are dead wrong, and again Antigua Week was impressive proof since the courses are all at least one-third to windward, and even on a sixteen-mile Olympic course in which windward work predominates, she did well. It's an odd misconception anyway when one thinks of the little Olympic Finn, or the Lasers or even a Sunfish, all of which get to weather notably well, and the claim goes contrary to the rather plain and well-accepted theory. After all, headsails are granted to be the most efficient sails in a sloop rig because they are up there in clear air and can take a good airfoil shape. The Freedom simply moves that efficiency aft to the main and the main driving forces which only makes sense.

Gary, himself, wasn't too certain about all that until he rigged out a little Sunfish with an unstayed mast, double luff and wishbone and discovered that she outmaneuvered and outran conventionally rigged Sunfish and even the Laser . . . and with ease.

But even more to the point, in 1977's Week, which was even windier than the usual windy Week, most of the crews dragged themselves ashore at the end, haggard with exhaustion and completely beat out. But Freedom's crew danced ashore, bright-eyed and bushy-tailed and ready for anything, because they really had done little but saunter from port to starboard with beer cans in hand when she tacked. The only exceptions were when they set the mizzen staysail or diddled with the centerboard, but most of the time that was more of a case of having something to do than pure necessity. One of them told me it had been the most relaxing, enjoyable race he had ever made, and the only problem was they ran out of off-color stories.

I can believe him after spending some days putting the Freedom 40 through her paces myself, which I will report in the next chapter. In the meantime, suffice it to say that she is the handiest, most tractable, and yet quick and responsive little vessel I have encountered. The amalgamation of those old ideas has produced a boat that really makes sailing a pleasure.

40 ❀ Freedom 40 II

SAILORS ARE REALLY a funny lot when you think about it. In the old days, by and large, they went all out trying to make life as easy as possible for themselves, but today we seem hell bent on the opposite tack, trying to make sailing as difficult, as attention absorbing, as frustrating as we can

The Telltale Compass, February 1978.

with multitudes of gadgets to tweak and pull and designs that have all the ill manners of an unbroken colt. I suppose that's progress, but it is a misnomer.

Sailing is one area where looking back can make some sense, and that's why Gary Hoyt's new Freedom 40 appeals so much to me—in effect he has gone back to the beginning to start over with a boat designed to take you from here to there quickly and with as little fuss and work as possible. He has succeeded.

I finally talked Gary into lending me his boat for a few days—a practice he regards in about the same light as lending his wife—and in those few days I put the boat through about every maneuver and test I could conceive and not once did she so much as stumble. I can't recall getting more plain pleasure out of simple sailing because there was practically nothing she wouldn't do quickly and quietly, when asked, and with little effort on our part.

Sailing the Freedom 40 turned out to be unbelievably easy. Starting at anchor, first set the mizzen wishbone at the proper height and haul up the mizzen, sheeting it flat. Then set the main wishbone and the mainsail, easing it slightly. Ease the mizzen, let her fall off and she starts sailing, so you tack up to the anchor, haul it aboard, and you are on your way. With the sheets trimmed, tacking is simply a matter of putting down the helm, nothing more.

Bear off, and ease the sheets. Again, nothing more . . . no sheet leads to move, no main traveler to adjust, no boom vang to connect up. Just plain ease sheets. As soon as she is far enough off to take the mizzen staysail, simply yank it up. It sets flying. That increases the sail area some 400 square feet. Anyway, with almost 1200 feet on a 40-foot boat, she has to fly.

Bear off still more until the staysail begins collapsing. Douse it, swing the main over to the other side, and you are wing on wing. But as the wind goes aft, you have much less worry about accidental jibes than with the conventional rig. The Freedom's sails can be overeased so far that she can luff even with the wind on the quarters or better. Without shrouds to interfere, the booms can swing in an arc of about 270 degrees as compared to the 160 degrees, more or less, of the stayed rig, and the boat can yaw 30 degrees on either side of a dead downwind course without fear of gibing. It makes it handy in foul water, or for the lousy helmsman.

That ability to overease everything also makes her about the handiest boat in tight spots I have sailed, not excepting my own *Iolaire* which has had only sail power ever since I gave up the battle with those damnable engines. I have sailed *Iolaire* in and out of all sorts of holes, but now, after the Freedom, it feels a bit like maneuvering a truck as opposed to a Porsche.

Street's Sketch: The Freedom 40.

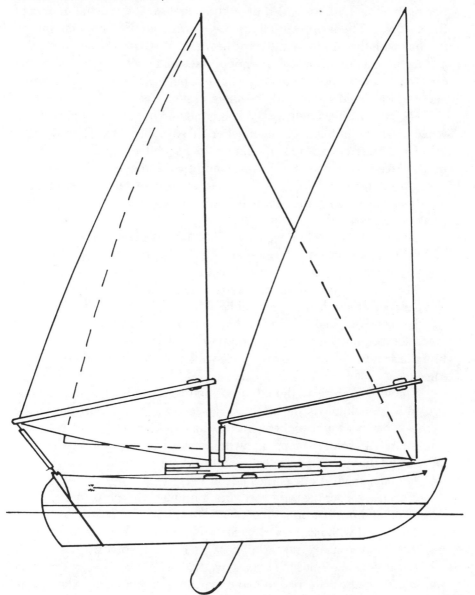

   As an instance, the first day I sailed the Freedom 40 with Gary—he was trying to make up his mind whether he would let me borrow her and insisted on a checkout demonstration—we sailed into Roadtown Harbor which is notable for a collection of fat sandbars as well as for a general congestion of anchored craft in about every inch of good water. We were having so much fun maneuvering the Freedom through the fleet under her main alone, that we ended up a little careless and ran full on one of the sandbars. The board was all the way down, and the Freedom ground to a halt with the wind well aft of the beam after we had slacked the sheet and let the sail luff forward. I was nonplussed and ready to put the dinghy over to take out an anchor to kedge her off, but Gary wasn't a bit worried and said we would sail her off, lee shore or no.

   He put my wife, Trich, on the helm and told her to hold it hard down while slowly trimming in the main when he gave the word. Then we both got on the board and started cranking it up. As it lifted and the main came in, the Freedom forged ahead slowly, and then sedately headed up, and we were off again. It is the only time I have seen a boat sail herself off a lee shore, and the only time such an incident hasn't created the complete panic party aboard.

   By itself, that incident gave me a lot of confidence in the Freedom, and the next few days did nothing to lessen it. We took her out and sailed up through the Virgins, challenging everything in sight, including several Morgan 41s that seem omnipresent down here. The first one we skipped by as though she were anchored, and clapped ourselves on her weather bow. She tacked, we covered, and she tacked back. We let that go on for a couple more rounds and then withdrew as we could see the Morgan's crew was panting over their winches while we had done nothing except to steer and drink our beers.

   The second Morgan, though, was a momentary shock to me because my crew, unbeknownst to me, had raised the centerboard during the night—it bangs a bit at anchor—and we had gotten underway with it still housed. While we were stepping by the Morgan alright, we were sagging off at about the same rate she was and I couldn't understand it since that had not happened in our earlier encounters. That is, of course, until I asked what the board setting was, and found we had none at all. So we turned off and put her on all points of sail without the board, and found she did as well without it—and faster—than most of the so-called cruising boats I have sailed, and certainly as well as the Morgan.

   In the course of those few days, we had about every weight of wind you would want, so we had ample opportunity to check out shortening the Freedom down, which is probably the second most frequent question about her rig. The answer is that you don't reef, even though some of the later owners have insisted on jiffy reefing rigs which are needless. The Freedom does well in winds up to a bit better than twenty knots under her full rig, we found, but she did begin to labor when the winds piped on.

Gary has an aversion to the mishmash and scrambling involved in reefing—as who doesn't?—and he and Herreshoff resurrected an old system of changing sail combinations to replace that workout. The Freedom carries, besides her two full sails, a smaller main and a smaller mizzen, both double luff, which are bent on loose-footed without the wishbones and sheeted directly to the travelers. These provide a fantastic assortment of combinations which I found worked extremely well despite my initial skepticism.

When the winds went beyond twenty knots or so, we dropped the mizzen and its wishbone, and set the smaller mizzen in its place. This carried her well up to about thirty knots at which point we doused the little mizzen and used the main alone. To begin with, I was sure that would make her almost unmanageable, but it doesn't. She sails well under main alone, albeit with a very slight lee helm that is almost unnoticeable . . . she still comes up, pays off, tacks, jibes, and reaches as handily as she does with her full rig.

When the breeze hit forty or so, we doused the main and replaced it with the smaller loose-footed sail along with the small mizzen. Under that combination she charged along very comfortably, and I expect it would carry through a whole gale of sixty knots, although we didn't get that much. Beyond that, no forty-footer is going to weather anyway, and the Freedom heaves to very nicely with only the small mizzen set . . . and also lies to her anchor very quietly under it.

One sailor I talked to took a dim view of having to change sails, but it really is much less a drill than fooling around with reef points. We found we could douse a sail, stow the wishbone and have the smaller sail set in its place in five to eight minutes total which certainly compares favorably with the time it takes to tuck in reefs. Incidentally, the wishbones are both extremely light and they have no tendency to rise or twist when trimming or jibing them as does the conventional boom.

From all this, it may sound as though I think the Freedom 40 is the "perfect yacht." Not quite. There isn't such a beast and probably won't be until you build six or seven of them yourself and even then it will only be personally perfect. The first thing I would do would be to take a Skilsaw and get rid of the Freedom's "great cabin," or whatever you want to call it. It makes a good boat look like a tub, whereas without it she is quite handsome as I proved to myself by sketching her out.

Then I would stretch the cabin six or eight feet aft which would give you some really handsome room below to play with, and I would put the cockpit right aft to the transom. I would dump the big box in the present cockpit and the somewhat Mickey Mouse-like steering gear, and install a plain and simple tiller. Why complicate things?

The running rigging would be next. On the present boat it is a great collection of misplaced cleats and bad sheet, halyard and lift leads. They need sorting out and I would bring everything to vertical sheet stoppers and a couple of self-tailing winches. That would make it simple to handle even for a small sailor.

The centerboard on the Freedom is 1,200 pounds of fiberglass-covered steel which contributes significantly to the boat's stability, but it is rigged with the pendant about a third abaft the pivot so that the pendant does not extend below the keel. That avoids drag, of course. But the pendant leads directly to a Barient winch with no purchase at all, and the thing is a bear to hoist. I would secure a pendant rod to the aft corner of the board and lead it to a three-part purchase before the winch. That would set up a little drag and would make hoisting or lowering the board slower but one hell of a lot easier.

The Freedom ice-box, which I cheer, is huge, but not well designed. It probably will hold 500 pounds of ice and is well insulated on the sides and bottom. But there is no insulation on the top, which makes no sense, and it would be better if it were broken into two or even three smaller boxes so that the ice can be used most efficiently, as I pointed out in the *Ocean Sailing Yacht*. A properly built three-part box probably would hold ice for four or five weeks, and it wouldn't be subject to the ills of a machine.

I can find no fault with Gary's solution to the electrical question. He installed all fluorescent lights—with kerosene back-ups—and a single battery. That lasts for about a week and will cover needs for most alongshore cruising which is where the Freedom shines . . . she wasn't meant to be a round-the-world vessel. I might add a couple of batteries, as I have on *Iolaire,* to give a couple more weeks' capacity, but those along with a Sears–Roebuck charger make a simple set-up that works and has few worries.

Similarly, there is nothing wrong with his water system—two one-hundred-gallon tanks, and hand pumps. He has contrived an ingenious shower system that works and has nothing to go wrong. On deck he has a tank that is three feet long, two wide, and four inches deep, covered with a clear lucite panel, that gravity feeds to the shower below. A couple hours of sunshine heats the water enough that you have to mix in some cold, but it couldn't be more foolproof.

Finally, I agree completely with the Freedom's original basic idea of no engine, although I have little doubt that few of them ever will be launched without some smelly monster below even though it will add something like $10,000 to the cost. She really doesn't need one, and the more so because she does have space topsides for a decent dinghy. Gary's 11½-footer is a little beauty which can be carried either in davits over one of the waterways, or stowed upside down on the cabin top for the long hauls. With one or two little Seagulls to power the dink, the Freedom can be pushed through any calm, if the sailor is that impatient, at something around four knots, or he can row her, as Gary does, with a pair of eighteen-foot sweeps. It's good for the constitution, and while it may raise a sweat, it reduces the mental torture.

If the sailor can't conceive of life without an engine, there is room for it. I am sure that plenty will be in that spot even though I think it simply shows a lack of confidence in his own sailing abilities and, sadly enough, it is a confidence he probably never will acquire with an engine crutch at hand. Anyway, I hope he keeps it as simple as possible.

Pearson suggests, as more or less standard, the Perkins 4.108 diesel of 50 horsepower, but I think that is more than is needed. If it were my choice, which it won't be, I would elect the little 2-cylinder, 22-hp. Saab, fitted with variable-pitch, mechanically feathering propeller. That is an extremely smoothly running diesel as has been indicated dramatically during several of the recent European boat shows. Saab usually has the engine running during the entire show with it just sitting on its bed and not a single bolt to hold it down. It mutters away without so much as a jiggle. It would be hard to find a diesel to match.

The variable-pitch prop lashup has been popular in Europe for years and has stood up extremely well to all tests of time and use, but for some reason, it hasn't yet come into its own on this side of the Atlantic. It should, because it is an excellent answer. The prop pitch can be adjusted to be most efficient at any sea state, while the standard solid wheel is really only efficient at one rpm setting in one kind of sea, and it can be fully feathered to provide the least drag. Not only that, but the engine and variable-pitch prop costs less than the engine and a standard gear box, so you get more for less, and there aren't many places you can do that.

Then there is the bottom line, as everyone seems to be saying these days, which can be almost anything, but if the sailor resists the worry-making goodies and sticks to a plain and simple sailing machine of Freedom's original conception, he can get it for $45,000. These days that is a remarkably low price, or so Everett Pearson told me. But if the sailor goes for the frills and furbelows, that line can run all the way up to $70,000. And that seems reason enough to keep it simple.

Postscript, December 1978

The original piece I wrote on the Freedom 40 was so complimentary that *Sail* magazine refused to publish it. After the above article appeared in *Telltale Compass*, it was followed by an article in *Yachting* by Bill Robinson and another by Hal Roth in *Motor Boating and Sailing*. The Freedom 40 continues to do extremely well, virtually having cleaned house while racing in the Eastern Caribbean in 1976, '77, and '78.

Many people do not like the raised poop deck, aft cabin version. Others wanted more space below. The result has been a flush deck, aft cabin version. The flush deck gives much room below, but we have lost the side decks with the deep bulwarks and thus, the ability to stow anchors, anchor-lines, and a dinghy in the waterways and to forget about them. The davits have also gone. Ventilation is not as good now that we have lost the ports in the cabin sides.

Some of the new Freedom 40s have two-wheel hydraulic steering which certainly seems a waste of the aft cockpit version, which can be so easily steered with a tiller and trim tab.

Further, the true Freedom 40 no longer exists, as a fifty-horsepower diesel (with no drip pan, so every time you pump the bilges you'll be polluting the harbor) has been installed. Accessibility to the engine is limited and it drives the shaft through a Vee-drive. This is expensive and does not have the world's greatest reputation for reliability. It has much more horsepower than necessary to drive the easily pushed Freedom 40 hull, and is complicated by its electrical and refrigeration systems.

The running rigging has been cleaned up, however. Sheets and halyards all lead through vertical sheet stoppers to a couple of winches, and the board to a self-tailing winch.

My dream-boat design would be a three-masted Freedom 40 with an aft cockpit, tiller steering with trim tab, cabin trunk, full lifelines, only a small bow pulpit, and davits for a fourteen-foot clinker-built dinghy that could be stored upright on skids in the waterways for short trips, and upside down on the cabin trunk for longer trips. To keep the kids busy when you're at anchor, a couple of wind surfers could be stored inside the dinghy.

Flat calm power would be provided by two Seagulls on the stern of the dinghy and these would push her along very nicely at 3½–4 knots. Electrical power would be provided by an Ampair wind generator mounted on the mizzenmast, backed up by a towed generator for down-wind work.

If, by the time I got round to affording this Freedom 40 of mine, I was too old and decrepit to sail a boat without an engine, I would go for the two-masted rig, with a two-cylinder Saab handstarting diesel with adjustable pitch, and a fully feathering propeller. This could be de-clutched and allowed freewheeling to drive an electric generator when one wanted to generate electricity, but otherwise would feather fore and aft to minimize drag.

To complete my dream Freedom 40, the ice-box would be divided into three sections so that three hundred pounds of ice would last for three weeks to a month.

As I say, if anything ever happens to my *Iolaire,* I know where I am going.

41 ❊ Out Island 41

A MONTH OR SO AGO, we sailed a Morgan Out Island 41 from Boston to St. Thomas via New York, Norfolk, the Intracoastal Waterway to Morehead City in North Carolina, and thence directly to St. Thomas in the Virgin Islands. It was a passage of about two thousand miles and three weeks' duration that left both my crew and myself with broad impressions on the suitability of the Morgan 41 for cruising.

A voyage of such length and over such a course provided an almost perfect test for a cruising boat since we had a bit of coastwise work, a little waterway ditch-crawling, and an offshore passage. We left Boston with the temperature at 36° and arrived in St. Thomas with the temperature at 86°, having had a variety of weather, wind, and sea conditions that any-one could expect to meet on a cruise.

The Morgan Out Islands are tremendously popular boats judging by the number you see around, but my crew decided that popularity proba-bly reflected more a good marketing program and able advertising cam-paigns, salted with catchy copywriting, than a measure of suitability. Cer-tainly, the name alone immediately conjures visions of strange and exotic

The Telltale Compass, March 1975.

places—the Outer Hebrides, the Lesser Antilles, the Out Islands of the Bahamas, the far distant islands of the Pacific—which some desk-bound copywriter obviously had very much in mind not only for the 41, but also for her new big sister, the 51, as well as for her smaller relatives like the 38, 36 and 28, all of which Morgan has given the flavorful title whether or not the boats have the ability to get to such places.

In our case, the 41 managed to get us there without major incident, but with little elan, style or even comfort. As we raised St. Thomas, the crew decided that the sailing abilities of the Out Island 41 were about on par with a square-toe frigate that had lost her centerboard. The 41 goes downwind beautifully. Going to windward, she still goes downwind beautifully. Beating to windward in a six-to-eight-knot breeze, it took us a full forty-four hours to make good sixty miles. In heavy weather, she simply would not go upwind, even with everything drawing and the motor beating a steady tattoo. Under both sail and power, the 41 tacked on 100° and, despite the engine made full 10° leeway, if not more. That provides a total tacking angle of 120°, which means that for every mile made good to windward, the 41 had to sail two miles. Without the motor and under sail alone, she tacked on 120°, and sagged off fifteen degrees on each board, giving a total tacking angle of 150°, which meant she had to sail three miles to make one good. All that puts the windward going abilities of an Out Island 41 about the same as the lumbering *Santa Maria*. We ran out of fuel between New York and Norfolk.

Eric Hiscock often has stated that the true cruising boat must be able to work her way offshore, beating to windward in a gale of wind under reduced canvas without the aid of an engine. I seriously question that the Morgan Out Island 41 can do it. In any case, there is no question in my mind that the Morgan needs a substantial centerboard which she does not have, but I note in studying the designs for her new sister, the 51, that she will have a centerboard. It would not surprise me to hear that the Morgan management has heard much on this point from owners, but to date they have shown no signs of doing anything about the existing design, even to holding to the big solid three-blade prop which helps her abilities not a whit. A variable-pitch prop could help.

By and large, we had an easy passage and none of the problems that usually pinpoint construction faults but it left us with plenty of time to pry into the corners, and, as usual, we wondered what a thoroughly competent fiberglass surveyor would have to say about the Morgan, a speculation somewhat extended by all the reports we have heard from the three and four-year-old Morgans in the charter fleet in the Caribbean which apparently still are badgered with deck, portlight and deck-hull joint leaks.

Generally, though, we were not impressed by the quality of the joiner work, and certainly not by the fiberglass finishing. One crewman, who should know better, ended up with a nasty cut from a sharp fiberglass edge in rummaging about in a locker, and we all were indignant over the loss of several cans of beer, punched open by a series of glass stalagmites in a locker bottom. None of the lockers had drain holes and would have to be sponged out, a job obviously not without its dangers.

Despite the easy passage, and quite unaccountably, the alley door fell off its hinges, and the only grab rail that was used below decks promptly came adrift, which left the remaining rails untested by a wary crew. The drawers beneath the chart table sagged open on the port tack, and other drawers, as well as the hanging locker doors, jammed shut. And in one spot of heavier weather, the engine room bulkhead made very strange and worrisome noises.

The so-called head liner, which is common aboard stock boats now, makes it almost impossible to find the location of any deck leaks, and it makes it most difficult to install winch pads, pad eyes, or the additional fittings a cruising yachtsman generally wants.

From the design standpoint, the boat does have some excellent characteristics. She has a good big rudder and a long straight keel. With them and her self-locking hydraulic steering system, she steered so easily that an auto-pilot was really unnecessary. And she should be an easy boat to haul. On the other side, though, her ballast is incased within the fiberglass hull, again a common but questionable practice these days. The practice greatly increases the likelihood that on even touching ground, the gel coat will be cracked, water will penetrate the fiberglass and eventually cause delamination. So even the most minimal grounding calls for immediate hauling and repair. Anyone poking about in the Out Islands is certainly going to touch bottom now and again, and had the ballast keel been bolted outside, there would be less cause for worry.

Although primarily rigged as a sloop, the Morgan 41 also has an optional ketch rig, and ours was so rigged. There are advantages to a ketch rig, if properly done, with one of the prime ones the fact that if one mast goes by the board, usually you will have one left standing. But with the 41, the masts are not independently stayed so that one going most probably will take the other with it, nullifying the advantage. And the main boom was much too long, nearly touching the mizzen, so there was little clearance and the mizzen most often was backwinded and completely ineffective. Even so, as with the ketch rig, we found the Morgan could be easily trimmed to self-steer, providing the boom vangs were carefully rigged. But that was no easy problem since there were no pad eyes for the vangs and no cleats. The only possibilities were the lifeline stanchion bases which on the Morgan looked much too light to take the load in any weight of wind. Consequently, we confined our experimenting on the point to those times when the wind went light.

The rigging itself was very poorly executed. In place of wire-to-rope splices on the halyards, the wire was eye-spliced and joined to an eye-splice on the tail. The halyards also were cut so long that the winches were overloaded with turns, making it most difficult to set sail. Swage fittings on the standing rigging also were poorly done, with a number of them obviously bent when rigged, and almost all showing heavy corrosion as did the wire itself although the boat was a scant six months out of the yard. The mast heel, too, showed corrosion, being stepped directly on top of the keel and continually in bilge water. It had not been either anodized or painted.

The sails were not particularly well made nor were they particularly well cut. On both the main and mizzen, there was a very substantial rubback dimension, but the sails obviously were not cut to fit it. Even though the Morgan 41 is a cruising boat, her sails were racing weight—7.25 ounce specified for main and mizzen—but they appeared even lighter. The tack, clew, and head were not heavily reinforced, and the stitching was doubled rather than triple stitched. The batten pockets showed no reinforcing which definitely will cause trouble in years to come.

The layout of sheets, cleats, and winches in the cockpit was such as to make you wonder if a sailor had anything to do with it. Only two sheet winches were provided, both at the after end of the cockpit, and so sited that on a reach, the lee jibsheet winch handle fouled the main sheet. All the sheet leads were concentrated around the helm so it absolutely was impossible to jibe the boat without having a Chinese fire drill with everyone jamming winch handles and elbows in each other's ribs.

Despite the great beam, the cockpit was extremely cramped and uncomfortable. Mostly this was because of the "walk-thru passageway," as Morgan spells it, connecting the forward and aft cabins below. Such passageways are another item in design that are seemingly reaching the fad stage in American boats and I suppose it is because the so-called market analysts find that buyers like the idea, whether it makes practical sense or not. Most likely, it reminds Mother of the hall at home. At any rate, our boat had a "walk-thru" although Morgan also has what they call a "Traditional Aft-Stateroom Model" that mercifully omits that misbegotten feature.

In order to get the headroom for the passage, the port seat in the cockpit is raised a full four feet above the cockpit sole. If you elect to sit there, your feet dangle and there is no backrest. You end up feeling as though you were perched on a coffin strung out on the cockpit bench.

Sloop-rigged Morgan Out Island 41 with the two accommodation plans offered.

L.O.A.	41'3"
L.W.L.	34'0"
Beam	13'10"
Draft (nominal)	4'2"
Displacement (approx.)	10,500 lbs.
Sail area (approx.)	774 sq. ft.

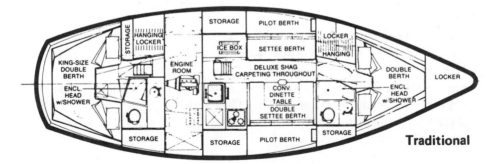

Traditional

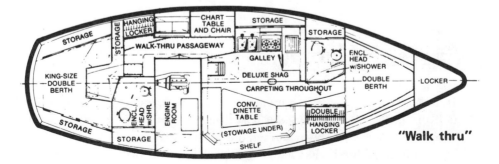

"Walk thru"

Come to think of it, it looks a bit like that, too. Below decks, the passageway uses up a tremendous amount of space in the best part of the boat for
the occasional use it gets although it does provide very easy access to the
engine room. Still, at the end of our three-week passage, my crew was in
accord that it was a feature they happily could get along without since it
all but destroyed what otherwise could have been a comfortable cockpit.

The amidship cockpit on a ketch is an excellent idea since it does get
one out from under the mizzen boom, but they definitely are wetter than
the more common aft cockpit. The amidship cockpit must have a good
watertight dodger, and ours did not. But even if a good dodger were built
to cover the forward end of the cockpit, the layout on the Morgan, particularly with its coffin, was such that it would be difficult, if not impossible,
to sit comfortably under the dodger.

Still, perhaps the most ridiculous part of the deck layout was the
deck ice-box. To me, that was especially disappointing because a good
deck box is a great idea in adding to the creature comforts, notably in
warm waters. But whoever laid out the one on the 41 either has never
gone sailing or possibly doesn't drink beer and was only including the box
because somebody upstairs told him it had to be there. In any case, just
getting to it was an operation that required the helmsman to stand up and
move out from behind the wheel before anyone could so much as crack
the box. Then on the one we had, the box was so badly insulated that
even in Morehead City, with the temperature in the mid-fifties, twenty-
five pounds of ice disappeared overnight. The ice would have lasted better if we had left it on the cockpit sole. The whole thing was a pity.

The more the pity when you consider the inherent frustrations of
sailing aboard something like the Morgan Out island 41. But the passage
did give us a sharp appreciation for what Columbus must have endured
aboard the lumbering *Santa Maria* so long ago. We only hope his winds
were fairer.

42 ❦ Heritage 38

IN OCTOBER 1977 we picked up in Florida a Heritage 38, hull No. 57 for
delivery to St. Thomas. Since it was hull No. 57, we assumed that the
worst of the bugs had been worked out of the design.

Both Les Hazell, head of Heritage Yachts Charters, and Charlie

Morgan of Heritage Yachts asked me to judge the boat not as an offshore cruising boat but rather as a boat designed for bare-boat chartering in the east Caribbean. Les Hazell of Heritage Yachts deserves a pat on the back for cheerfully supplying all the safety equipment, spares, tools, etc. we requested. All too often when one picks up a new boat for delivery to the islands the delivery crew has to fight tooth-and-nail to get anything more than a pair of pliers and a screwdriver. Judging bare-boats as bare-boats, not offshore cruisers, is perfectly legitimate but does put delivery crews on their toes as the boat designed for bare-boat day sailing in the Caribbean is obviously not designed and equipped to fight its way to windward against the northeast Trades and equatorial current. But that, in itself, is another story. We ended up having an easy trip.

Needless to say the boat was late from the builder's yard. It was delivered on a flatbed truck, and the final payment had to be made before the boat went in the water. There was no thought of a check-out by an independent surveyor prior to delivery. We were delayed in our departure by a big Irwin that was tying up the lift. She was going in and out of the water like a yoyo. Although she was new, she was leaking like a sieve from undiscovered sources.

The Heritage 38 was delivered and a crash commissioning program commenced. Undoubtedly I would *still* be trying to commission the boat were it not for the fact that one of my crew, Bill McGill, was a Chief Warrant Officer, Canadian Army, a maintenance specialist on leave. He ran into some difficulties getting the refrigeration system working; finally he surmounted that problem and then attacked the wiring.

We were supplied with a beautiful wiring diagram. The boat was completely color coded; but not only did the wiring diagram not agree with the actual installation but the color coding of the wiring in the hull did not match the color coding of the wiring in the mast. Bill finally got the electrical system working but said "Woe betide the poor guy trying to figure out what I've done." In many places he had to connect red to green, brown to yellow, and various other strange and apparently wrong, but in practice correct, combinations.

This boat was specifically altered and equipped for bare-boat chartering in the Caribbean, yet we discovered she had a bare, unanodized aluminum spar which will undoubtedly cause massive corrosion problems. The standing rigging was all rod, which basically has a dubious reputation for reliability, and, in any case, how do you ship a replacement forty-five foot rod head-stay to the Caribbean? The mast boot consisted of a piece of cloth poorly secured to small wooden strips around the mast partners, absolutely guaranteed to leak. What was needed was a proper, oval-shaped partner made of aluminum, bronze, or stainless plate (or casting) with a good, high, two-inch lip. This coupled with a neoprene mast boot secured with hose clamps produces a combination which is absolutely watertight. To find a proper mast boot and mast partners today on a stock boat is rare indeed.

The topping lift was poorly designed. It led from the end of the boom up over the top of the mast then down alongside the mast, where it was guaranteed to slap all night long, both at anchor and while sailing. The boat did not have roller reefing, so why did not the topping lift come from the top of the mast to the end of the boom then through the center of the boom to a cleat on the side of the boom?

The reefing system within the boom was good, but the sail was old-fashioned; it had reef points. In this day and age why was jiffy reefing not installed? This would certainly simplify reefing for the average charter party and would also minimize the chance of a reef being shaken out with one of the points still secured!

The headsail was what I would call a three-quarter genoa (about a no. 3) secured to a foil roller furling system which left a lot to be desired.

In the eastern Caribbean a good deal of the time the boat will have to be sailed with the genoa half rolled-up. This is hard on the sail, and when one shortens sail by rolling the sheet lead must move forward; yet there was no onboard track nor any onboard pad-eyes for sheeting the genoa in a half rolled-up position. This is a standard failure on practically all stock bare-boats. We ran into the same problem, the lack of an inboard sheet lead for either a partially rolled up head-sail or a smaller working jib on both the Columbia 45 and the Morgan 41, boats we had previously delivered. An inboard sheet lead for a working jib is seldom found on the stock boats I have sailed on or inspected.

There were only two winches in the cockpit, yet there was a definite need for a third. The geriatric charter party will certainly need a winch to roll up the genoa in heavy weather. On starboard you could use the windward sheet winches; however, on port tack by the time you threw off the genoa sheet, took the roller furling line around the winch and rolled up the genoa, the sheets had tied themselves one around the other in such a ball of knots it took an hour to disentangle them.

Like most modern cruising boats which have the windward-going qualities of a haystack, a Heritage 38 has its upper and lower shrouds chainplates at the extreme outer edge of the hull, despite its ample beam. As a result it is impossible to sheet any overlapping headsail in to the proper angle. Were the chain plates to be moved onboard a foot to eighteen inches on either side I am sure the windward-going qualities of the boat would be greatly improved.

A small electric anchor windlass was installed to reduce the number of bad backs. The unit was no better or worse than others but its chances of operating over a long period of time were minimal. The wires were led through the deck to a terminal block no more than six inches away from the naval pipe. Within a few months the terminal block would be so corroded by the salt water coming down the naval pipe that no electricity would reach the winch. Further the naval pipe was without any sort of a hold-down to make a watertight seal. In heavy weather a lot of water would come through the naval pipe corroding the terminal blocks and filling the bridge.

A perfectly good Grunert refrigeration system was installed, but whoever installed it certainly never read Grunert's manual. A most critical part of any refrigeration system is the installation of the small twelve-volt circulating water pump. It was specifically noted in the instructions that the pump should be mounted as low as possible with the shortest run possible from the intake to the filter, to the pump, to the cooling coils, with the pump placed below the water-line. However the unit was installed the new Goiot double-opening hatches, which open fore and aft pump and filter above the water-line: no hope!!! The pump would continually get air bound on port tack.

The hatches were single opening; i.e. they opened forward only and, thus, could only be used in port and had to be closed for every rain squall. This was not all. The forward hatch was so warped that the only way it could be dogged down was to have Bill, the heaviest member of the crew, stand on the hatch during the dogging. Why had the mechanics not installed the new Goiot, double-opening hatches, which open fore and aft and can be switched from the forward opening to the aft opening position or vice versa from below decks? If the Goiot hatches were installed and covered by good watertight dodgers open at the after end, it would allow them to be left open while under sail. The Heritage 38 would then be changed from a sweatbox into a well-ventilated boat under sail.

The boat's ventilators were worse than useless. Tiny, soft plastic affairs from Nico Frico that were so low they could not possibly produce any quantity of air below decks (see *Ocean Sailing Yacht,* pp. 276,277, for further elaboration). The ventilators were not securely fastened into the dorade boxes and, consequently, were frequently knocked out by the jib sheets while tacking.

Despite the fact that there was a sign in the engine room warning of a $500 fine for polluting the harbor there was no engine drip pan. Thus, within a short time, the bilge would become foul with oil.

As is often the case on stock boats, all the below-water through-hulls were equipped with gate valves which were of dubious quality and slightly above the water-line on the starboard side there were positioned two through-hulls with no valves at all. As in almost all stock boats, specifications show seacocks on below-water through-hulls only, not on above-water through-hulls—I suppose the standard stock boat is supposed to stay tied up in the marina and never to go to sea and heel over! Further, there was no shut-off on the engine exhaust. No matter how well designed an exhaust system is, no matter how many loops, vents, and fancy arrangements one installs (I am a belt-and-braces man, myself), in heavy weather I want to be able to turn off the engine exhaust valve. More engines have been drowned by water working its way up the exhaust pipe than by any other source.

The above are basic design errors, other things we encountered were mere pains in the neck which revealed simple lack of thought. The galley sink drained beautifully on either tack. However, both heads were on the starboard side of the boat, both head sinks drain overside; thus, on port tack they cannot be used. Why do they not drain directly into the head? Then they could be used on either tack. Soapy water could be pumped out through the head every time one used the sink. I have never found a marine head yet that suffered from having too much water pumped through it.

The fresh-water system did have three separate tanks, but valves were hidden here, there, and everywhere making filling extremely complicated and making the switching of tanks difficult. Why did the designers not lead all lines from all the tanks to one single manifold with individual stop-cocks?

They did have one fresh-water hand pump in the galley. When the pressure system was turned off (or broken down) the only place one could get fresh water was in the galley. Why were fresh-water hand pumps not installed in both heads?

Furthermore, there was no salt-water pump (or tap) in the galley. Whenever we wanted to wash the dishes it was a case of getting a couple of buckets of water from overside, passing them up through the cockpit down into the sink, and spilling the water over the entire galley in the process. It would have been so much simpler to have a salt-water pump in the galley or a gravity-feed tap down near the cabin sole (as is described in *Ocean Sailing Yacht,* Volume I, p. 385). We have had this system on *Iolaire* for the past twenty-two years. It has caused no problems.

The ice-boxes (which were superbly insulated) drained into the bilge, thus assuring a smelly bilge within a few months. The hull was so shallow that there was no sump for the bilge pump. Once a little water would enter the bilge it sloshed around everywhere. It was impossible to pump the bilge really dry unless the boat was dead level.

It is a well-known fact that while going to windward a mid-ship cockpit is wet and a good watertight dodger is needed. Not only was a good watertight dodger not provided but because of the way the forward end of the cockpit coaming circles across the cabin-top, it would be most difficult to install one—and this was a hull No. 57! I wonder if the designers ever beat to windward in heavy weather in a Heritage 38?

Evidently yachting customs have changed. I was always brought up on the routine of owners and guests come on board on the starboard side, crew and tradesmen on port side. Naturally the companionway ladder is rigged on the starboard side, thus everyone normally swims from the starboard side. But you'd better not try that on the Heritage 38, for both heads are on the starboard side and if one is flushed while the crew is swimming . . .

Digital instruments you can have—it is admittedly a personal view but it was shared by the entire crew; we all hated them. Secondly, on the speed gauge it is necessary to have two paddle wheels as the paddle wheel either lifted out of the water or cavitated on the windward side. At ten degrees angle of hull the speed gauge became erratic; at fifteen degrees it gave up completely. This provided the navigator with a bit of extra work.

The accommodations below had good points and bad. The forward cabin was no better or worse than one would expect on this sized boat. The main cabin was fine except for the lack of a gimbaled table and the fact the starboard side settee was only five-feet six-inches long. With a little bit of thought a removable panel could have been installed, allowing one's feet to fit into a cubbyhole in the head compartment. This would allow two people to sleep in the main cabin, instead of one. The after cabin was excellent.

The passageway berth was abandoned and used as a really large and magnificent chart table. I have grave doubts if any charter party will use the passageway berth, for it is just too poorly ventilated for use in the tropics. Yet the sad truth is that this boat was designed for use in the tropics!

The cushion coverings were wonderful, with a fabric that felt warm and soft in cold weather and cool in hot weather and was much like a non-itchy wool. However, the covers were permanently secured to the cushions; exactly how one removed them for cleaning was beyond us. They should have been secured with zippers, Velcro, or snaps. Further, the backs of the settees in the main cabin were made in single length;

thus, whenever anyone wished to get into the storage compartments behind the settees, everyone else had to move over to the other side. It would have been better if the storage compartments had been split at each side, the cushions split accordingly, and thus, only one person would have had to move out of the way when a locker behind the settee needed to be opened.

As is the case on most delivery trips, we had to install lee canvasses. I cannot understand why lee canvasses are not installed as a matter of course on all boats. Without lee canvasses it is hopeless trying to rest below decks under sail, which charter parties often will want to do, in order to get out of the burning tropical sun.

People will say that a gimbaled table is not needed on a boat if it is only day-sailing in the Caribbean and not making overnight passages. This boat will be used in the southern end of the Caribbean where numerous passages are all-day passages. Lunch must be eaten underway. With a gimbaled stove and a gimbaled table it is relatively easy for the cook to make up soup and sandwiches; or to make soup and place the sandwiches on the table and allow everyone to help themselves. However, if the poor cook has to go down and make sandwiches in the absence of a gimbaled table, the result is a quite difficult battle. In general if you are going to leave the Marina you must have a gimbaled table if you want to have a happy cook rather than a mutinous galley slave. However, non-skid plates enabled us to eat regularly in the absence of gimbaled table.

The stove, of course, was a typical gimbaled unballasted stove (see *Ocean Sailing Yacht, Volume II* for a complete discussion of this matter) which tried to capsize as soon as a big pot of stew was put on it. We solved this problem by scrounging around the yard and finding thirty pounds of scrap-iron and lead and placing it in the bottom of the stove. To prevent the stove from oscillating over in heavy weather we installed shock cord (see *OSY, Volume I*, p. 394, sketch 161).

The galley layout left much to be desired; I've seen worse, but I've seen a lot better. You had to be six feet or over to comfortably reach into the refrigerator and the outboard lockers behind the stove. There was adequate locker space but of course, since this was a new boat, everything was just thrown in helter-skelter. Considering the fact that knives, forks, spoons, plates, bowls, cups, pots, and pans are all of fairly standard size, I do not understand why proper stowage for these items was not organized by the builders. Leaving open shelves and having each individual owner fight the stowage problem is expensive, time consuming, and frustrating for the owner.

Although the refrigeration was incredibly poorly installed, the ice-boxes (she had systems for both refrigeration and ice-boxes) were superbly insulated. We iced up in Tampa with 300 pounds of ice the day before we left. We did not use the ice too efficiently, i.e., the refrigeration system was packed up and we had to transfer the ice in the ice-box to a warm refrigerator; thus the ice-box drain clogged, and we had trouble with clearing it. Consequently, everything was less than efficient. Yet, when we arrived in St. Thomas ten days later we still had plenty of ice.

A pump connected directly to the ice-box which can be pumped into a bucket three times a day would be most useful. The bucket could then be dumped down the galley sink. This is infinitely more reliable than relying on a gravity drain. The gravity drain clogs all too easily and is difficult to clear once clogged.

If a pump is connected directly to the ice-box drain, when the drain clogs it is merely a matter of pulling the hose off the bottom of the pump, putting a short length of hose on to the discharge end of the pump, connecting the discharge to the ice-box drain, and holding a bucket of water underneath the ice-box pump. This procedure will blow the clogged line clear with hydraulic pressure. It works every time.

Given an ice-box as well insulated as that of the Heritage 38 (i.e. properly designed and broken up into three separate boxes), I am sure that 300 pounds of ice would last a full three weeks even in the tropics—in that case why spend $3,000 installing a refrigeration system?

The gas bottle installation left much to be desired. The bottles were installed on deck, well protected by moulded covering; an electric shut-off was installed so that the gas could be turned off on deck without going on deck; and an indicator light was installed to show when the gas was gone. However, boxes for the bottles were ugly, rising above the cabin top like a pair of mule's ears, and were located so that one tended to stand on them when furling the main. Since they had no non-skid strips on them one was likely to slip and go flat on one's tail. Further, the location necessitated a fairly long run-in of copper tubing to reach the stove.

If slightly different sized gas bottles were used, vapor-tight lockers could be moulded into the starboard coaming, where the gas bottles would be easily accessible, would have a short run of copper tubing to the stove, would be completely invisible, and thus would improve the appearance of the boat. It would also leave the cabin-top free for stowage of a dinghy or for just plain lounging and (weather permitting) sunbathing.

The athwartship trim of the boat left much to be desired since the batteries, fuel tank, and refrigeration system were all on the starboard side. Loaded up, she had a substantial starboard side list. With little bit of forethought in the placement of these heavy weights the list could have been eliminated.

Regularly sailing with a half-rolled-up genoa is undesirable—it may be a great advertising gimmick but it does not work well in practice. Rather, in areas like the eastern Caribbean where a considerable amount of heavy weather is to be expected, bare-boats should be equipped with a double head rig, either both roller furling with a loose-footed staysail, as on *Iolaire,* or a roller furling jib and club staysail rigged similarly to the newest CSY boats. With this rig in heavy weather or when a squall approaches, the jib can be rolled up, and one can sail under full main and staysail. If she does not balance under that rig she should certainly balance under reefed main and staysail.

As to sailing qualities the Heritage 38 is probably not much better than other sailing barges that are sold to the yachtsmen today as cruising boats. We definitely noted that the Heritage 38 was very difficult to steer on a beam reach when it piped up unless a boom vang was not rigged, and the boom bowed down hard. This was a difficult problem since there were no strong points along the deck to secure the boom vang. Nor was a boom vang provided. We improvised one with spare block and lines, secured it to a stanchion base and hoped for the best. Anyone who owns a Heritage 38 would be advised to install the gear necessary for a heavy boom vang and use it continually. It will improve the performance of the boat.

There are good points about the Heritage 38. The lead keel was bolted to the *outside* of the hull, so that the inevitable minor groundings one experiences in a cruising boat should not be a source of future trouble; the engine is well mounted. It ran very smoothly, quietly and efficiently. We set some sort of a world record in that we ran the engine 120 hours on 70 gallons of fuel. We motor-sailed in light air much of the time arriving in St. Thomas strictly on leftover fumes. Other boats that had left ahead of us were becalmed off St. Thomas for two days with no wind, no fuel, no ice, and no beer.

The accessibility to the engine was poor; there was no drip pan; the oil filter was relatively inaccessible; and since there was no drip pan, when changing the oil filter, oil would inevitably spill into the bilge. There was no sump pump on the engine—on the whole it is clear that no one planned ahead before designing this engine installation.

The engine was installed with a hydraulic gear box which permitted continuous freewheeling. The noise was enough to drive one batty, and the wear on the bearings is unnecessary. If it was decided to allow the shaft to freewheel why didn't the designers use some of this power by belting an alternator off the shaft to charge the batteries when sailing? One could connect all batteries in parallel for charging. If blocking diodes were installed the batteries could not feed one to the other while discharging; only the selected battery would discharge. If this were done the continual problem bare-boat charterers have with flat batteries would be eliminated. Every day when they were going to sail, whether they ran the engine or not, the batteries would be topped up. In fact if they did succeed in running the batteries down by leaving all the electrical equipment on, all that they would have to do is pick up the anchor and go sailing for a few hours. The batteries would soon be charged enough to start the engine.

It should be noted here that *Agube,* from South Africa, had an alternator belted off the freewheeling shaft which generated 30 amps at 6 knots from an 18″ × 10″ 3-bladed propeller!

One wonders, as well, about the engine-size, gear, and propeller. We never had to drive her under power into a head sea so we can not speak, with absolute certainty, about her powering capabilities. However, from previous experience, I would say that 4/108 with a two-to-one reduction will not allow the boat to be pushed dead to windward in a head sea, something the bare-boat charterers are very likely to want to do. If the Heritage 38 was using a standard two-to-one reduction and a seventeen-by-eleven propeller, the engine would develop roughly 815 pounds thrust. However, if they switched to a three-to-one reduction and installed a 22″ × 14″ propeller the thrust figures would go up to about 938 pounds—a decided improvement. This would be much easier and cheaper than doing what many operators of bare-boats of similar size have done, i.e. installing a 4/154. They usually use a two-to-one reduction throwing an 18″ × 12″ prop producing 1,115 pounds of thrust. Rather than installing a larger engine, with an engine of the same size you could increase the reduction gear, propeller size, and thrust, and you would be home free.

The designers of the boat obviously had not really thought the problem out; thus they made many basic errors: too wide a staying-base, which destroyed what few windward-going qualities the boat may have had, lack of proper inboard sheet leads prevented the headsail from being properly sheeted, poor dodger installation, poor hatch design, poor ventilation, a poor boat bilge pumping system, a basically unacceptable plumbing system with hulls at the water-line, with no seacocks, and with gate valves (instead of proper stop-cocks) throughout the boat. Further problems include: An engine installation which is certainly going to cause much trouble in the future due to inaccessibility, lack of shaft brake, and oil-fouling of the bilge; a gas bottle installation that leaves much to be desired; a rig that is going to cause many problems in future; and a mast partner situation which will inevitably result in a leak. All this on a boat costing about $70,000.

As I have already written, it is essential if one wants to get a good boat to have a surveyor check the boat throughout every stage of construction. If this were done many of the problems we encountered would not have existed.

I will not condemn the Heritage 38 outright, but I would say that to make a standard stock to set the Heritage 38 right and make it a fine vessel, it would probably cost $20,000 over and above the standard purchase price. Of course if Heritage builders got themselves organized, and made the necessary alterations as stock, the cost to the buyer of the alterations would be considerably lessened. Many of these alterations should not be regarded as customizing for rather they are correcting basic design errors. If the design were to be significantly changed then possibly we would be more enthusiastic about the boat.

Looking at the boat as a whole I come back to my earlier conclusions. The Heritage 38 was better than some, and worse than others with which I have been involved; but, most certainly, it was no world beater. Quality control was either poor or nonexistent, and the detail was poorly done. I wonder what the state of the layup moulding of the hull was?

43 ❧ Use a Surveyor Even When Buying New Construction

FEW YACHTSMEN will deny the necessity of hiring a good surveyor before purchasing a secondhand boat. The old English common-law principle of *caveat emptor* is enforced with a vengeance when buying a seondhand boat. It should be clear that the surveyor is the buyer's agent, not the broker's or seller's. The buyer should be aware of the fact that brokers often have their favorite surveyors who tend to give the seller the benefit of the doubt.

What is less generally realized is that it is just as essential that a surveyor, and perhaps a design consultant, be retained when purchasing a new boat.

The first essential is to make sure the boat suits the buyer's needs;

second, that it is basically well built; thirdly that it is truly built to the designer's specifications. Furthermore, the buyer's surveyor should be permitted to look over the builder's shoulder during construction. Only if the surveyor is given freedom to roam the plant can the buyer be sure that his yacht is being built properly.

A design-consultant-surveyor can earn his pay simply by advising the buyer about the suitability of various designs to the buyer's needs. It is an expensive folly to purchase a boat that can cross oceans and beat to windward around Cape Horn if the owner never expects to leave Chesapeake Bay, Long Island Sound, or Lake Mead. It is equal folly to purchase a boat that is suitable only for sailing in Chesapeake Bay, Long Island Sound, or Lake Mead if its purpose is to sail offshore.

I was hired by a yachtsman in Puerto Rico who wanted to buy a boat in the 32-foot to 35-foot category to be based at the eastern end of Puerto Rico. What he needed was a boat built to take the stress of the trade winds in that area, as well as a boat that would both go to windward and run downwind well, since one is sailing either dead to windward or dead downwind in that area. In addition, the boat had to be well ventilated, the ice-box or refrigerator well insulated, and there should be good deck-space and a comfortable cockpit to meet the needs of the tropics where so much of one's time is spent on deck. The owner thought he wanted a particular, brand-name 32-footer and asked that I advise him. I was moderately familiar with the boat and with its good points as well as some reported bad points.

Luckily there was in Grenada at the time an owner who allowed me to go over the boat in great detail. Further, he discussed his trials and tribulations with the Westsail Corporation, and the boat and its sailing qualities.

I filed a sixty-six-page report for the owner—the first six pages being surveyor's instructions, the remainder being suggested changes in details and specifications.

Some who read the report felt that I was trying to customize a stock boat. Their comments were partially true, but it is debatable as to how many of the changes required were customizing and how many were corrections of poor, or even bad, design features in the boat. As a result of this report the buyer decided not to purchase the 32-footer in question.

Needless to say, the above operation did not endear me to the manufacturer, but it did save the owner from spending about $60,000 for a boat that was not suited to his needs. To pay the price for the wrong boat, or to be burdened with a boat that needs massive changes after delivery not only costs money but means at least part of a season of sailing lost.

Too many boats are poorly built or poorly designed. I suggest as reference the back issues of *The Telltale Compass* and Ian Nicholson's *Surveying Small Craft,* published by International Marine Publishing Co., Camden, Maine. In this book Mr. Nicholson presents more than enough evidence for the need to have even new boats surveyed. One case he describes is significant. An unnamed production boat originally was excellent; then the company was reorganized and quality control deteriorated; then the company reorganized again and its production quality improved. For the uninitiated, the quality of any one of its seemingly identical boats was all but impossible to determine.

It should be remembered that plant production managers often are caught in a tight bind. They are trying to produce good boats, but the returns are not generous. For a $50,000 boat the manufacturer is lucky to realize $25,000. The balance is spent on advertising, brokers' commissions, and overhead. Frequently, after a boat goes into production it is discovered that the selling price is not enough; the cost of construction is too high. The managers of the corporation insist that the boat be built for less. Unfortunately, one of the easiest ways to save money is to skimp on the amount of glass going into the hull because glass itself and the costs of lay-up are high.

As evidence of the variable quality of hull lay-up, witness this account from the 1974 Stamford boatshow. A cold northwest front blew through, making the main exhibit building and outdoor stands nearly uninhabitable. Knowledgeable people began to gravitate toward those boats in the water that were equipped with both heating and liquid refreshments. As the day wore on and good alcohol liberated many a tongue, numerous stories regarding boat construction, even from good yards, came to light. One of the most instructive stories came from a yacht broker who also installed fathometers and speed gauges on the boats he sold. He had in his possession a cardboard box full of circles and plugs cut from hulls and deckhouses of various makes of fiberglass boats. Each was labeled with the model it had come from. Many were from supposedly identical stock boats built over a period of years. The plugs showed a wide variation in hull thicknesses. It was a positive illustration of changes in construction quality that would be impossible to ascertain were not a surveyor present during the lay-up of the boat.

Even the very best yards are kept on their toes by having numerous visits from an independent surveyor or owner's representative during construction of the boat. A good yard will be happy to have its work inspected. Avoid the yard which resists an outside observer.

The prospective buyer of a new boat, then, should be guided either by an experienced friend or hire a design consultant to check the market and find a boat in his price range that is suitable to his needs. Then, if it is a stock boat with sister ships already on the market, he should find a good surveyor and have him go over the existing boat to ascertain whether or not the design is standing the test of time and to make recommendations for changes in the boat to be built.

Further, the owner should obtain from the builder a complete set of specifications for the boat. The surveyor should approve the specifications and visit the plant to make sure the boats coming off the production line are in fact built to the specifications. If the surveyor recommends going ahead with the project the buyer should be allowed in the factory to inspect the boat whenever he wishes. In addition, the builder should agree that he will notify the surveyor of the various stages of production so that the surveyor can be present during critical stages. Finally, it should be agreed that the surveyor may take the boat out on a series of trials and that the final payment on the boat (probably ten percent of the total value) not be paid to the builder until the boat has completed builder's trials and all deficiencies made good to the surveyor's satisfaction.

To ensure a fair and amicable relationship between purchaser and builder it is often wise to select a mutually acceptable, independent arbitrator whose decisions will be legally binding on both parties. Then, if the surveyor claims that something is not as per specifications and the builder claims it is, the arbitrator can be called in. His decision is final.

What the surveyor should look for would make a book in itself but in brief a few major points come to mind:

First and foremost, the surveyor should insist that the boat be built to the specifications of the designer.

The surveyor should be available to inspect the quality and care of the hull lay-up.

The surveyor must inspect the ballast to make sure that it is of the proper material and weight before it is dropped in the mold and glassed over. All too often ballast keels are considerably below weight or sometimes of a form not specified. What is stated on the specifications as vast chunks of iron or lead may turn out to be nothing but scrap-iron, sash weights, et al. This usually is discovered years later when the boat has grounded, knocked the bottom off the keel, and the bits and pieces start falling out.

The method of joining the deck to the hull is critical. The surveyor should make sure that the design of this joint is sufficiently strong to stand the test of time. When the deck mold is joined to the hull, the surveyor should be on hand to make sure the job is properly done. Even with correctly designed boats, poor quality control can ruin an otherwise good boat. The failure of the deck joint is a major problem of fiberglass boats.

The yard should notify the surveyor when the through-hulls are to be drilled. The surveyor should be present when these are cut, collect the plugs and give them to an independent lab. They should be analyzed to ascertain if there is a proper cure and proper ratio of glass to cloth in the lay-up.

The surveyor should check the electrical system while it is being installed. All too frequently the electrical system as installed bears little or no resemblance to the wiring diagram.

Deck fittings must be checked to see that they are properly bedded, that the correct diameter holes are drilled in the deck, and that proper back-up plates are installed. The surveyor should equip himself with a magnet to ascertain that all the stainless is really stainless. (I realize some stainless is magnetic. If he finds magnetic stainless he can check the specifications and ascertain if it really belongs on board.) He will immediately discover if chrome-plated steel has been substituted for stainless or chrome-plated bronze.

The rig, of course, should be checked at all stages to make sure everything is done to the designer's specifications.

When the builder maintains that the boat is all ready to go, the surveyor should then take the boat out on builder's trials. Exactly how long the builder's trials will last is a subject to be agreed upon, with prior agreement between the owner, builder, and surveyor. It has been pointed out by the distinguished naval architect, Frank MacLear, that builder's trials are really not worthwhile unless they are a full twenty-four hours; that many things which go unnoticed during the day will show up at night.

Upon completion of the builder's trials and completion of recommendations made by the surveyor, the final ten percent can be paid with confidence.

Since builders will not want to delay the final payment, they are likely to expedite rectification of all deficiencies found by the surveyor. On the other hand, builders do not want to have the boat sitting on their hands waiting for the purchaser to raise this last ten percent. Thus the builders are well within their rights if they demand that the final payment be placed in an escrow account in a bank of their choosing to be released upon acceptance of the boat by the surveyor. It would thus mean that the builder would not be waiting for his final payment beyond the date when the boat is finished and ready for delivery.

All too often none of the foregoing precautions are taken and the boat is delivered on a flatbed truck, the owner pays the entire fee, the boat is launched, and inevitably, on boats from even the best yards, all sorts of deficiencies, some minor and some major, are discovered. The owner then spends many months, sometimes years, making good the deficiencies and in trying to collect the money spent from the builder.

A good surveyor is worth his fee. If he is in the area and can drop in on the yard once or twice a week, the money spent on these inspections will be saved many times over in the long run.

To sum up, then: The buyer should select his dream boat with care, then retain a surveyor to see it through construction, agree with the builder on an independent arbitrator whose decisions will be legally binding on both parties, and insist that ten percent of the purchase price remain in escrow until the boat has completed its builder's trials and been declared acceptable by the surveyor.

● ● ●

NOTE As of this writing there seems to be little or no reliable surveyor service available in some key areas. Tampa Bay is one, and since there are numerous builders there, including CSY, Irwin, Morgan, Heritage, and Gulfstar, this is a serious matter for both the buyer and the builder. There is reason to believe that the same problem exists in Taiwan, Japan, and Hong Kong—all yacht-building centers.

Index